VICTORY

★ ★ ★ WORLD WAR II IN REAL TIME ★ ★ ★

VICTORY

★ ★ ★ WORLD WAR II IN REAL TIME ★ ★ ★

THE ASSOCIATED PRESS

EDITED BY ALAN AXELROD

DEVELOPED BY LES KRANTZ

FOREWORD BY DAVID EISENHOWER

STERLING
New York

STERLING
New York

An Imprint of Sterling Publishing Co., Inc.
122 Fifth Avenue
New York, NY 10011

STERLING and the distinctive Sterling logo are registered trademarks
of Sterling Publishing Co., Inc.

ISBN 978-1-4549-4116-3

Distributed in Canada by Sterling Publishing Co., Inc.
c/o Canadian Manda Group, 664 Annette Street
Toronto, Ontario M6S 2C8, Canada
Distributed in the United Kingdom by GMC Distribution Services
Castle Place, 166 High Street, Lewes, East Sussex BN7 1XU, England
Distributed in Australia by NewSouth Books
University of New South Wales, Sydney, NSW 2052, Australia

For information about custom editions, special sales, and premium and corporate purchases,
please contact Sterling Special Sales at 800-805-5489 or specialsales@sterlingpublishing.com.

Manufactured in Canada

2 4 6 8 10 9 7 5 3 1

sterlingpublishing.com

Cover design by David Ter-Avanesyan and Elizabeth Lindy
Interior design by Kevin Ullrich

Picture Credits - see page 204

**Page i: A group of U.S. soldiers pose for a picture with an Englishwoman
during exuberant celebrations in London's Piccadilly Circus after
Germany's surrender was announced, May 7, 1945.**

To the 1,600 war correspondents who risked or lost their lives during World War II.

ABOVE: Don Whitehead of The Associated Press writing his story of landing with Allied troops behind enemy lines at Anzio Beach in Italy, Feb. 16, 1944. **BOTTOM:** A group of AP photographers and correspondents at the Normandy front, mid-July 1944. From left to right: photographer Harry Harris; photographer Bede Irvin (killed in action north of Saint-Lô, July 25, 1944); correspondent Hal Boyle; Robert Bunnelle, chief of AP's London Bureau; Whitehead, unidentifed man at the wheel, and AP executive Lloyd Stratton.

Contents

NOTE: The dates in this table of contents correspond to the actual dates of events and do not always match the dates in the corresponding newspaper headings or article bylines in this book. Those dates are often a day later than the event or sometimes even a week or more later if an operation was censored.

Foreword

Like most people born in the years after 1945, I grew up surrounded by the stories and histories of World War II, trying to understand the war, its impact on our parents, and its impact on the world. In my lifetime, World War II has been an inexhaustible subject, one that commands universal interest, due in part to ever new and creative ways of presenting its story. *Victory: World War II in Real Time* does just that.

Victory is fun to read. More importantly, it presents the story in an unforgettable way, in "real time," which permits the reader to imagine how contemporaries—specifically, newspaper readers of our parents' generation—learned of and reacted to the events that enveloped America and the world. *Victory* is a primary source: real-time broadcasts, diaries, dispatches, and other firsthand accounts of the amazing events as they unfolded. As a primary source, the book has special meaning because of the significance of the stories that it tells: of history's greatest and most destructive war; of the epic clash of right and wrong; of the transformation of America, which in the span of this book rose from eminence to preeminence.

The editors of *Victory* have chosen The Associated Press dispatches and pictures of highlights and turning points between 1939 and 1945. As readers are reminded in the introduction, prior to 1939, isolationism was the dominant current in American thinking about the world, a response to the horrors and perceived futility of World War I. What drew Americans out of this mood? Evident in *Victory* is that the news from abroad, combined with America's ability to act, produced the fortitude and resolve necessary to join a worldwide conflict.

The alarm bell sounds in March 1939, when German forces occupy the portions of Czechoslovakia not ceded to Germany by the so-called Munich Pact. AP reportage covering the event plainly confirm that diplomacy has failed and that the Nazi menace is, in fact, unappeasable. Successive AP dispatches over the next weeks and months report the German-Italian military pact, Hitler's relentless campaign of pressure on Poland, the shocking news of the Nazi-Soviet pact, the German invasion of Poland, and the outbreak of general war.

AP dispatches have several striking characteristics from the start. First, familiarity. They are the earliest eyewitness accounts that we have of these events, and the best—scarcely to be improved on; they are the foundation of all subsequent films, movies, and books about the war. Second, for want of a better word, candor. As a European-theater historian, I am struck by the detailed accuracy of AP dispatches covering the stories I know. Plainly, AP policy throughout the war was to report truth, evidently believing that truth was on our side. Third, characteristic of AP reporting from the start is its immediacy. AP assumed that its readership recognized that global crisis was not some faraway event, but a matter of direct concern to Americans. The inexorability of America's involvement builds throughout Chapter 2, as AP dispatches of 1940 chronicle the Nazi victory in France and their removal of the French army as the last barrier to German conquest of Europe, Churchill's elevation to prime minister, the Blitz, the Anglo-German naval war, and the accelerated start of America's industrial and military mobilization.

Between 1939 and 1945, Americans embarked on a great mission and adventure, and the AP highlights published in *Victory* chronicle the most important moments of the war that drew in and raised up the United States as the greatest international power in history. By Chapter 3—1941—America's entry is a matter of time, finalized by news of the German invasion of Russia, and formalized by the Japanese attack on Pearl Harbor. Other traits emerge in the AP dispatches of that year: a matter-of-factness in the reporting of astounding events; a cheerful acceptance of the burdens imposed by the war; an unblinking awareness of dangers, of enemy cruelty and ruthlessness; and an unfailing—pervasive—sense of optimism and confidence. In the four succeeding chapters, covering 1942, 1943, 1944, and 1945, Americans cross two oceans, Americans double Axis military production, and American forces take on the two greatest regional military powers of the era at the points of greatest enemy strength. Along the way, AP matter-of-factly notices the transformations at home: actions taken against racial discrimination at work, the mobilization of black servicemen, the vast expansion of American industry made possible by women in the workplace. The darkest aspects of the war at home and abroad are covered in "real time" as well—America's internment of Japanese Americans; the dire and credible warnings of the Holocaust reaching the West in late 1942; the fact of total war, culminating in Germany's crushing defeat on the ground and in the air in early 1945; and the atomic bombardment of Japan.

President Harry S. Truman awards the Distinguished Service Medal to General Dwight D. Eisenhower at a White House ceremony held in the Rose Garden, June 18, 1945. Mamie Eisenhower stands to the left of the president.

Victory enables readers to appreciate the sheer scale and impressiveness of the American war effort, and hence the great renewals and affirmations we experienced, on which so much that we call positive about this country has been based. More than anything, the confidence inspired by victory was the critical psychological boost for decades of ever-expanding postwar prosperity. America's crusade against fascism and racism abroad could not but inspire an unfinished crusade at home to strengthen a society dedicated to liberty and justice for all. For, in the final analysis, the thread of self-confidence that runs through *Victory*, covering America's war for human rights, has been the indispensable ingredient necessary for the startling postwar advances in civil rights and human rights, the indispensable ingredient of a national postwar culture that has become a kind of global culture. It is, too, the critical element in our technological achievements, ranging from landings on the moon to the inventiveness of the American private sector on which the hopes and dreams of peoples around the world still depend.

And the war surely demonstrated the kind of kinship possible among faraway peoples. As *Victory* shows, Americans saw their own future bound up in the futures of Asia and Europe and Africa. Americans perceived a like-mindedness in the opponents of Axis aggression. To paraphrase Dwight D. Eisenhower's famous 1945 address at the Guildhall in London, Americans accepted as fact that peoples separated by distance, size, and history were linked by a common dedication to freedom of worship, equality before the law, and the liberty to act and speak as one saw fit, subject only to provisions that one not trespass on the similar rights of others—and we stood ready to fight for these things. Such was proven by the events covered in *Victory*: facts proven in North Africa, in Italy, in the Solomon Islands, on D-Day, and in the dozens of other battles fought in dozens of theaters around the globe.

With the passage of 75 years, as large and as immediate as World War II seems, that conflict has receded into history. The generation of wartime leaders has long since passed away and the generation that fought the conflict is all but gone; gone also are many of the political and strategic verities of the era. Yet the fascination remains, because the lessons endure: the lesson by—or reminder of—the America covered in *Victory* that given a choice, people will choose freedom and the opportunity to live by the principles of freedom, and free societies, because of their dynamism and their principles, will always prevail.

—**David Eisenhower**
September 2020

Preface
REPORTING THE WAR

Herewith is the epic story of World War II: the story that civilians on the home front read day by day in their newspapers as reported by war correspondents and photographers of The Associated Press.

At the outset of this project, historian Alan Axelrod provided us with an outline of important, pivotal events in the war, which I used to compile the articles from wartime newspapers that make up the bulk of this book. While pulling the articles, I was struck by the fact that the historical outline and the newspaper stories often differed (something I was aware of intellectually, but never realized to what degree until working on *Victory*); some of the stories hardly made the papers at the time of the events. This wasn't poor journalism, it was *wartime journalism*, and it was done that way for a good reason—which is a story in itself:

On Jan. 15, 1942, a month after America's entry into the war, a Code of Wartime Practices for the American Press was issued by the Office of Censorship, and in June of that year, the U.S. Office of War Information (OWI) was created. Together, these developments set forth guidelines for the content of the news that stated that no coverage of the war should benefit the enemy. The code noted that "the security of our armed forces and even of our homes and liberties will be weakened . . . by every disclosure of information"—be it related to the activities and identities of Allied troops or even weather reports that covered more than four adjoining states outside of a 150-mile radius—for fear that such disclosures might facilitate enemy military operations. In general, the news was supposed to accentuate the positive and minimize the negative both for the sake of GIs on the battlefront and for civilians on the home front consuming war news.

These news-reporting guidelines, for the large part, were voluntary, heavily relying on reporters' and editors' patriotism. Among the concessions were delaying battle reportage for 24 hours, eliminating casualty counts and banning photographs of Allied war dead, censoring troop movements, and maintaining confidentiality of the whereabouts of important Allied leaders, including Gen. Dwight D. Eisenhower, President Franklin D. Roosevelt, and Prime Minister Winston Churchill. Other provisions ranged from the very specific, such as not reporting factory output, to the broadest, including handling the obvious—and not so obvious—enemy propaganda aimed at GIs and the folks at home.

While the accuracy of the news was a concern for all, it was fortunate that at its forefront was one of America's top journalists, Byron Price, the executive news editor of The Associated Press and the pre-war head of its Washington news bureau. Twelve days after Pearl Harbor, Price was appointed by President Roosevelt's administration as the U.S. Director of Censorship. He quickly established advisory panels in an effort to reasonably balance news reportage without misleading the public, including administering newspaper and radio codes of conduct. In 1944, Price earned a special Pulitzer Prize for his diligence and was later presented the Medal for Merit by President Harry S. Truman in 1946 for his wartime efforts.

The day after the Japanese surrendered on Aug. 14, 1945, Price happily hung a sign in front of his censorship office that read: "Out of Business."

—Les Krantz, Facts That Matter, Inc.
Producer and Developer, *Victory: World War II in Real Time*

ABOVE: Byron Price, right, wartime chief of censorship, is congratulated by President Harry Truman at the White House after receiving the Medal for Merit for his services during the war, Jan. 15, 1946. OPPOSITE, TOP: A poster issued by the WPA War Services of Louisiana c. 1942, warning against careless correspondence between civilians and military personnel; BOTTOM: AP war correspondent Daniel De Luce, attached to the Chinese army and the U.S. Army Air Forces in China, walks through a street in Yenangyaung, Burma, July 20, 1942. Dark smoke in the background billows from burning oil fields.

"CENSORED"

EXAMINED BY 42

Pvt. John Doe
U.S. Army.

FREE

Mrs. John Doe
1000 Silence St.
New Orleans, La.
U.S.A.

LET'S CENSOR OUR CONVERSATION About the WAR

W.P.A. WAR SERVICES of LA

Publisher's Note

The newspaper articles in this book date from 1939 through 1945. We have largely reproduced the transcriptions of the newspaper articles as they first appeared in publication, however we have corrected some typographic errors and standardized the formats of some parts of the texts.

Also please be aware that because we are presenting the newspaper articles and photographic reproductions of newspaper front covers in their original state, some of the articles and headlines contain language that today is considered racially or ethnically insensitive or inappropriate.

Finally, note that some of the articles have been slightly abridged for space considerations.

—**Barbara Berger**
Executive Editor, Sterling Publishing Co., Inc

LEFT: The scene in an improvised bomb-proof field HQ in North Africa, April 1, 1943—AP war correspondent Hal Boyle (center, at typewriter) writes a dispatch on North African fighting while AP photographer Harrison Roberts (second from right) removes film from his camera. Lt. Joseph E. Schmidt (left foreground), a public relations officer, puts copy into a dispatch bag as Capt. Jay R. Vessels (left rear), on military leave from the AP, checks air transport command on a field phone. Irving Smith (right) prepares caption material for his film.

ABOVE: Bill Boni, AP war correspondent, types out his firsthand account of the American landing at Saidor, New Guinea, in the "press room"—the jungle on the beach—January 1944. RIGHT: AP photographer Edward Widdis sits on top of his jeep, camera at the ready, during troop exercises in New Guinea, May 30, 1943.

ABOVE: On June 11, 1944, staff in the AP's Washington, D.C., bureau view a layout of 153 pictures sent over wirephoto during the first four and a half days of the D-Day invasion (June 6–June 10, 1944).

LEFT: AP war correspondent Bill Boni grins at the photographer while being carried on a stretcher, New Guinea, Aug. 5, 1943. He was wounded by Japanese shell fragments while in a landing craft off New Guinea, for which he was awarded a Purple Heart.

RIGHT: AP staffer Ed Ball jumps over a muddy road in an unidentified location in the European theater, Feb. 12, 1945.

ABOVE: Five AP war correspondents profiled in a March 1943 issue of *Cosmopolitan* magazine that paid tribute to war correspondents "scattered throughout the world's fighting fronts." Pictured here, from left to right: Vern Haugland, whose 43-day trek through the jungles of New Guinea is an epic of the war; Edward Kennedy, who ducked bombs in the Balkans and in Egypt (and who would later break the story of Germany's surrender, see page 178); Charles McMurtry, who was severely burned while pulling several sailors to safety during a kamikaze attack on USS *Hornet* in the Pacific; Larry Allen, who was captured by the Italians from a sinking British destroyer during a raid on Tobruk; and Clark Lee, who "saw action in more different theaters of war than any other man."

BELOW: AP war correspondent Don Whitehead, known as "Beachhead Don," is seen on a panzer tank en route to the U.S. 9th Armored Division in Saxony, Germany, Aug. 18, 1945, more than three months after the Germans surrendered. Whitehead covered almost every important Allied invasion and campaign in Europe.

Introduction

OTTO VON BISMARCK was a power in German politics before there even was a Germany; he served as Prussia's foreign minister (1862–90) and minister president of Prussia (1873–90). From these positions he guided the nineteenth-century wars that rallied the disparate German states to consolidate around Prussia as the first unified German empire since the Middle Ages. Having achieved imperial preeminence in Europe, Bismarck wove an intricate web of alliances to maintain it. Some of these were grand public affairs. Others were top secret. Both, Bismarck believed, would bind all Europe to Germany.

Many contemporaries credited Bismarck with making Europe more peaceful and prosperous than it had ever been. Late in life, however, Bismarck himself was said to have expressed doubts about lasting peace; perhaps apocryphally, he is said to have exclaimed that if a general war began, it would be because of "some damned foolish thing in the Balkans." Because Bismark died in 1898, he himself did not witness the final work of the web he had woven. He was gone before Gavrilo Princip, a young Bosnian Serb nationalist, murdered the heir to the Austro-Hungarian throne, Archduke Franz Ferdinand, and his wife, Sophie, in Sarajevo on June 28, 1914. He was not alive to see that event set into motion a sequence of ultimatums, mobilizations, and acts of war, which, through the very system of treaties and secret side agreements his diplomacy had created or inspired, plunged Europe and then much of the world into global conflagration.

That conflict of 1914 to 1918 began as the "Great War," but by the time the United States joined the battle in 1917, it had become a world war. It was ended by armistice on Nov. 11, 1918, having killed approximately 20 million troops and civilians. The thought of another such war, a *second* world war, was too awful to contemplate. So, the political leaders of the four major powers that had defeated Germany and its allies gathered in Paris to hammer out a peace treaty intended to ensure that *this* war would be "the war to endall wars"—a phrase most closely associated with novelist H. G. Wells and U.S. president Woodrow Wilson but widely uttered throughout the conflict.

Tragically, what Wilson, Britain's David Lloyd George, France's Georges Clemenceau, and Italy's Vittorio Orlando created was the 1919 Treaty of Versailles, a document intended to punish and permanently cripple Germany and the nations that had supported it. Thanks to this, the 1914–18 conflict became the war to end all peace.

Versailles did not just humiliate Germany, it impoverished it, creating conditions that strangled the struggling new Weimar Republic democracy in its cradle and bred the desperate political and economic environment in which a hate-mongering political opportunist named Adolf Hitler rose to power. In 1920, the National Socialist German Workers' Party—the NSDAP, or Nazi Party—was one of scores of obscure cultish political organizations in a chaotic Germany. Hitler joined it, dominated it, and, by the elections of 1932, had led it to a plurality in the

Members of the Nationalist Socialist German Workers' (Nazi) Party cheer their leader, Adolf Hitler, as he leaves the Hotel Kaiserhof in Berlin, following his appointment by President Paul von Hindenburg as chancellor of Germany, Jan. 30, 1933.

Reichstag, forcing eighty-five-year-old president Paul von Hindenburg to appoint Hitler chancellor on Jan. 30, 1933.

In the parliamentary elections of March 5, 1933, the Nazis skyrocketed to 44 percent of the vote, which Hitler used to usurp total control of the Reichstag. On March 23, he pushed through that body the Enabling Act, by which the government he now controlled was "enabled" to issue decrees independently of the Reichstag and Hindenburg. Becoming Germany's dictator, Hitler used his absolute authority on July 14, 1933, to proclaim the Nazi Party the nation's only political party. Upon Hindenburg's death on Aug. 2, 1934, Hitler appointed himself the Führer—absolute leader—of Germany.

Business and industry effectively became the Führer's strategic and political partners. In defiance of the Treaty of Versailles, Hitler rearmed the nation, not only expanding Germany's military—even as the world's democracies reduced theirs—but obscenely enriching the industrialists while also lifting the nation's economy out of its postwar recession and the global depression of the 1930s. He also united Germans against what he relentlessly portrayed as their common enemy: the Jews.

On April 1, 1933, the Nazis instituted a nationwide boycott of Jewish businesses, followed days later by the expulsion of Jews from the civil service and, days after this, restrictions on Jewish attendance at public schools and universities. On Sept. 15, 1935, the Reichstag enacted the Nuremberg Laws, which provided the legal framework for systematic anti-Semitic disenfranchisement throughout Germany. The pre–World War II culmination of this persecution came on the night of November 9, 1938, in a Nazi-orchestrated national riot throughout Germany, Austria, and the Sudetenland, during which hundreds of synagogues and more than 7,500 Jewish-owned businesses, homes, and schools were burned down, plundered, or destroyed. So much window glass lay shattered in the streets that the event became known as Kristallnacht ("Crystal Night," or the Night of Broken Glass), and was marked by the mass arrest of some 30,000 Jewish men, who were summarily packed off to concentration camps. Early reports estimated 91 deaths, although the actual number is believed to be much higher.

A cozy relationship between business and state prevailed in Fascist Italy, as it did in Nazi Germany, bringing an unaccustomed prosperity to the country and reinforcing support for Benito "Il Duce" (The Leader) Mussolini—who had been absolute dictator since 1922. Mussolini had visions of recreating in modern Italy the glory that had prevailed in the ancient Roman Empire, and invaded Ethiopia on Oct. 2, 1935. The country's exiled emperor,

German troops in Vienna parade past Maj. Gen. Fedor von Bock, one of the commanders of the Nazi occupation and annexation of Austria, March 24, 1938.

Haile Selassie, made an impassioned plea for aid to the League of Nations, which denounced Italy but soon proved powerless to stop the conquest.

AMERICANS SENSED THE STIRRINGS of a new major war. This time, however, they were determined to keep out of it. Congress passed the Neutrality Act of 1935 on August 31, imposing a general embargo on trade in arms and war materials and warning American citizens who booked passage on ships of belligerent nations that they traveled at their own risk.

Throughout most of the 1930s, Americans were focused mainly on the ongoing crisis of the Great Depression at home. When they did look abroad, their glance was mainly toward Europe, which they saw as a stage on which a contest between Soviet communism on the one hand and fascism and Nazism on the other was being played out. The epicenter of this drama was Spain, where the Spanish Civil War erupted on July 17, 1936, and would not end until April of 1939. President Franklin Roosevelt declared absolute U.S. neutrality in the conflict, but some 3,000 idealistic young Americans enlisted in the International Brigade to fight against the fascists. Most of these volunteers were members of the American Communist Party.

A minority of Americans turned from Europe to the rising militarism of Japan. The focus was on the Japanese invasion of China and especially on the brutal Battle of Shanghai (Aug. 13 to Nov. 26, 1937), which was covered by numerous Western newsreel and newspaper photographers. Images of the Japanese bombardment of Shanghai in August and October of 1937 were shattering.

Despite graphic coverage of the fighting in China, few Americans seriously believed the United States would ever become involved. The more imminent threat came from Europe, where, on March 12, 1938, Germany annexed Austria in the Anschluss ("connection" or "union"). As many Americans saw it, the Anschluss empowered both Austria and Germany, effectively nullifying the Allied victory in the World War.

THE ANSCHLUSS WAS FOLLOWED by Hitler's demand that Czechoslovakia, a nation created by the Treaty of Versailles, cede to Germany its German-speaking region, the Sudetenland. Both France and England were bound by the treaty to defend Czech sovereignty, but neither nation wanted to risk war with Germany. On Sept. 29/30, 1938, British prime minister Neville Chamberlain joined Édouard Daladier of France and Benito Mussolini of Italy in Munich to negotiate with the Führer. Notably, Czech leaders were not invited.

When Hitler proved adamant in his demand for annexation, Chamberlain decided to "appease" him by giving him the Sudeten region in exchange for his pledge to seek nothing further. With that, the prime minister returned to London, stepped down from the airliner, waved a scrap of paper in the air, and announced that he had returned with "peace for our time."

Winston Churchill, then no more than a Conservative backbencher in the House of Commons—an unheeded agitator for British rearmament—delivered a speech to the House on Oct. 5 condemning Chamberlain's so-called peace as a "total and unmitigated defeat." Yet no less a figure than Franklin Roosevelt himself, on the eve of Chamberlain's departure for Munich, sent the prime minister a telegram encouraging his clear intention to appease Hitler. It consisted of just two words: "Good man."

In fact, during Roosevelt's first two terms in the 1930s, Congress passed four Neutrality Acts, including the 1935 act (see left column on this page). The 1936 act prohibited extending loans or credit to any belligerent in a foreign war, and the 1937 act barred trading arms with Spain during the civil war there. But Roosevelt came increasingly to see U.S. interests as aligned with the opponents of fascism and Nazism. Accordingly, he began enforcing the Neutrality Act of 1937 very selectively, to favor China against Japan. More important, he supported the provision in the 1937 law that authorized him to permit arm sales on a strict cash-and-carry basis. When the fourth Neutrality Act was passed in 1939, FDR lobbied Congress to renew the cash-and-carry provision but was refused.

President Roosevelt lived with the new restrictions of the 1939 law but began a covert correspondence with Churchill in September 1939, immediately after German forces invaded Poland and started the war. At the time, Churchill was First Lord of the Admiralty in the Chamberlain War Cabinet, but the correspondence intensified beginning in May 1940, when Churchill replaced Chamberlain as prime minister.

June 1940 brought the fall of France, which rapidly accelerated the decline of isolationism in America. About to run for an unprecedented third term, FDR named two prominent pro-intervention GOP leaders, Henry L. Stimson and Frank Knox, as his secretaries of war and the navy, respectively. With bipartisan support, the president secured congressional funding for a crash military buildup and, in September, signed the nation's first peacetime draft into law.

FDR also deliberately violated the 1939 Neutrality Act by supporting Britain with his Destroyers for Bases Agreement (see page 15). On Dec. 29, he broadcast a speech in which he announced his intention to make America the "Arsenal of Democracy" for Britain and other allies. This was followed on Jan. 6, 1941, by his articulation of the "Four Freedoms" in his State of the Union Address. Freedom of speech and of worship, and freedom from want and from fear, he declared, were American rights and should be regarded as human rights "everywhere in the world."

Throughout 1941, FDR moved closer and closer to war and repeatedly secured more military funding. Indeed, although the Japanese attack against Pearl Harbor on Dec. 7, 1941, was a surprise, it propelled the United States into war far better prepared to fight than it had ever been in its 165-year history.

FROM THE MOMENT of the nation's entry into World War II, President Roosevelt cultivated a frank approach to the American people. "We are now in this war," he explained in his Fireside Chat broadcast of Dec. 9:

We are all in it—all the way. Every single man, woman, and child is a partner in the most tremendous undertaking of our American history. We must share together the bad news and the good news, the defeats and the victories—the changing fortunes of war.

So far, the news has been all bad. . . .

And so he shared the war news, bad and good, just as the free people of the United States expected him to do and just as they demanded and expected the free American press to do, day after day and in real time.

President Franklin D. Roosevelt in the Oval Office during his Fireside Chat "On the Declaration of War with Japan" on Dec. 9, 1941. FDR wears a black mourning armband for his mother, who died on Sept. 7.

CHAPTER ONE

1939

"**P**eace for our time," British prime minister Neville Chamberlain had promised in September 1938, on returning from his conference with Hitler in Munich. There, desperate to at least delay a war for which Britain was woefully unprepared, he "appeased" Hitler by handing him the Czech Sudetenland in exchange for the Führer's promise to seek no further conquest.

On March 15, the Reich bit off and gulped down what remained of Czechoslovakia, annexing Bohemia and Moravia-Silesia in blatant violation of the Munich Agreement. The very next day, Germany created the Protectorate of Bohemia and Moravia, obliterating with the stroke of a pen the short-lived Second Czechoslovak Republic.

Also on March 16, German-aligned Hungary annexed Carpatho-Ukraine, and four days later, Germany's foreign minister Joachim von Ribbentrop demanded that Lithuania cede the Baltic port of Klaipeda and the surrounding region (the Memel Territory, which the Germans called Memelland). Though obligated by treaty to defend Klaipeda, Britain and France made no response to the German demand. Memelland was annexed to East Prussia on March 23.

One day after the Memel ultimatum, on March 21, Hitler demanded that the strategic Baltic port of Danzig (present-day Gdansk, Poland), proclaimed an autonomous city-state after World War I, be returned to Germany. The League of Nations, sworn to protect the independence of Danzig, made no response, and pro-Nazi German residents of Danzig agitated for annexation. By the end of March, however, France had joined the U.K. in a guarantee of Polish independence, thereby making any German aggression against that country a cause for war. On April 3, Hitler ordered his generals to prepare Fall Weiss (Plan White), the invasion of Poland.

In the meantime, the Fascist "Duce" (leader) of Italy, Benito Mussolini, ordered an invasion of Albania during April 7–12, which led to that country being annexed to Italy. On April 14, an alarmed U.S. president Franklin D. Roosevelt sent letters to Hitler and Mussolini calling for peace. Four days later, the USSR approached France and Britain with a proposal for a three-way pact. It was rejected, even as Hitler, on April 28, renounced the German-Polish Non-Aggression Pact of 1934 and the Anglo-German Naval Agreement of 1935, a treaty limiting the size of the Nazi navy, the Kriegsmarine.

On May 17, Hitler offered nonaggression pacts to Sweden, Norway, and Finland, all of which rebuffed him; but on May 22, he and Mussolini concluded the "Pact of Steel." Publicly, it proclaimed nothing more than "trust and cooperation" between the two nations, but a "Secret Supplementary Protocol" created a military and economic union.

After much delay, Britain's Neville Chamberlain responded on July 10 to Hitler's March 21 demand to annex Danzig by rejecting the Führer's contention that the fate of Danzig was an internal German-Polish affair and reaffirmed that the U.K. would come to

Poland's aid in the event of German aggression against that nation. It was now clear that battle lines had been drawn, and Europe was on the verge of the second great war in a generation. But few expected what came next.

On August 23, headlines of news stories breathless with disbelief announced that the foreign secretaries of the Soviet Union and Germany had signed the Molotov-Ribbentrop Pact, in which the two nations pledged mutual nonaggression. The shock was that Soviet Communism and German Fascism/Nazism were ideologically, politically, and (as many saw it) morally irreconcilable. The anti-fascist leaders and peoples of the world, especially in the democracies, had counted on Stalin's unshakeable opposition to Hitler, which they believed would ultimately check German aggression. The pledge of nonaggression dashed this hope.

How much greater the shock would have been had the democracies known the content of the pact's secret provisions, which called for the division of Eastern Europe between the Soviet Union and Germany, with joint occupation of Poland and Soviet occupation of the Baltic States as well as of Finland and Bessarabia. Those secret portions of the pact were nothing less than a joint venture agreement for European conquest.

Secret, too, was a document drawn up earlier in the month, on Aug. 2. It was a letter drafted by Leo Szilard, a physicist newly fled from Hungary to the United States to escape anti-Semitic perse-cution. It was elaborated upon and endorsed by Albert Einstein, a Jewish refugee from Hitler's Germany who, ensconced at Princeton University, was the world's most famous and revered living scientist. The addressee of the letter was President Franklin D. Roosevelt, and its subject was an urgent warning that German scientists were hard at work harnessing the explosive power of the atom to make nuclear weapons. Roosevelt heeded the warning and, later, authorized one of history's costliest, most massively complex scientific and technological endeavors, the Manhattan Project, which produced the weapons used against Hiroshima and Nagasaki.

On Aug. 30, Hitler issued an ultimatum to Poland, demanding the return of Danzig and a plebiscite on possession of the "Polish Corridor" that would give Germany access to the Baltic. Absent a response from Poland, Gestapo agents staged an attack on a German radio transmitter at the German town of Gleiwitz (modern-day Gliwice, Poland), on the Polish frontier. They arrested a Silesian Polish-sympathizer outside of Gleiwitz, and, on the night of Aug. 31, dressed him in the uniform of a Polish soldier and gave him a lethal injection. He was then taken to the transmitter station, where he was shot. The next day, Sept. 1, Adolf Hitler announced to the Reischstag and to the world that "Polish soldiers" had been shot during an unprovoked attack by the Polish army on German territory.

Thus, Hitler justified a titanic invasion of Poland by some 1.5 million troops, unimpeded by the Soviet Union. They were hopelessly opposed by the 800,000 men of the Polish army, whose valiant resistance, outmanned and outgunned, was doomed. The country was soon overrun by blitzkrieg (lightning war), which hit with unparalleled speed, violence, and the brilliant coordination of infantry, armor, and aircraft. On Sept. 3, with Poland all but defeated, France and Britain declared war on Germany. World War II had begun.

Hitler (left, under the end of the long-range gun barrel) inspects fiercely contested Oxhoeft (Oksywie), near Gdynia, Poland, one of the last areas of resistance after the Nazi invasion of that country, Sept. 21, 1939.

Corsicana Daily Sun, Corsicana, TX, Wednesday, March 15, 1939

HITLER GRABS CZECH NATION

German Commander Taxes – Executive Power in Bohemia

PRAGUE, March 15 (AP)—General Johannes Blaskowitz, commander of group three of the German army, proclaimed to the people of Bohemia today that he had taken the executive power into his hands on orders from Chancellor Hitler.

General Blaskowitz appointed the Sudeten Nazi Leader Konrad Henlein as chief of the civil administration of Bohemia.

Henlein, instrumental in bringing about the German annexation of Sudetenland last October, asked the whole Bohemian administrative machinery—police, postal, railway and state affairs—to continue its work.

German troops of occupation were hissed and cheered today as they moved into positions of control in the once proud capital of free Czecho-Slovakia.

Cheers of German welcomers were interspersed with the hissing of Czech patriots and cries of "pfui, pfui, go back home!" Some patriots sang the Czech national anthem. Two persons were reported struck by German military automobiles. There were no serious disorders, however.

End of Czech Sovereignty

The entry of Adolf Hitler's battalions marked the end of Czech sovereignty in the shattered republic which dissolved yesterday after [the] Hitler-inspired secession of Slovakia which followed in the wake of the Munich dismemberment.

The easternmost division of Czecho-Slovakia—Carpatho-Ukraine—was being occupied by Hungarian troops. German occupation of the Czech western part, Bohemia and Moravia, was agreed upon in Berlin last night when Emil Hacha, former Czech president, placed the area under Hitler's protection.

Hitler was on the way to join his marching legions.

Huge crowds were massed along the central streets of Prague as the troops, in four groups, moved in.

Get Bronx Cheer

At times the "Pfui's"—continental version of the Bronx cheer—were so loud they could be heard blocks away. The crowds grew more demonstrative as the troops increased in number.

Here and there the troops were encouraged by cries from German crowds wearing swastika armbands.

Before the ancient Rathaus (city council building) a large German delegation had gathered, bearing a swastika banner of heroic size which the Nazis like to hang from their public buildings. But it was the only one in sight.

No flags of any sort decorated the houses or streets. Some street cars flew various flags but they were the Czech colors, such as would be flown on a national holiday.

It was the most lifeless and colorless reception that Reichsführer Hitler's troops had received since the Führer started his expansion program.

The contrast between today's reception and the flowers and kisses with which Nazi troops were welcomed when they occupied Sudetenland last October was most striking.

LEFT: Mechanized units rumble across the Czech border, March 17, 1939, several days after Hitler claimed executive power in the Czech Lands and established it as a Nazi territory, the Protectorate of Bohemia and Moravia.

Czech subjects watch in despair, booing "Pfui, pfui, go back home!" as German motorcycle units
roll into their capital, March 15, 1939.

Nashville Banner, Nashville, TN, Thursday, March 16, 1939

ABSTRACT OF HITLER PROCLAMATION ON STATUS OF NEW PROTECTORATE

PRAGUE, March 16 (AP)—Following is an abstract of Chancellor Hitler's proclamation of protectorate over Bohemia and Moravia, delivered by German Foreign Minister Joachim von Ribbentrop.

For a thousand years Bohemian and Moravian lands were part of the living space of the German people. But force and lack of reason tore them arbitrarily from their old historic environment and finally, through their inclusion in the artificial formation of Czecho-Slovakia, created a center of disturbance.

At any time from this space a new and formidable threat to European peace was bound to arise. This had happened once before. That is because the Czecho-Slovak state and those in charge of it did not succeed in the sensible organization of the common life of national groups, which were arbitrarily united within its borders, and thereby in awakening and maintaining the interests of all concerned in maintaining this common state.

Thereby the Czecho-Slovak state proved its inability to live and actually fell to pieces.

The German Reich, however, could not tolerate lasting disturbances in these regions which are so important to its own peace and security as well as to the general welfare and the general peace.

Sooner or later Germany was the power most strongly interested, through its historical and geographical position and, as the power most seriously affected, was destined to bear the most serious consequences.

"Law of Self-Survival"

It is therefore by the law of self-survival that the German Reich is determined to intervene decisively again to erect the foundations of reasonable Central European order and proclaim decrees accordingly.

Germany already has proven in its 1,000-year-old historical past that, by reason of its size and the characteristics of the German nation, it alone is predestined to solve these problems.

Filled with an earnest desire to serve the true interests of the peoples dwelling in this living space, to safeguard the national and individual characteristics of the German and Czech peoples, to serve the peace and social welfare of all, I therefore decree in the

German troops march into Brno, Czechoslovakia, March 16, 1939.

name of the German Reich as the basis for the future cooperation of the inhabitants of this territory the following:

FIRST—Those lands of the former Czecho-Slovak Republic which were occupied by German troops in March of 1939 belong henceforth to the territory of the Greater Reich and come under its protection as "the Protectorate of Bohemia and Moravia." Insofar as the defense of the Reich demands, the Fuehrer will decree regulations for individual sections of this area.

SECOND—German inhabitants of the protectorate become German subjects and, under the stipulations of the Reich's citizenship law of September 1935, they become citizens.

Accordingly, provisions for the protection of German blood and German honor also apply to them. They are under the jurisdiction of German laws and courts.

Remaining inhabitants of Bohemia and Moravia are made subjects of the protectorate of Bohemia and Moravia.

Protectorate Autonomous

THIRD—The Protectorate of Bohemia and Moravia is autonomous and administers its own affairs. It exercises sovereign rights appertaining to a protectorate in harmony with the political, military and economic needs of the Reich. These rights of sovereignty are exercised by organs of its own, by offices of its own, and by officials of its own.

FOURTH—The supreme head of the autonomous administration of the Protectorate of Bohemia and Moravia enjoys the protection and honors accorded a head of state. For execution of the duties of his office, the supreme head of the protectorate must enjoy the confidence of the Führer and Chancellor.

FIFTH—As guardian of the Reich's interests, the Führer names a Reich's protector, in Bohemia and Moravia. His official seat is Prague. This Reich's protector, as representative of the Führer and as Commissioner of the Reich's Government, has the task of seeing to the observance of the guiding political policy of the Führer. . . .

Foreign Affairs

SIXTH—Foreign affairs of the Protectorate, especially the protection of its subjects in foreign countries, are under the care of the Reich. The Reich will conduct foreign affairs in such a manner as they will harmonize with common interests. The Protectorate is accorded one representative accredited to the Reich's Government with the title of Minister.

SEVENTH—The Reich accords the Protectorate military protection. In accordance with this protection, the Reich maintains garrisons and military establishments within the Protectorate. For safeguarding domestic security and order, the Protectorate may set up its own formations. The organization and its strength in numbers and arms are determined by the Reich's Government.

EIGHTH—The Reich has direct supervision over communications and transportation, as well as the postal, telegraph, and telephone service.

NINTH—The Protectorate belongs to the customs territory of the German Reich and is under the jurisdiction of the Reich's customs sovereignty.

TENTH—Legal tender until further notice will be the Reichsmark and the Crown. The Reich's Government will determine their relative value.

ELEVENTH—The Reich may issue legal regulations for the Protectorate insofar as common interests demand. Insofar as mutual needs exist, the Reich may take over parts of the administration and for that purpose set up necessary Reich's authorities. The Reich's Government is empowered to put into effect measures necessary for maintenance of security and order.

TWELFTH—Laws now prevailing in Bohemia and Moravia remain in force insofar as they do not run counter to the spirit of the German Reich as protector of the territory.

THIRTEENTH—The Reich's Minister of Interior, in agreement with the Reich's ministers concerned, will issue the legal and administrative orders necessary for executing and implementing this decree.

(The decree was signed by Hitler; Wilhelm Frick, Minister of Interior; Joachim von Ribbentrop, Foreign Minister; and Dr. Hans Friedrich Lammers, Chief of the Reichschancellery.)

An official hangs a sign on Brno's Liberty Square with its new name, Adolf Hitler Platz, March 17, 1939.

Daily Messenger, Canandaigua, NY, Monday, May 22, 1939

GERMANY, ITALY SIGN MILITARY ACCORD

BERLIN (AP)—Germany and Italy became out-and-out military allies today with signature under the eyes of Chancellor Hitler of a "pact of alliance and friendship" decided upon in Italy two weeks ago.

Foreign Minister Joachim von Ribbentrop, who signed the pact with Italian Foreign Minister Count Galeazzo Ciano in Ambassadors' Hall of the new chancellery, immediately proclaimed the two countries "an indissoluble community of interests."

In a radio address Hitler's foreign minister declared the pact was "our determined answer" to "encirclers" of Britain and France. With Ciano he declared the agreement was aimed at world peace but meant the axis powers were ready for anything.

After the ceremony Hitler bestowed Germany's highest decoration, the golden grand cross of the German eagle, upon Count Ciano. It was the first time this decoration "in gold" had been bestowed upon a foreigner.

Applaud Pact

Enthusiastic heils for the pact appeared to have drowned out the sound of shots which heightened tension on the Danzig-Polish-German border. Nazis, however, watched the incident attentively if silently.

Apparently anxious to have the signing of the treaty completed without too much agitation of Danzig and Polish questions, the foreign office withheld immediate official comment on the border trouble in which Gustav Grueber, a Nazi butcher, was slain in Danzig territory.

Prominent among those who witnessed signing of the agreement were General Alberto Pariani, Italian undersecretary of war and army chief-of-staff; Bernardo Attolico, Italian ambassador to Berlin; Field Marshal Hermann Wilhelm Göring; and Colonel-General Walther von Brauchitsch, German army chief-of-staff.

Terms Not Published

Terms of the pact were not published immediately.

In short radio addresses after the signing, the two foreign ministers declared Italy and Germany had come to an agreement directed at preserving the peace of the world.

"We are two nations of 150,000,000, now joined together and marching toward peace," Ciano said. "But we are ready for any eventuality."

"May the world take note that this is our answer to efforts of the democratic powers to encircle Germany and Italy," said von Ribbentrop. "At the beginning of May, the Führer and Il Duce decided to conclude a political and military pact to join the two states.

"In Milan, I and the Italian foreign minister, applauded by the whole Italian people, prepared the basis for such an agreement.

"Today, about two weeks later, the whole German people welcomes the representative of Il Duce, who just now has signed this pact with me.

"This historic act is the culmination of developments growing out of the spiritual similarity between the National Socialist and Fascist revolutions.

"Germany and Italy are now one in their general interests.

"The world must take note of this fact. No power on earth and no hatred directed at us can change this fact. If the democratic warmongers attempt to create complicated and ambiguous pact systems to encircle Italy and Germany, we can say that here we are making our answer.

"This is our determined answer.

"The language is unmistakable. In the future the two nations will stand together, come what may, always ready, always extending hands towards peace, but determined with an iron will to guard and preserve our vital interests."

OPPOSITE: Huge crowds hail German and Italian leaders on the balcony of the Reich Chancellery in Berlin, May 22, 1939,
after the Pact of Friendship and Alliance ("Pact of Steel") between the two countries is signed. ABOVE: On the balcony,
front row, left to right: German foreign minister Joachim von Ribbentrop, Italian foreign minister Galeazzo Ciano, Führer Adolf Hitler,
Field Marshal Hermann Göring, and Italian undersecretary of war Alberto Pariani; back row: German navy grand admiral
Dr. H. C. Erich Raeder, German army commander in chief Walter von Brauchitsch, and German chief of the Armed Forces
High Command Wilhelm Keitel.

Chicago Tribune, Chicago, IL, Thursday, August 24, 1939

NAZIS AND RUSSIA SIGN PACT; HITLER DEFIANT ON POLAND

Berlin, Moscow Pledge to Keep Peace 10 Years

MOSCOW, Aug. 24 [Thursday] (AP)—Germany and Soviet Russia early today signed a nonaggression pact binding each of them for ten years not to "associate itself with any other grouping of powers which directly or indirectly is aimed at the other party." By the pact Reichsführer Hitler and Dictator Stalin also agreed to "constantly remain in consultation with one another" on their common interests, to adjust differences by arbitration.

The nonaggression clauses bound each power to refrain from any act of force against the other and to refrain from supporting any third party which might engage in warlike acts against either of the parties.

Contains No Escape Clause

The pact did not include an escape clause providing for its denunciation in case one of the contracting parties attacked a third power. This provision has been written into most nonaggression agreements signed in the past by Moscow.

An official communiqué announced that Foreign Minister Joachim von Ribbentrop of Germany, who arrived in Moscow by air yesterday, had a three-hour conference yesterday afternoon with Foreign Commissar Vyacheslav Molotov and Dictator Stalin. The German ambassador to Moscow, Friedrich Werner von der Schulenburg, also was present.

Von Ribbentrop and Molotov signed the pact in the presence of Stalin.

Text of Pact

The text of the pact follows:

"The German Reich's government and the Union of the Socialist Soviet Republics, moved by desire to strengthen the state of peace between Germany and the U.S.S.R. and in the spirit of the provisions of the neutrality treaty of April 1926, between Germany and the U.S.S.R., decided the following:

"ARTICLE ONE—The two contracting parties obligate themselves to refrain from every act of force, every aggressive action and every attack against one another, including any single action or that taken in conjunction with other powers.

"ARTICLE TWO—In case one of the parties of this treaty should become the object of warlike acts by a third power, the other party will in no way support this third power.

Clause for Consultation

"ARTICLE THREE—The governments of the two contracting parties in the future will constantly remain in consultation with one another in order to inform each other regarding questions of common interests.

"ARTICLE FOUR—Neither of the high contracting parties will associate itself with any other grouping of powers which directly or indirectly is aimed at the other party.

"ARTICLE FIVE—In the event of a conflict between the contracting parties concerning any question, the two parties will adjust this difference or conflict exclusively by friendly exchange of opinions or, if necessary, by an arbitration commission.

Pact Runs Ten Years

"ARTICLE SIX—The present treaty will extend for a period of ten years with the condition that if neither of the contracting parties announces its abrogation within one year of expiration of this period, it will continue in force automatically for another period of five years.

"ARTICLE SEVEN—The present treaty shall be ratified within the shortest possible time. The exchange of ratification documents shall take place in Berlin. The treaty becomes effective immediately upon signature."

The signing of the pact occurred only a few hours after von Ribbentrop reached Moscow in Reichsführer Hitler's private, swastika-emblazoned airplane. "Heil Hitler," a strange sound in the capital of Red Russia, resounded across the airport as the German embassy staff greeted their chief.

Russians gazed curiously at the swastikas. They are emblems they have been taught for years to scorn.

Soviet foreign minister Vyacheslav Molotov signs the Treaty of Non-Aggression between Germany and the Union of Soviet Socialist Republics (the Molotov-Ribbentrop Pact); Joachim von Ribbentrop and Soviet leader Josef Stalin stand behind him, Moscow, Sept. 28, 1939.

★ ★ ★ GERMANY INVADES POLAND, SEPTEMBER 1, 1939 ★ ★ ★

Paris News, Paris, TX, Friday, September 1, 1939

GERMANS OPEN WAR ON POLAND WITH ATTACKS BY LAND AND AIR

NAZIS NOT TO HAVE SUPPORT OF ITALIANS

War Not Formally Declared, But Germany Claims Victories at End of Day

BERLIN, Sept. 1 (AP)—Germany, at the end of the first day of her undeclared war on Poland, claimed victories all along the line, but especially insisted on having complete control of "Polish air."

Authorized sources insisted there was no war—but merely that a counterblow had been struck in retaliation for Thursday night's alleged Polish attack on Glewitz and for border incidents which have been occurring for weeks.

Start War Thursday

The German attack on all Polish fronts had begun at 5:45 a.m. (10:45 p.m. Thursday C.S.T.) or almost a quarter of a day before Chancellor Hitler in an impassioned 36-minute speech before the Reichstag, once more pleaded his case before the nation and the world.

In that memorable session, the Reichstag members not only unanimously pledged allegiance to their Führer, who now is also their war lord, but formally annexed Danzig to the Reich.

Hitler further declared Germany would fight against Poland alone, at least without the help of Italy, her partner in the Rome-Berlin axis.

Russia May Join

Hitler's warm endorsement, however, of Germany's non-aggression pact with Soviet Russia, and official admission a Soviet military mission is expected soon in Berlin, probably Friday, left the interpretation open that Soviet Russia may yet join Germany in a "counter-bloc" against Poland.

Germany was speedily getting down to a war basis. Through-out the day the radio instructed the populace what to do under completely altered conditions.

One of the first of many far-reaching orders was a complete blackout of the capital. The orders, effective at dusk, stand for an indefinite period.

Day Is Crowded

The day was crowded with fast-moving events. Orders of the day to the army, navy and air force admonished the nation's fighters to do all for the Fatherland. An appeal by the Reich's women's leader, Gertrud Scholtz-Klink, vied with similar appeals for support by leaders of civil servants and other organizations.

At noon Friday an official announcement said the Nazi air force had gone into action over Polish territory and that the German army was "counter-attacking" all along the German-Polish frontier.

(Warsaw was among several Polish cities that were bombed.)

German land forces, the announcement said, were determined to break all resistance.

The official statement that war was on came shortly after Führer Hitler left the Reichstag amid cheers for his declaration that he would enforce a Polish settlement or die fighting in the army gray uniform he wore.

Not Counting on Italy

In his passionate 36-minute Reichstag speech the Führer declared significantly that Germany does not count on Italian help. On the other hand, he pictured Soviet Russia as Germany's eternal friend. Hitler spoke as if war already was under way, but he did not go through the old-fashioned procedure of formally declaring war.

He inferred that the Rome-Berlin axis had been smashed. Germany, he said does not count on Italian help.

He vowed eternal friendship for Soviet Russia.

The supreme Nazi leader declared to his nation and the world that Germany would fight until the Polish government yields or is supplanted by a government that will yield.

He threatened to answer "bomb with bomb" and "gas with gas"—depending on the sort of warfare Poland wages.

Reichstag Shouts Approval

The Reichstag unanimously shouted its approval of a law annexing Danzig—original bone of German-Polish contention.

The German radio announced the League of Nations Commissioner for Danzig, Prof. Carl Burckhardt, and his staff had left Danzig.

The German swastika immediately was raised over the red brick house which had been headquarters of League Commissioners since after the World War. Danzig became a free city, under League protection and a unit of the Polish customs administration.

Hitler declared his intention to lead his forces at the front and named Field Marshal Göring as his first choice for succession to the Nazi leadership if he were killed.

He called Germany's army the best-equipped in the world and confidently assured Germany "there will not be another November 1918."

"Meet Force With Force"

A few hours earlier Hitler had ordered his mighty army to "meet force with force" and artillery fire was heard near the Polish-Silesian border.

The sound of cannonading rumbled over the Silesian fields near Gleiwitz on the Polish frontier.

The German fleet swung into action on the Baltic. It blockaded the Polish port of Gdynia, neighbor of Danzig.

German warships started clearing neutral shipping off the Baltic.

The German air defense ordered the grounding of all but military planes and threatened to shoot down the others—German and foreign.

Germany tensed herself to repel air attacks. Schools were dismissed. War conditions prevailed all along the Eastern frontier.

Numerous overnight skirmishes ushered in the heavy fighting along the Polish-German border.

Withholds Order to Strike

But Hitler withheld his order to strike in force until after dawn. Then in an order of the day to his massed force, he declared German patience had been exhausted by Polish "provocations."

Danzig, meanwhile, was cut off from telephone communication and it was assumed Poles had cut communication lines in Pomorze, the Polish Corridor, which Hitler has demanded as Germany's own.

There were no reports of Polish resistance in Danzig and it remained uncertain whether the Poles would fight for the Free City.

The proclamation by which Albert Forster, chief of state for the Nazified Free City, handed Danzig back to the Reich took immediate effect in Danzig.

Poland was declared dangerous territory for foreigners.

Despite the tension Berlin was outwardly calm. Stores were open. Housewives stood in line before the meat shops.

Many persons remained close to radios to hear the frequent news bulletins and official statements.

German soldiers tear down a barrier at the German-Polish border, Sept. 1, 1939, as the German invasion of Poland begins.

Adolf Hitler delivers his speech at the Reichstag in Berlin, Sept. 1, 1939, several hours after the Nazi invasion of Poland, declaring "to his nation and the world that Germany would fight until the Polish government yields or is supplanted by a government that will yield."

ABOVE: A crowd in Washington, D.C., outside the U.S. State Department building reads newspaper headlines of "War! Bombs Rain on Warsaw," while diplomats hold a conference on war conditions in Europe, Sept. 1, 1939.

Berlin Citizenry in Dark

But the citizenry was completely in the dark as to developments outside Germany and the zone of hostilities. "What are France and England doing?" This was a frequent question.

A government spokesman denied reports by Warsaw radio that the German air force was bombing open Polish cities, including Krakow, Katowice and Grodnow.

"Our planes bombed military objectives near these cities," the spokesman said, "but no attack was made on defenseless towns or on the Polish population."

Two War Bulletins Daily

The Propaganda ministry announced two bulletins would be issued daily, at noon and 4:30 (5 a.m. and 9:30 a.m. C.S.T.).

After telling the air force its "great hour has arrived," Field Marshal Göring, in his orders, continued:

"Fliers—in lightning attacks you will annihilate the enemy wherever he presents himself for battle or retreats in full rout! . . .

"Men of the ground organization—you will be happy conscientiously to make preparations for attacks and for the safety of your comrades in the air!

"Anti-aircraft artillerymen—you will bring down every attacker!

"Radiomen—upon you devolves the responsibility of insuring the quick and frictionless cooperation of our Air Force!

"Comrades! I look each of you in the eyes and pledge each of you to give all for the people and the Fatherland. At your head, our beloved Führer; behind you, the entire German nation united in National Socialism.

"Then there can be but one slogan for us: Victory!"

Forward with God!

General von Brauchitsch's orders said: "In the certainty of our just cause we enter the fight for a clear aim: the lasting security of German folkdom and German living space against foreign attacks and claims to power. Forward with God for Germany!"

Admiral Raeder stated: "The Führer's call has reached us. The hour of decision finds us ready to give our all for the honor, justice and liberty of our Fatherland.

"Remembering our glorious tradition, we will conduct the fight in unshakable confidence in our Führer and in firm belief in the greatness of our people and the Reich.

"Long live the Führer!"

★ ★ ★

OPPOSITE: German officers (left foreground) and Soviet officers (right foreground) salute the Nazi swastika flag during their joint parade in Brest-Litovsk, Poland (present-day Brest, Belarus) marking the withdrawal of German troops to the demarcation line secretly agreed to in the Molotov–Ribbentrop Pact, and the handover of the city to the Soviet Red Army, Sept. 22, 1939.

CHAPTER TWO

1940

The German-Soviet invasion of Poland took little more than a month in the early autumn of 1939 and killed, wounded, or captured some 875,000 Polish troops. The Soviets turned to Finland next, invading on Nov. 30, 1939, and fighting until March 13, 1940. This "Winter War" saw some of the bitterest fighting of World War II, and although the outnumbered Finns were forced to cede territory to the Soviets, they inflicted disproportionate casualties on the Red Army, killing or wounding 321,000 for a loss of 70,000 Finns.

In the Asian theater at this time, Japan intensified what historians call the Sino-Japanese War, which began on July 7, 1937, and lasted throughout World War II. Back in Europe, the British and French navies tightened their blockade of Germany, but activity on the western front was characterized by the French as the Drôle de guerre (Funny War), by Germans as Sitzkrieg (Sitting War), and by Britons as the Phoney War. In contrast to the eastern front blitzkrieg and the brutality of the Finnish and Chinese theaters, western front land operations were limited until Germany invaded France and the Low Countries beginning on May 10, 1940.

On April 9, Germany launched an airborne-led combined-arms invasion of Denmark and Norway, capturing numerous Norwegian port towns and the capital city of Oslo despite King Haakon's resistance, which did manage to delay German victory by two months. The Danish invasion moved much faster, with the nation capitulating in six hours—though a daring resistance movement was established. A Franco-British campaign to liberate Norway collapsed in May, a defeat that toppled the government of Neville Chamberlain, who was replaced as prime minister on May 10 by the far more aggressive Winston Churchill.

On the very day that Churchill assumed office, Germany invaded Belgium, France, Luxembourg, and the Netherlands. German troops crossed the French border on May 12. Two days later, the Luftwaffe obliterated the Dutch port of Rotterdam in a massive air raid, and Churchill began a desperate campaign to win alliance with Franklin Roosevelt, president of the as-yet neutral United States. The Dutch army surrendered on May 15, but the barbarity of the raid on Rotterdam persuaded Churchill to order the Royal Air Force (RAF) to begin the war's first strategic bombing campaign. RAF bombers targeted Gelsenkirchen, Hamburg, Bremen, Cologne, Essen, Duisburg, Düsseldorf, and Hanover. Simultaneously, Churchill risked a perilous flight into Paris to strategize with French prime minister Paul Reynaud, who phoned him the night before to announce that "we have been defeated."

Churchill endeavored to rally Gen. Maurice Gamelin, the French army's commander in chief, imploring him to put his "strategic reserve" into action. When Gamelin quietly admitted to having no such reserve, Churchill's heart sank. France, abjectly defeated, had the largest and best-equipped military among the Allies!

At the time, virtually the entire British professional army, some 340,000 troops, was fighting and losing alongside the French. The Germans had pushed the British Expeditionary Force (BEF) to Dunkirk on the English Channel. With nowhere to go but into the sea, Churchill authorized Operation Dynamo, a trans-Channel flotilla of hundreds of warships, commercial vessels, tugboats, yachts, and civilian pleasure craft, to evacuate the BEF to Dover. Between May 26 and June 4, the simultaneously ragtag and epic operation saved most of the BEF and occasioned Churchill's most famous parliamentary speech, in which he declared, "We shall fight on the beaches, we shall fight on the landing grounds, we shall fight in the fields and in the streets, we shall fight in the hills; we shall never surrender . . . "

While Churchill cautioned that "wars are not won by evacuations," the Dunkirk deliverance did win the cabinet's support to continue the war, despite protests from Foreign Secretary Viscount Halifax and Chamberlain, who counseled a negotiated surrender.

Pressure mounted as Italy joined the war on June 10. On the sixteenth, Marshal Philippe Pétain, aged hero of World War I, became French premier after Reynaud resigned. Two days later, a dissident brigadier general, Charles de Gaulle, formed the Comité français de la Libération nationale, a government-in-exile headquartered in London. Under Pétain, France concluded an armistice with Germany on June 22, and the nation was divided between a German-occupied northern and western region and an unoccupied southeastern rump portion nominally governed by Pétain from the spa town of Vichy.

Still under the constraints of neutrality, Roosevelt on July 10 asked Congress for massive increases in military funding; six days later, Hitler issued a directive for the plotting of Operation Sea Lion—the invasion of Britain. His plan called for air raids to destroy the RAF on the ground prior to an amphibious invasion. This aerial Battle of Britain commenced on Aug. 13. It loomed as a terribly one-sided struggle, the Luftwaffe outnumbering the RAF 2,830 to 650 aircraft. But the British pilots were tremendously skilled and flew such great fighters as the Supermarine Spitfire and the Hawker Hurricane; they also possessed patriotism matched only by their courage.

Luftwaffe chief Hermann Göring was stunned by unexpectedly heavy losses. Worse, a vengeful Hitler forced him to depart from the sound strategy of targeting RAF bases and instead ordered strategic bombing raids against London and other British cities. Beginning Sept. 7, "the Blitz" pounded the British capital and other major cities day and night for eight months and five days, killing some 43,000 British civilians, injuring at least 100,000 more, and destroying some two million British homes. Yet it failed to break Britain's war will and instead resulted in catastrophic losses to the Luftwaffe. The invasion was never launched.

In the meantime, on Sept. 2, Churchill and Roosevelt negotiated the Destroyers-for-Bases Agreement, by which neutral America "loaned" the Royal Navy fifty obsolescent destroyers in exchange for ninety-nine-year rent-free leases on Caribbean naval bases. Then, on Sept. 16, FDR signed the Selective Service Act of 1940, the first peacetime draft in U.S. history.

As America and Britain inched closer together, Germany, Italy, and Japan signed the Tripartite Pact on Sept. 27, creating the Berlin-Rome-Tokyo "Axis."

While looking toward world conquest, Hitler and his ministers also plotted the destruction of the Jews throughout that world. On Oct. 3, Warsaw's large Jewish population was forcibly concentrated into the city's medieval ghetto.

Hope in democratic Europe was at a low ebb. But when U.S. ambassador Joseph P. Kennedy Sr. told a newspaper reporter on Nov. 10 that "Democracy is finished in England," FDR, reelected to an unprecedented third term, secured his resignation. British and Indian troops had won their first major victories against Axis ground forces in Operation Compass, which spanned Dec. 9, 1940–Feb. 9, 1941; it drove Mussolini's best soldiers out of Egypt.

German troops march under the Arc de Triomphe in Paris, Aug. 2, 1940.

Decatur Herald, Decatur, IL, Friday, May 10, 1940

GERMANS INVADE LOWLANDS

100 Planes Roar Over Brussels; Troops Land

BRUSSELS (Friday) (AP)—Belgium and her lowland neighbors, the Netherlands and tiny Luxembourg, were invaded today by Germany.

Waves of German bombers and transport planes launched the newest Nazi blitzkrieg in the dark hours before dawn, realizing Belgium's worst fears since the European conflict started Sept. 1.

More than 100 German planes roared over Brussels, the capital. The Brussels airport was subjected to heavy bombing.

German troops were landed by parachute at Hasselt, in eastern Belgium, while reports of other troop landings could not be confirmed immediately.

The situation still was unclear at 6 a.m. (11 p.m. C.S.T.) and it was not known whether Belgium was at war.

The sound of anti-aircraft fire made it appear war had begun.

The Brussels radio announced that German troops crossed the frontier of Belgium at four points. The Belgian foreign ministry said the invasion was launched by bombardment of the Brussels airport. Great clouds of smoke could be seen rising from the airport while anti-aircraft batteries kept up continual pounding against the invaders.

The defense ministry immediately declared a "state of alarm" throughout the nation which in the world war learned the tragic cost of a German invasion.

Unconfirmed reports said that the neighboring grand duchy of Luxembourg, wedged between the warring powers, also had been invaded.

Parachute troops landed at Hasselt, in eastern Belgium.

The Belgian cabinet went into emergency session as soon as the first news came through that the Netherlands was invaded.

Reports from the Netherlands said the Dutch quartermaster general had announced German troops crossed the Netherlands frontier at 3 a.m. (8 p.m. C.S.T.).

Several houses around the Brussels airport were destroyed.

BERLIN (Friday) (AP)—D.N.B., official German News agency, announced today that the "Reich's government has submitted to the Royal Belgium and Royal Netherlands governments a memorandum where in the Reich's government announced that she

ABOVE: A military map from the *San Pedro News Pilot*, San Pedro, California, depicting the German invasion of the Low Countries, May 11, 1940.

OPPOSITE: German soldiers cross the Meuse River at Maastricht in May 1940, during the German invasion of Holland.

German motorcycle troops drive around street barricades during their advance into Luxembourg, May 10, 1940.

GERMANS OVER ENGLAND

LONDON (Friday) (AP)—British anti-aircraft batteries went into action early today at several points on the Thames Estuary when five planes, believed to be Heinkel bombers, were seen flying in an easterly direction.

Flashes of bursting shells were plainly visible to thousands of persons in townships near the river who were awakened by sounds of the guns. The planes were flying at an altitude of about 10,000 feet.

The firing awakened residents at 4:40 a.m., 9:40 p.m. (C.S.T. Thursday). Airplanes were heard over the vicinity and puffs of smoke were seen in the sky over the estuary.

'has evidence' that the British and French are planning to attack through their territory immediately."

D.N.B. said the evidence "unequivocally proved" that the Allied attack would be toward the Ruhr through Belgium and the Netherlands.

"The Reich's government therefore ordered German troops to safeguard the neutrality of these countries with all the military means of the Reich."

It was announced that Germany had expressed another memorandum to the Luxembourg government.

According to the agency, Germany established in her memoranda to the Netherlands and Belgium that "she is reliably informed that England and France, in pursuance of their policy of expansion of the war, have decided to attack Germany in the near future via Dutch and Belgian territories."

PARIS (AP)—The second longest air raid alarm of the war, one hour and 48 minutes, roused sleeping Paris early this morning. Anti-aircraft fire was heard above the sound of wailing sirens.

The alarm first sounded at 4:48 a.m. and ended at 6:36 a.m. (12:36 a.m. C.S.T.). It was the first alarm in Paris since Feb. 27, and the 10th of the war. Alarms also were sounded in Northern France.

★ ★ ★

The center of Rotterdam, Holland, after Germans bombarded the city on May 14, 1940. The Nazi blitzkrieg flattened buildings and sparked an inferno that destroyed most of downtown Rotterdam.

Salem News, Salem, OH, Friday, May 10, 1940

CHAMBERLAIN QUITS, CHURCHILL GIVEN JOB

Vigorous Hand Takes Helm of British State

Colton Courier
INDEPENDENT HOME PAPER FOR 10,000 PEOPLE
WORLD WIDE NEWS FROM THE ASSOCIATED PRESS

The Weather

Southern California: Fair and warm today and Saturday. Slightly cooler in the west portion.

VOL. LXIV   COLTON, CALIFORNIA,   FRIDAY EVENING, MAY 10, 1940   No. 57

CHURCHILL MADE PRIME MINISTER

NAZIS LOOSE BLITZKRIEG

Hard-hitting Lord of Admiralty Succeeds Chamberlain as Tragedy Of "Appeasement" Brings Change

Low Countries Rally Defenses Against German Invaders As Allied Forces Rush To Military Aid of Belgium and Holland

Hitler Smashes Neutral Nations With War Machine

German Air Force Spans Water Defense To Take Rotterdam

Chamberlain in Valedictory Address Appeals For United Support of Churchill and Scores Hitler for Adding to His "Horrible Crimes"

Nazi Thrust Said Halted Near Belgium Border And Holland Claims 70 German Planes Shot Down; Hitler Tells of Sweeping Advances

Fuehrer Says Fate of Nation for 1,000 Years Hinges on Campaign

Big Holland City Falls Before Surprise Attack From Nazi Air Armada

Winston Churchill leaves the Admiralty, London, May 12, 1940, two days after becoming prime minister, to go meet with King George VI at Buckingham Palace.

LONDON, May 10 (AP)—Winston Churchill, belligerent first lord of the admiralty and longtime target of Adolf Hitler's wrath, tonight became Britain's man of destiny, succeeding Neville Chamberlain as prime minister as war surged over western Europe.

The government announced "the Right Honorable Neville Chamberlain resigned the office of prime minister and first lord of the treasury this evening and the Right Honorable Winston Churchill accepted his majesty's invitation to fill the position."

"The prime minister desires that all ministers should remain at their posts and discharge their functions with full freedom and responsibility while the necessary arrangements for the formation of a new administration are made."

Chamberlain, the apostle of appeasement who saw his policy fail, and when war came expressed the hope he could carry on long enough to see Hitlerism destroyed, had been in office since May 28, 1937.

Churchill, whose mother was an American, has been first lord of the admiralty since the outbreak of the war, returning to the post he held during the world war. He is 65 years old.

Bakersfield Californian, Bakersfield, CA, Tuesday, June 4, 1940

NAZIS CAPTURE 40,000 PRISONERS, SEIZE DUNKIRK

335,000 ALLIES' TROOPS SAVED IN FLANDERS

Churchill Vows Nation Will Battle to Death, Admits 30,000 Died in Nazi Trap

LONDON, June 4 (AP)— Attacks by Royal Air Force bombers on munitions works at Mannheim, Germany, and on German troops advancing into Dunkirk and on Nazi batteries shelling the port last night were announced today by the air ministry.

LONDON, June 4 (AP)—Britain will fight from the outposts of empire, if need be alone, until "the new world" comes to her rescue, Winston Churchill told the House of Commons today. In a long war statement, during which he listed the British dead, wounded or missing in Flanders at 30,000 and the Allied rescued at 335,000, Churchill asserted Britain must carry on at all odds "until in God's good time the new world in all its strength and might sets forth to the rescue and liberation of the old."

Should England or a part of it be subjugated, he said, "then our empire across the seas, armed and guarded by the British fleet," will continue the struggle. This was seen as a possibility Canada may be used as a base against Germany.

Churchill made it plain that he "did not for a moment believe" that the Nazis could subjugate England, and he declared that Britain and France would work on together "like good comrades." However, he looked ahead to the darkest eventuality.

"We shall go on to the end," the prime minister said. "We shall fight in France. We shall fight on the seas and oceans. We shall fight with growing confidence and growing strength in the air.

"We shall defend our island whatever the cost may be. We shall fight on the beaches. We shall fight on the landing grounds. We shall fight in the fields and streets and in the hills.

"We shall never surrender and even if, which I do not for a moment believe, this island or even a part of it is subjugated and starving, then our empire across seas, armed and guarded by the British fleet, will carry on the struggle until in God's good time the new world and in all its strength and might sets forth to the rescue and liberation of the old."

He said the Allies had suffered "a colossal military disaster," that the French army had been weakened and Belgium lost.

The deliverance of the troops from Dunkirk, he said, was largely due to the work of the Royal Air Force, guarding the 220 light warships and 620 other vessels, employed in the work.

Churchill disclosed that the RAF used "part of the main metropolitan fighter strength" assigned to guard London to strike at German bombers and their protecting fighters who were harassing the movement of the troops across the channel.

He told the cheering House that Britain "shall not be content with a defensive war" and said the nation would never surrender and never give up the struggle against German tyranny.

"We will reconstitute and build up the BEF once again under its gallant commander-in-chief, Lord Gort," he said.

Against the loss of the 30,000 men, many of whom he predicted would return home safely, Churchill said, "Far heavier losses were inflicted on the enemy."

Turning to the question of home defense he said:

"We have more military forces in this country at this moment than ever before in this war or in the last."

He added, however, that "this will not continue. We shall not be content with a defensive war."

The fighting prime minister said that although some good judges had told him that 20,000 or 30,000 men might be re-embarked "it certainly seemed" as though the whole of the French First Army and the BEF north of Amiens and the Abbeville gap might be lost.

When he set the time for withdrawal a week ago, he continued, "I feared it would be my hard lot to announce the greatest military disaster in our long history."

However, he said, the Allies must be very careful not to assign "to this deliverance the attributes of a victory."

"Wars are not won by evacuations," the prime minister said.

He said the British resistance at Calais had enabled the Allies to keep the port of Dunkirk open.

Churchill said the BEF lost nearly 1,000 guns in Flanders, and said the men who were withdrawn were "brought back from the jaws of death by a miracle of deliverance."

"The whole root and core and brain of the British army around which we were to build—and are to build—the greater British armies of later years appeared about to perish or to be led into ignominious and starving captivity," said Churchill.

He acknowledged that all channel ports are in Hitler's hands and warned that "we must expect another blow will be struck almost immediately at us or at the French."

★ ★ ★

ABOVE: British Expeditionary Force (BEF) troops view the Nazi bombardment of Dunkirk from a transport after their evacuation from the French coast, June 1940.

BELOW: Allied troops wait on the beach of Dunkirk, France, for rescue ships to take them to England, June 4, 1940. Over 300,000 soldiers, cut off from retreat on land by the German invasion, were evacuated in a heroic emergency sealift code-named Operation Dynamo.

RIGHT: Captured British soldiers are led away by German troops at Dunkirk, June 1940.

BELOW: A hospital ship takes wounded from the armies of the North away from Dunkirk as columns of smoke and flame rose in the background, June 4, 1940. The ship is plainly marked with the Red Cross but has to run the gauntlet of Nazi machine-gunning planes just the same.

GERMANS IN CONTROL OF KEY CHANNEL CITY

Great Land Offensive Expected to Open on Western Front by Hitler's Legions

BERLIN, June 4 (AP via Radio)—Adolf Hitler, in a special message from his western headquarters broadcast tonight on the German radio, was declared to have "sworn to carry through the war to the final and complete annihilation of all Allied forces."

This message from the Führer's field headquarters spoke of the great battle of Flanders as "finished" and declared Allied losses in the war so far amounted to about 1,200,000 men.

By The Associated Press

BERLIN, June 4—The German high command today claimed capture of Dunkirk, Allied escape port from the Nazi trap in Flanders, and with it complete mastery of the entire French and Belgian channel coast as far south as the Somme River. The port fell after heavy fighting, a communiqué said, and the German troops captured 40,000 prisoners and "a vast amount of booty."

The communiqué said: "The fortress of Dunkirk has been taken after heavy fighting. Forty thousand prisoners and a vast amount of booty fell into our hands.

"As a result of this action, the entire Belgian and French channel coast up to the mouth of the Somme has been completely occupied by German troops."

Wait to Strike

The report that Dunkirk has been captured, following swiftly after an announcement that German troops had entered it, came as the Nazi air force, back from an "experimental" bombing of the Paris region, waited for orders to strike again in conjunction with a great land offensive which most Germans expect to start in the west any day.

Puncture of the Allied rearguard defending the withdrawal from the German pocket in Flanders was achieved in hard fighting, the high command acknowledged.

"The fight for Dunkirk is nearing its end," the communiqué declared. "Our troops penetrated into the town and captured Fort Louis from the desperately fighting enemy. House-to-house fighting is still going on with French troops whose task it was to protect the flight of the British soldiers to their vessels."

The German air raids yesterday destroyed between 300 and 400 Allied planes in hangars and on airfields in addition to shooting down 79, the communiqué reported, superseding an earlier special announcement. . . .

While getting set for the next blow, Germany took extraordinary steps in an effort to convince the United States that she has no desire to see the western hemisphere involved in the war and that she is taking unusual measures to avoid even accidental affront to America.

Charlotte Observer, Charlotte, NC, Saturday, June 22, 1940

FRANCE FACES HOUR OF BITTER DECISION

Acceptance or Rejection of Hitler's Truce Terms Hinge on Central Demand for French Facilitation of Germany's War on Her Ally Britain

BY KIRKE L. SIMPSON
Associated Press Staff Writer

The cup of defeat brewed by Nazi Germany and Fascist Italy is at the lips of France, all but helpless to thrust aside the bitter draught.

Whether she meekly accepts, or in a last gesture of defiance sends a symbol of her sovereignty into exile overseas to prolong the struggle, the immediate result must be the same for continental France herself.

She is out of the war that rages on between Britain and the Italo-German allies, except that her conquered ports and industrial centers are to be regeared by her German masters to attack England.

That is the substance of the armistice terms that Hitler personally laid before the sad-faced peace emissaries of France in historic Compiègne forest. He saw them as not humiliating to France, as granting the "soldier's peace" for which France's aged hero, Marshal Pétain, had asked.

Still a Nation

Only the heart of France, the spirit of her people that has withstood the storms of centuries to make and keep her a nation, can fittingly answer that Hitler fiat. While that spirit is resolute, France is still a nation, even in German chains.

Details of the armistice terms are not needed to illuminate the tragic hour to which France has been brought. The preamble alone tells the story of Hitler's purpose.

France is not only to be reduced to military impotency herself; she is to be hitched to the Nazi war chariot to "facilitate" Germany's war on her ally, England.

What that means in specific terms must await fuller revelation of German plans, and the reaction of Pétain and his cabinet colleagues. What it seems to mean is that France may end the bloodshed not alone by surrender of what remains of her shattered armies; she must also pledge the co-operation of her government and people in Germany's war on Britain, still France's ally.

Labor Domination Seen

It seems to spell out German operation of French industry with French labor to fashion new weapons of war against England. It seems to imply a demand that the French government mobilize for German use all French economic resources.

It hints at the spectacle of French police under Nazi domination driving French labor into French dockyards and French airplane and munition plants to turn out the ships of sea and air, and the shells and bombs, that Nazi legions will loose against England. It might even mean—as a final step to compel French enslavement to the Nazi war aims—the stark specter of starvation for non-cooperating French laborers and their families.

Whatever may be the Nazi blueprint for a new Europe to right world war "wrongs" done to Germany, it is around that central demand for French facilitation of Germany's war on England that the French decision must turn, and perhaps the destiny of Europe and the world. It is a bitter decision for proud old Pétain to make, faced by the reality that France, at most, could make only a futile gesture of defiance.

France had prepared herself for surrender. She is confronted instead with the prospect of virtual enslavement to the needs of the German-Italian war machine. Her fate is written into that terrible Point Two of the preamble of the armistice terms which Hitler holds are not humiliating.

ABOVE: Adolf Hitler (seated, second from left) and Nazi officials meet with a French delegation led by Gen. Charles Huntziger (second from right), in a railroad carriage in Compiègne Forest, France, June 21, 1940, to discuss terms before signing the Armistice of June 22, 1940.

LEFT: Hitler shakes hands with Marshal Philippe Pétain, chief of state of Vichy France, in occupied France, Oct. 24, 1940.

Greenwood Commonwealth, Greenwood, MS, Saturday, September 7, 1940

LONDON BLASTED BY GERMAN BOMBS

Hitler's Bombers in Attacks on Center of English City; Many Civilians Are Killed

LONDON, Sept. 7 (AP)—Huge waves of German bombers, attacking in groups of more than a score each, swept in against London late today and the dull boom of bombs reverberated over the city.

The sky directly over the Associated Press building, in the heart of London, was speckled with anti-aircraft bursts as nine of the raiders roared high over the center of the capital in the first attack within 16 hours. Buildings shook with the thud of bombs and the crash of anti-aircraft fire.

The waves of attackers spotted from the Associated Press office broke up into formations of five to more than 20.

The reverberations from the bombs shook the tables from which this dispatch is being written. The Associated Press building is two blocks from the Thames and a mile east of Charing Cross.

Anti-aircraft bursts spotted the sky immediately overhead like mushrooms. One group of a half dozen planes was caught in a solid ring of shell bursts from London's inner defenses. It was the heaviest attack thus far on London.

The constant chatter of the anti-aircraft batteries ceased for a few seconds and one could hear people in the streets below shouting with excitement. There must have been at least 50 dive-bombers attacking in groups of 10 over one section, while others wheeled and waited their turn in the evening sky. As the air raid continued a blanket of smoke rolled out of the east. Out of this dull canopy 35 German planes emerged in a group, wheeled leisurely to the northeast and continued on their way. Behind came 15 more planes, at about 12,000 feet.

The streets which for a time were crowded with the curious by now virtually had been deserted.

One formation of German planes flying above a balloon barrage was seen to drop 15 bombs. A moment later three British spitfires dived into them. Other bombs were heard as the aircraft disappeared. In the distance, big columns of smokes were visible.

A parachute blossomed out from one winged German machine.

By The Associated Press

LONDON, Sept. 8 (AP)—German air raiders, now shuttling back and forth across the Channel on a 24-hour-a-day schedule, smashed intently at England's northwest coast early this morning after subjecting London to its worst day and night of the war.

High explosive and incendiary bombs were showered on the coast by a formation which swept overhead just before dawn in a thunder of anti-aircraft fire.

London itself, which experienced six air raid alarms—a record—between dawn yesterday and midnight last night, was quiet during the early morning hours as Adolf Hitler's war birds struck at scattered objectives elsewhere. . . .

LEFT: Bombs dropping on Oct. 4, 1940, on the Port of Tilbury, the largest shipping center for food supplies for London during the war.

LEFT: This image captures the wreckage and enormous crater created by a bomb that fell directly in front of the main entrance to The Associated Press building on Tudor Street, London, Sept. 26, 1940; the piled sandbags outside the building saved it from sustaining much damage.

BELOW: Civilians shelter through the night in a London underground station during the Blitz, Sept. 26, 1940.

Fires started during the previous raid were still burning when the Germans swept over the city for the sixth time in less than 18 hours. Several additional blazes were set by bombs which the last wave of raiders dropped in a crowded area, but the casualties were believed relatively small.

The Germans employed a new technique in their attacks on the London area during the night, dropping flares in chains to illuminate the capital with an eerie light before unloading their bombs.

Several scream bombs were dropped by the raiders, their high-pitched shriek rising above the hammering of anti-aircraft guns. One bomb, which fell in a district hitherto untouched by the raiders, exploded near the entrance to an air raid shelter, but none of the several hundred persons within were injured.

A number of streets in one residential area were badly battered by high explosives and incendiary bombs. A resident said the Germans first set off fires with incendiaries and then used the glare to guide them in further attacks.

The almost continuous raids launched against the London area were begun at 4:50 a.m. yesterday, the first time since Sunday that the pre-dawn darkness had been broken by attack. The raiders came in masses of 300 or more, with waves of 20 or 30 planes flying over the city in relays. So fast did the raiders come that on one occasion two bombs were dropped on the edge of the metropolitan area before a warning was sounded. This occurred just before the fourth alarm, which came at 8:53 p.m.

British observers said the Germans apparently were devoting their night attacks to urban objectives and striking at Royal Air Force bases during the day in an attempt to gain supremacy of the air by knocking out the British fighter force.

★ ★ ★

OPPOSITE: King George VI, center, in uniform, and Minister of Home Security Herbert Morrison, left front, in glasses, inspect the ruins of Coventry Cathedral on Nov. 16, 1940, after the devastating raid on the Midland town.

ABOVE: A long line of mourners passes alongside the graves of those killed in the Nazi raid in Coventry, during a mass burial service, Nov. 20, 1940.

BELOW: The people of Coventry go about their business in the damaged streets of the town, Nov. 16, 1940.

★ ★ ★ SELECTIVE SERVICE ACT, September 16, 1940 ★ ★ ★

Jackson Sun, Jackson, TN, Monday, September 16, 1940

DRAFT BILL SIGNED
WITH 16,500,000 ELIGIBLE TO SERVE

U.S. Secretary of War Henry L. Stimson is blindfolded as he draws the first number from the "gold fish" bowl
for the nation's first peacetime military draft lottery at the Interdepartmental Auditorium in
Washington, D.C., Oct. 29, 1940. President Roosevelt stands behind the podium at left.

Washington, Sept. 16 (AP)—President Roosevelt signed today the peacetime draft bill making 16,500,000 men 21 through 35 years of age subject to military service.

The first contingent of 75,000 to be called up under the measure will go into uniform about a month after all the 16,500,000 are registered. Subsequent quotas will be called in blocks of 100,000 or 125,000 to a total of 400,000 about Jan. 1, and 900,000 in the spring of 1941.

Historic in its significance, the nation's first peacetime conscription was enacted finally Saturday, after extended and often bitter debate in Congress, as part of President Roosevelt's announced goal of "total defense."

The men drafted will receive initially 12 months of training. They will be liable for service anywhere in the Western Hemisphere, in the United States possessions outside the hemisphere, and in the Philippine Islands. They will get the regular army pay, which the measure raises from $21 to $30 a month for privates.

In addition to the main manpower provisions, the draft law also gives the government new and greater powers over industry in the interest of keeping armament production abreast of need. In effect the law provides that the government may take over and operate, with payment of just compensation, the factory of any manufacturer who rejects government orders or declines to give them priority. Such a manufacturer also would face possible maximum penalties of five years imprisonment and $10,000 fine. . . .

In his proclamation Mr. Roosevelt called upon "the governors of the several states and board of commissioners of the District of Columbia to provide suitable and sufficient places of registration and to provide suitable and necessary registration boards to effect such registration."

. . . He also called upon "all local officials and other patriotic citizens to offer their services as members of the board of registration."

"In order that there may be full cooperation in carrying into effect the purposes of said act," the proclamation declared, "I urge all employers, and government agents of all kinds—federal, state and local—to give those under their charge sufficient time off in which to fulfill the obligation of registration incumbent on them under the said act."

Macon Chronicle-Herald, Macon, MO,
Thursday, September 19, 1940

MOVIE STARS WILL NOT GO

Several Within Age Limits But Government Says They Are Needed

WASHINGTON, Sept. 19 (AP)—It's a good guess that none of the Hollywood handsome leading men will be drafted for the selective service list into army training camps.

The selective experts privately expressed their unofficial opinions that stage, radio, and movie stars would probably be deferred from service because of their importance to a so-called "essential industry"—essential in that it maintains civilian morale by entertainment.

Among the better Hollywood figures within the draft age are: James Stewart, Wayne Morris, Eddie Albert, Jeffrey Lynn, Lew Ayres, John Carroll, Dennis O'Keefe and Cesar Romero.

Actor Jimmy Stewart is fingerprinted at his induction into the U.S. Army Air Corps in Los Angeles, March 22, 1941.

Members of the first group to be drafted under the peacetime Selective Service Act raise their right hands as they are sworn into the U.S. Army in a ceremony performed front of Los Angeles City Hall, Nov. 18, 1940.

The president said that the registration on Wednesday, Oct. 16, would be between the local hours of 7 a.m. and 6 p.m. (local time).

On that day, he declared, every male citizen between 21 and 35, inclusive, "will be expected to report" to a neighborhood precinct to fill out a registration card and a registration certificate.

The certificate which will thereupon be issued to the individual, Mr. Roosevelt continued, will be carried by him "as a testimonial to his acceptance of the fundamental obligation of citizenship." The registration card, he explained, will be forwarded to the county clerk or similar official and delivered by him to the local selective service board. These boards, consisting of three men each . . . will be set up in more than 6,000 communities.

Then when the states notify the national director of selective service that all local boards have completed their work, the chief executive said, "a national drawing by lot will determine the order or priority of the registrants in each local board area."

The priority established by the drawing, Mr. Roosevelt added, will determine the order in which draft questionnaires will be mailed to the registrants in each community. Upon receipt of these questionnaires the registrants will enter on the questionnaires "pertinent facts" to be used in making final classifications of the registrants according to their qualifications for service.

The president said that advisory boards for registrants, "composed of patriotic citizens, civilian volunteers," will be organized in every community in the land.

Upon return of the questionnaires, Mr. Roosevelt said, the local boards, "after due consideration," will place the registrants in one of four classes. "In class one," he said, "will be those who are available for immediate service; in class two, those who are deferred because of the essential character of the service they are rendering in their present occupations; in class three, those individuals who should be deferred because of individuals dependent upon them for support; in class four, those specifically deterred by the terms of the act."

★ ★ ★

Richmond Times-Dispatch, Richmond, VA, Thursday, September 19, 1940

100 Questions Are Included in Registration

Washington (AP)—Are you a patient of an asylum? What is your income? How is your wife's health? Are you a licensed marine pilot? Do you have a hobby? Are you in jail?

These and 100 or so other questions will be asked of the 16,500,000 men of 21 through 35 who will be required to register for military service on October 16.

Although the questionnaire has not been drafted in final form, the War Department says it will follow closely the pattern of a sample questionnaire prepared some time ago for use in case of war. The sample states flatly that the "nation is at war and every registrant is thus put on notice to know his position and duty." Since this is to be a peacetime draft, the War Department says the "nation-at-war" phrase will be eliminated.

Present plans call for distribution of the questionnaires soon after registration day and for their return within five days. On the basis of the replies, the local selective service boards will determine the classification of registrants. Some will be deferred and others will be marked as eligible for immediate service.

Sample Questions

Some of the sample questions follow:

1. Have you any physical defect?

2. Are you single, married, widowed or divorced?

3. In what calling, if any, is your wife trained or skilled?

4. State your total income from all sources during the last 12 months.

5. Do you or any of your family or dependents own the house in which you live?

6. What is your usual occupation?

7. Are there any other things (including hobbies) that you do well?

8. Of what well-recognized religious sect or organization opposed to war are you a member?

9. From what port do you regularly sail? (If a licensed marine pilot).

10. Are you now authorized to preach or promulgate the doctrines of your religion? (This section applies to ministers who intend to claim deferred classification.)

Farm Substitute

11. How many years have you been engaged in agriculture (if you have) and what special training have you had?

12. Why cannot any one or more of your relatives, or some other person, continue your farm operations during your absence? (Persons employed in agricultural pursuits may claim deferred status, but the questionnaire covering this claim must be accompanied by a supporting affidavit.)

13. To what country do you owe allegiance? (If you are not a citizen of the United States you will be asked various other questions concerning the country in which you formerly resided, whether you have taken out first citizenship papers, whether your parents are naturalized, etc.)

14. Have you ever been convicted of a crime?

15. Do you claim deferred classification? If so, on which of the following grounds: physical condition, dependency, occupation, alien status, or moral unfitness.

A section of the 5,000 men who "graduated" into active duty with the motorized Fourth Division at Fort Benning, Georgia, May 3, 1941, stand in parade formation during a review. The men, from New York, New Jersey, and Pennsylvania, are the largest group of selective service trainees ever turned to duty in the U.S. Army at one time.

Decatur Herald, Decatur, IL, Saturday, September 28, 1940

JAPAN SIGNS MILITARY PACT WITH AXIS

Pact Provides Aid for All If War Expands

By LOUIS P. LOCHNER
Of The Associated Press

Berlin

Germany, Japan and Italy banded together their totalitarian arms and the energies of their quarter million people yesterday in a 10-year pact of military and economic character which means plainly that all three will help each other against the United States if any one of them becomes involved with America.

This thunderbolt of authoritarian diplomacy, conceived and stage-managed down to the names on the dotted lines by Adolf Hitler, was signed yesterday afternoon in Berlin's sumptuous new chancellery by the foreign ministers of Germany and Italy and the ambassador of Japan.

(Authoritative Associated Press sources foreshadowed the pact two days ago.)

Soviet Mentioned

The treaty itself does not mention the United States.

But this much is clear: No European power, save Soviet Russia, can ever think of attacking the signatories.

Soviet Russia, however, is specifically named in the treaty's Article 5, which says carefully that the "political status which exists now" between each of the contracting powers and the Soviet Union is in no wise affected. Germany now has a non-aggression pact with Russia.

Therefore, the United States is the only other power envisaged by Article 3 of the pact, as follows:

"Germany, Italy and Japan . . . undertake to assist one another with all political, economic and military means when one of the three powers is attacked by a power at present not involved in the European war or in the Chinese-Japanese conflict."

Russia Still on Spot

As for Russia, however, and in spite of the treaty provision, she still may find herself between two fires—Japan and Germany, with Italy on the sidelines.

The pact leaves unsaid that any contracting party can change its "present" political status in reference to the Soviet Union. In that case such a power would be free to act as it wished. Indeed, the Russian article then might not be binding on the other signatories, as well.

Hence there is no guarantee that Russia can remain out of the conflict.

Hitler, center, talks with Italian Premier Benito Mussolini, left, and Galleazo Ciano, in an armored train at Brenner Pass on the Austrian-Italian border, Oct. 22, 1940. It was the third meeting of the two dictators in that year.

Japan to Engage Fleet

In the eyes of neutral observers the clearest effect of the treaty was this: If the United States enters the European war she will be engaged immediately in the Pacific by a Japanese navy which is the third largest in the world; and so involved that the United States fleet would not be able to be of material assistance to Britain in either the Atlantic or the Mediterranean.

In the words of Foreign Minister von Ribbentrop of the Third Reich the pact also is directed against "inciters to war" over the world. A foreign office spokesman said flatly that among these "war inciters" is "a certain group in the United States."

Formally, the pact recognizes spheres of interest on the two sides of the world: Japan's "new order in Greater East Asia" and the German-Italian "new order in Europe." German spokesmen declined to give a precise definition of "Greater East Asia."

But apparently Japan is left free to determine what are to be the deciding factors in the fate of the Dutch Eastern colonies and French Indo-China. It is not clear whether Japan is to be recog- nized as the master power in so far as the Philippine islands are concerned. Africa is not mentioned.

Spain Not Mentioned

Contrary to many expectations, Spain was not even mentioned in yesterday's ceremonies. Conjecture varied between the belief that Spain is not yet ready to mortgage her future and the conviction that both the Axis and Spain are merely waiting for a psychologi- cal moment at which to spring an announcement of alliance.

It is possible that Germany, Italy and Japan are waiting to see how the South American States react to the pact of Berlin before they formally install Spain as a "bridgehead" in that direction.

The pact is effective immediately.

The Japanese ambassador to Germany, Saburo Kurusu (left, standing), reads a statement aloud during the signing ceremony of the Tripartite Pact at the Reich Chancellery, Berlin, Sept. 27, 1940. Italian foreign minister Galeazzo Ciano, center, and Adolf Hitler, right, listen.

CHAPTER THREE

1941

The year began with the aftermath of a catastrophic nighttime air raid against London, which destroyed or heavily damaged such landmarks as the Old Bailey, the Guildhall, and no fewer than thirteen Christopher Wren churches. Nevertheless, Churchill knew that every bomb dropped on London was one less bomb used against the bases of the RAF, which was shooting the Luftwaffe out of the skies while also pummeling German cities. On January 19, Churchill first publicly flashed the iconic V-for-Victory hand sign.

Earlier in the month, on January 10, the Lend-Lease bill was introduced in Congress. It would empower President Roosevelt to send food, oil, and weapons to any nation he deemed vital to America's own defense. On the twenty-third, aviator-hero and rightwing isolationist Charles Lindbergh testified before Congress, calling for a neutrality pact with Germany. Despite such isolationist opposition, FDR signed Lend-Lease into law on March 11.

In the meantime, with Europe continuing to fall under the relentless German advance, Britain mounted offensives on the war's periphery, including against Italian forces in Ethiopia and Kenya. By the end of January, the Italians were on the run. However, in North Africa, on Feb. 14, Germany's most esteemed military commander, Field Marshal Erwin Rommel, began driving the British army out of Libya and back into Egypt—for a time, at least.

Still, America continued its march from neutrality to commitment. On March 22, against conservative political opposition, the first African American unit of the U.S. Army Air Corps was activated. These so-called "Tuskegee Airmen" would form the 332nd Fighter Group and the 447th Bombardment Group, defeating foes both foreign and domestic to earn a legendary reputation in the skies of North Africa and Europe. In the next month, on April 10, U.S. forces occupied Greenland, a possession of German-occupied Denmark, securing the coast for U.S. naval and air bases. On the eleventh, the U.S. Navy began patrolling the North Atlantic, ostensibly to defend U.S. merchant vessels. Later, in July, American troops replaced British and Canadian soldiers stationed in Iceland.

Churchill welcomed these moves as hopeful portents of FDR's increasingly rapid evolution away from neutrality. In North Africa, beginning on April 10, Rommel attacked British positions at Tobruk, Libya, but was repeatedly beaten back. Also heartening was the triumphal return to Ethiopia of the exiled emperor Haile Selassie. On May 19, the Italian viceroy in that country surrendered to British forces.

The clash on the soil of many lands was counterpointed to the grim Battle of the Atlantic, in which German U-boats took a heavy toll on merchant convoys bound for Britain. The Royal Navy captured one U-boat, *U-110*, and took from it an Enigma cipher machine, enabling a breakthrough in British codebreaking that was instrumental in turning the tide of the Atlantic struggle.

Another U-Boat, *U-69*, sank the U.S. merchant vessel *Robin Moor* on May 21, prompting FDR to declare an "unlimited national emergency." Three days later, Britons were stunned by news of the sinking of the battle cruiser HMS *Hood*, with the loss of all but three of its 1,418-man crew. It fell victim to the new German battleship *Bismarck*, moving Churchill to order its destruction. The Royal Navy sank *Bismarck* on May 27.

On June 14, FDR froze all German and Italian assets in the United States. This did nothing to discourage Hitler, who, on June 22, launched Operation Barbarossa, shattering the Molotov-Ribbentrop Pact with a massive surprise invasion of the Soviet Union. As his nation now withered under blitzkrieg, Stalin, on July 3, ordered his people to carry out a "scorched-earth policy," and destroy everything of any use to the invader. On July 12, Britain and the USSR signed the Anglo-Soviet Agreement, a mutual defense pact.

President Roosevelt turned his attention from Europe to Asia on July 26, when, in response to Japan's occupation of French Indochina (modern-day Vietnam), he froze all Japanese assets in the U.S. and then, on Aug. 1, imposed an oil embargo. On Aug. 9, he met with Churchill aboard the heavy cruiser USS *Augusta* anchored in Placentia Bay, Newfoundland. Here, the leaders drew up the Atlantic Charter, a joint statement of objectives to pursue following victory in the war. The charter became the foundation of the postwar United Nations.

On July 31, Hermann Göring, on Hitler's orders, directed SS general Reinhard Heydrich to prepare to implement the Nazi's plan for "carrying out the desired final solution of the Jewish question." With this, the genocide of European Jewry became a leading German war aim.

On Oct. 31, a U-boat sank the U.S. destroyer *Reuben James*. America was now well into the Battle of the Atlantic, with or without a declaration of war.

Meanwhile, the USSR was being savaged. German forces began to lay siege against Leningrad (present-day St. Petersburg) on Sept. 8, the start of an 872-day ordeal that would cost the lives of 1,000,000 Leningraders, mostly from starvation. To the south, in Ukraine, Kiev was captured on Sept. 19, and, on Oct. 2, Operation Typhoon, the offensive against the Soviet capital, Moscow, was launched. At the end of October, President Roosevelt extended Lend-Lease to the Soviet Union.

In the Pacific war, Japan's fate was sealed when, on Oct. 18, Prime Minister Fumimaro Konoe was replaced by the militarist general Hideki Tojo. On Nov. 17, U.S. ambassador to Japan Joseph Grew cabled Washington that Japan had plans for a sudden attack on the U.S. Pacific Fleet at Pearl Harbor, Hawaii. The warning was disregarded, partly because of poor communication between the State Department and the military and partly because such an attack seemed simply inconceivable.

The attack on Sunday morning, Dec. 7, 1941, came as a total surprise. Twenty-one ships were sunk or damaged, including 8 U.S. battleships, 3 light cruisers, 3 destroyers, and 4 other naval vessels, and 188 American aircraft were destroyed. The death toll was staggering: 2,403 Americans killed. The next day, Roosevelt asked Congress for a declaration of war, even as Americans received the news that Japan had also made devastating attacks against Thailand, British Malaya, Guam, Hong Kong, the Philippines, Shanghai, Singapore, and Wake Island—which was valiantly defended by a tiny force of U.S. Marines and civilian workers.

On Dec. 22, some 40,000 Japanese troops landed north of Manila in the Philippines, prompting American general Douglas MacArthur to lead a retreat to Bataan on Christmas Eve. On Christmas Day, the British Crown Colony of Hong Kong surrendered to the Empire of Japan.

Smoke rises from the battleship USS *Arizona* as it sinks into Pearl Harbor, Dec. 7, 1941.

Petaluma Argus-Courier, Petaluma, CA, Tuesday, March 11, 1941

PRESIDENT SIGNS BRITISH AID BILL; WILL ASK CONGRESS FOR 7 BILLIONS

Britain Ready to Man Entire U.S. Fleet for Battle of Atlantic

By The Associated Press

A high London naval source declared today that Britain wanted all the ships she could get from America and that enough trained British personnel was ready to man the whole United States fleet if it were turned over to Britain for the developing "battle of the Atlantic."

On the diplomatic front, Axis propaganda guns assailed the United States—hinting at trouble in the Pacific—as Japan's foreign minister, Yosuke Matsuoka, prepared to leave the Far East for important talks with Adolf Hitler and Benito Mussolini.

The British comment on preparedness to take over the United States Navy was made after questions by American correspondents in London. So far, however, the British have not officially suggested that United States naval assistance was needed in combatting Hitler's sea raiders, and in Washington yesterday British ambassador Lord Halifax discounted reports that the two countries would exchange naval vessels as part of the British aid program.

A Japanese newspaper had asserted the United States planned to send U.S. destroyers in exchange for British capital ships for use in Far Eastern waters against Japan.

Halifax said he did not consider such an exchange was likely now or in the future.

Fascist sources in Rome hinted at an impending Japanese move under the triple alliance in reaction to the United States' British aid bill.

The Italian newspaper *La Tribuna* declared bluntly that Matsuoka's trip was "the immediate answer to Washington's threatening move."

"Yesterday America spoke," the newspaper said, evidently referring to senate passage of the British aid bill Saturday. "Soon Japan will say its word. It is for this that Matsuoka is coming to Berlin and Rome." . . .

In the war at sea, the London admiralty acknowledged the heaviest toll of shipping since October, with loss of 29 British, Allied and neutral vessels totaling 148,038 tons in the week ended March 2.

"The spring blitz which Hitler promised has begun," a British spokesman said, but he declared British countermeasures were improving.

The admiralty said German and Italian claims for the week totaled 432,500 tons—nearly triple the British figure. Weekly losses, excluding the withdrawal from Dunkerque, have averaged 63,342 since the war began. . . .

The Japanese press viewed U.S. Senate passage of the aid-to-Britain bill as putting the U.S. a step nearer war and said the possibilities for American pressure on Japan were increased.

One newspaper, *Asahi*, said "New York information" indicated the first step under the bill would be a deal whereby American destroyers would be traded for British capital ships which the U.S. "can send to Far Eastern waters against Japan in order to aid (Chinese) Generalissimo Chiang Kai-Shek more aggressively."

One widely read Japanese naval critic, Rear-Admiral Gumpei Sekine, defined Japan's "co-prosperity sphere" in Asia to include India, Australia and the Philippines.

OPPOSITE: At an unnamed British port, Lord Frederick Woolton, the British Minister of Food (right, with outstretched hand), and W. Averell Harriman, President Roosevelt's Lend-Lease special envoy (in dark coat to the left of Lord Woolton), greet the first food ship to reach England under the Lend-Lease Act, May 31, 1941.

BELOW: An American Lend-Lease warship sails out of New York Harbor, June 1, 1941.

British sailors carry their seabags aboard a Lend-Lease vessel in an American port, ready to sail her across the Atlantic, June 1, 1941.

Gazette and Daily, York, PA, Saturday, March 22, 1941

ARMY ORGANIZING NEGRO UNIT OF THE AIR CORPS

By The Associated Press

WASHINGTON, March 21—The army called today for volunteers on a "first come, first served," basis for the Negro unit of the air corps.

The unit, the 99th Pursuit Squadron, will have about 33 pilots and a ground crew of 276. It is to be formed at Tuskegee, Ala., in the fall after training is completed.

Like other men recruited for the air corps, the 276 men required for the maintenance crews must have at least a high school education. Enlistments will begin next week, and the men will be trained at Chanute Field, Ill.

The pilots for the Negro squadron, like other air corps flyers, must have two years college education or its equivalent and must undergo more than six months of training.

LEFT: A poster created by Betsy Graves Reyneau for the U.S. Treasury Department depicting Robert W. Diez, a Tuskegee Airman, asking Americans to buy war bonds, 1943.

BELOW: Maj. James A. Ellison reviews the first class of Tuskegee cadets on the flight line, Tuskegee, Alabama, 1941.

Detroit Free Press, Detroit, MI, Monday, June 16, 1941

ROOSEVELT DECRIES BAN ON NEGRO ARMS WORKERS F.D.R'S STATEMENT

By The Associated Press

WASHINGTON, June 15—Asserting that he had received complaints of nationwide discrimination against Negroes in defense industries, President Roosevelt called upon the Office of Production Management today to take immediate steps to deal "effectively" with this "grave" situation.

In a memorandum to William S. Knudsen and Sidney Hillman, co-directors, Mr. Roosevelt said that "no nation combatting the increasing threat of totalitarianism" could afford to bar large portions of its population from defense industries. He stressed the importance, also, of strengthening "our unity and morale by refuting at home the very theories which we are fighting abroad."

President's Statement

"Complaints have repeatedly been brought to my attention that available and much-needed workers are barred from defense production solely because of race, religion, or national origin. . . . Also that discrimination against Negro workers has been nation-wide, and other minority racial, national and religious groups have felt its effects in many localities. This situation is a matter of grave national importance, and immediate steps must be taken to deal with it effectively. . . . Our government cannot countenance continued discrimination against American citizens in defense production."

Luedell Mitchell and Lavada Cherry, a riveting team, at work in the El Segundo Plant of the Douglas Aircraft Company in Los Angeles, c. 1942.

Santa Cruz Sentinel, Santa Cruz, CA, Sunday, June 22, 1941

NAZIS TAKE ON RUSSIA

Nazi Troops Ready from Rumania to Finland for Fight

By The Associated Press

NEW YORK, Sunday, June 22—Adolf Hitler hurled his German armies against Soviet Russia in one of the greatest turnabouts in history today, declaring all-out war against the erstwhile friend whom he called a liar, double-crosser and secret ally of Great Britain.

Supporting the Germans, declared Hitler, were the vengeance-hungry forces from Finland and Rumania, both eager to regain territories lost to Russia. The British radio strongly intimated that embattled Britain would welcome Russia as an ally against the Nazis.

Hitler, who boasted by radio when his men invaded Poland on September 1, 1939, that his back was secure by reason of his non-aggression pact with Russia seven days earlier, today accused Russia of having sought to stab Germany in the back ever since. Russia has done this, he mourned, despite Germany's generous gift to her of half of fallen Poland.

Fighting on Two Fronts

Casting aside his oft-repeated declaration that Germany never again would fight a war on two fronts as she did in the World war, Hitler told the world—again by radio—that his deal with Russia was all off, and that the war between Red and Brown socialism was under way on a 1,500-mile front from the Arctic to the Black Sea.

His denunciation of Russia, bristling with a hatred nurtured in silence for nearly two years, was read over the air by his propaganda minister, Dr. Paul Goebbels.

Benito Mussolini and Adolf Hitler travel by motorcade to visit Italian troops in the Ukraine, Aug. 28, 1941.

Foreign Minister Joachim von Ribbentrop followed with the actual declaration of war.

In London, stunned almost into silence by this unexpected fruition of long-held but doubted dreams, the BBC said a Moscow statement had declared Russian and British accord on the international situation. These bulletins were picked up in New York by the NBC.

Direct from Germany, in a telephone call to the Associated Press headquarters in New York, the AP bureau in Berlin reported that German troops already were on the march along with the forces of Finland and Rumania. East Prussia and Norway were mentioned specifically as points from which the high-powered German army was moving.

The German radio declaration of war called the movement "the greatest march the world has ever seen."

That actual contact had not yet been established was intimated, however, by the German radio, in a subsequent news bulletin picked up here by NBC. It said the German troops along the 1,500-mile border were "moving into their last-minute positions."

The Italian radio chimed in quickly with word that Italy was standing by to aid her Axis partner.

The German radio, following up the Hitler-Ribbentrop blasts calling Russia a blackguard and enemy of world civilization, said proof would be offered in 24 hours that Russia came to a secret agreement with England behind the Reich's back.

The Berlin radio, heard here by NBC, also warned all Germans to keep a sharp lookout for Russian parachutists who would undoubtedly be dressed in civilian clothes and bent on sabotage.

Hitler accused the Russians of a tremendous double-cross, or having signed in bad faith the German-Russian non-aggression pact of August 23, 1939. He himself, Hitler asserted, had entered into that pact with sore misgivings, but had to do it because of Britain's policy of encircling Germany.

Bitterly he excoriated Russia for the Finnish and Baltic land grabs, the slicing up of Rumania. He blamed the Communist diplomats for playing England's game and stirring up the Yugoslav coup d'état of March 27 and the Rumanian Iron Guard revolt of last January.

Campaign of Sabotage

Von Ribbentrop added to the list of charges, declaring that Russian diplomats had been guilty of espionage against Germany and that Russia long had conducted a campaign of sabotage against the Reich.

The Axis victory in the Balkans momentarily foiled the deep-laid Communist scheme, Hitler said, of involving Germany in a long war and then, with English aid and American supplies, throttling the Reich.

At last, he said, the moment has come when Germany can tolerate no more.

The shrill-voiced Goebbels concluded with these stern words of his master: "The march of the German armies has no precedent. Together with the Finns we stand from Narvik to the Carpathians. At the Danube and on shores of the Black Sea under Antonescu (Rumanian premier Ion Antonescu) German and Rumanian soldiers are united. The task is to safeguard Europe and thus save all.

In Soldiers' Hands

"I have therefore today decided to give the fate of the German people and the Reich and of Europe again into the hands of our soldiers."

Adolf Hitler, like Napoleon before him, had turned to the east.

Hitler was back on one of the tracks he so long ago outlined for himself in *Mein Kampf*—enmity for Russia and for Communism. But he still was at war with Britain—a situation he professed in *Mein Kampf* to abhor.

Britain was apparently stunned by the German step which her wishful thinkers had so long forecast and which so often in the past has proved to be but a figment of unhappy imagination.

The only word that British sources would give was that apparently Hitler was convinced he could not quickly beat Britain and that he had decided to mop up Russia so as to gain a vast new amount of raw materials to equalize Britain's aid from the United States.

Washington Surprised

Washington, like London, was caught in surprise by the German-Russian war, which had been shaping up for a fortnight in a series of uncredited and almost unbelievable rumors of troop concentrations, border incidents and overpowering German demands on Russia for bread and oil and the territory containing them.

President Roosevelt, who has proclaimed the United States the arsenal of the democracies, was abed when the news came, and it was said he was not awakened.

Only last week Undersecretary of State Sumner Welles had brushed aside as hypothetical an inquiry whether Russia would qualify for American lease-lend aid if she became the victim of aggression.

★ ★ ★

ABOVE: German infantrymen, supported by tank units, move into a burning Russian village somewhere along the eastern front, June 26, 1941. INSET: Soviet prisoners of war in an unidentified Russian town after it was occupied by the Germans, Aug. 26, 1941.

Fresno Bee, Fresno, CA, Sunday, December 7, 1941

JAPANESE BOMB HAWAII; DECLARE WAR ON U.S.

British Also Attacked; Hundreds Killed in Raid on Air Base, Pearl Harbor

By The Associated Press

Imperial headquarters at Tokyo declared war late today against both the United States and Britain after Japanese bombers had attacked the great Pearl Harbor naval base at Honolulu and the Philippines.

An NBC broadcast said Japanese planes—estimated as high as 150 in the opening assault—struck at Ford Island in Pearl Harbor, the U.S. Navy's mighty fortress of the Pacific, and dropped high explosive and incendiary bombs on Honolulu itself.

Despite an official White House announcement that Japanese warplanes had also attacked Manila, an Associated Press dispatch from Manila timed at 4:25 p.m., E.S.T., Sunday, said the city was quiet with no signs of war.

Hickam Field Hit

NBC reports from Honolulu said 350 men had been killed by a direct bomb hit on Hickam Field and that the United States battleship *Oklahoma* had been set afire in Pearl Harbor. Two other United States warships also were reported attacked in the harbor.

Army officials said at least two Japanese planes had been shot down in the Honolulu area, where the death toll was listed at seven, including three whites, two Japanese and a 1-year-old Portuguese girl.

Indicate U.S. Victory

Latest reports indicated the United States had won the first battle in the new World War.

"The army and the navy, it appears, now have the air and sea under control," said an NBC broadcast from Honolulu, a few hours after the Japanese opened the assault.

Adopting Adolf Hitler's surprise tactics of striking over the weekend—ignoring President Roosevelt's personal last-hour appeal for peace to Emperor Hirohito last night—the Japanese attacked the two keystones of American defense in the Pacific at approximately 9:20 a.m., Honolulu time (3:20 p.m. E.S.T.).

WASHINGTON, Dec. 7 (AP)—Japanese airplanes today attacked American defense bases in Hawaii and President Roosevelt ordered

This photograph, from a Japanese film later captured by American forces, was taken aboard the Japanese aircraft carrier *Zuikaku*, just as a Nakajima "Kate" B5N bomber was launched off deck for the second wave

the army and navy to carry out undisclosed orders prepared for the defense of the United States.

The White House said Japan attacked American's vital outpost in the Pacific at 3:20 p.m. (E.S.T.). So far as is known the attacks were still in progress.

Attack Without Warning

Announcing the president's action for the protection of American territory, Presidential Secretary Stephen Early declared that so far as is known now the attacks were made wholly without warning—when both nations were at peace—and were delivered within an hour or so of the time that the Japanese ambassadors had gone to the state department to hand to the secretary of state Japan's reply to the secretary's memorandum of the 26th.

350 Soldiers Killed

A radio broadcast from the station of the *Honolulu Advertiser* at 1:50 o'clock this afternoon said 350 soldiers were killed in the attack on Hickam Field, bombs hitting the barracks. The attack was at 8 o'clock Honolulu time.

The same broadcast said three ships in Pearl Harbor were attacked by the bombers and the battleship *Oklahoma* was set on fire. Considerable damage was done to Hickam Field and planes. An attorney flying over Honolulu in his private plane was the first to learn of the attack when the bombers machine gunned his plane. He landed safely and in haste.

Navy officers in Washington said long-prepared counter measures against Japanese surprise attacks were ordered into operation and were "working smoothly."

And within a few minutes the war department ordered all military personnel in this country into uniform.

There was a disposition in some quarters here to wonder whether the attacks were ordered by the Japanese military authorities because they feared the president's direct negotiations with the emperor might lead to an about face in Japanese policy and the consequent loss of face by the present ruling factions in Japan.

A picture taken by a Japanese photographer shows the air attack on Pearl Harbor well underway. Billowing smoke in the top center of the image is from the burning hangars and planes at Hickam Field. White streaks from the wakes of two torpedos can clearly be seen in the harbor water headed toward USS *West Virginia*, which is already leaking fuel oil from previous torpedo hits.

A little later, the White House reported an army transport loaded with lumber had been torpedoed 1,300 miles west of San Francisco. This is well east of Hawaii. The first announcement did not say whether the ship was sunk or whether there was loss of life.

No Doubt of War

No official used the word *war* in reporting any of the developments, but with the series of events there could be no doubt that the Far Eastern situation has at last exploded, that the United States is at war, and that the conflict, which began in Europe, is spreading over the entire world.

The White House announced heavy damage has been inflicted in the Japanese attack on Hawaii and there probably has been heavy loss of life.

Bloch Reports Damage

The report of damage and casualties came to the White House from Admiral C. C. Bloch, commanding the 14th Naval District which embraces Hawaii.

The White House asserted, too, that Japan sent her bombers over the islands in dawn of early morning.

Asked about reports broadcast from Honolulu of a naval engagement off of Hawaii, Presidential Secretary Early said he could not confirm them.

President Dictates Message

Roosevelt concluded conferences with war, navy and state department chiefs late in the day and began dictating a special message to Congress.

Asked when the White House first had received word of the Japanese assault on America's key Pacific bases, Early said he did not know exactly but that it was only a few minutes before word was relayed to the press. Secretary of State Hull, he said, had no information of the attack at the time he was talking with Japan's ambassador and special emissary to the United States.

Early said he had asked the Secret Service to take up the credentials of Japanese correspondents. To a question whether they would be arrested, he replied that was up to defense officials and the justice department.

A Japanese reporter had been at the White House a few moments previously, belatedly gathering information second hand on the announcements which Early had been issuing with machine gun rapidity.

USS *California* lists to port after being struck by two Japanese torpedoes. The smoke in the background is from burning fuel oil leaking from USS *West Virginia* and USS *Arizona*.

Honolulu Star-Bulletin 1st EXTRA

8 PAGES—HONOLULU, TERRITORY OF HAWAII, U. S. A., SUNDAY, DECEMBER 7, 1941—8 PAGES · ★ PRICE FIVE CENTS

WAR!

OAHU BOMBED BY JAPANESE PLANES

(Associated Press by Transpacific Telephone)

SAN FRANCISCO, Dec. 7.—President Roosevelt announced this morning that Japanese planes had attacked Manila and Pearl Harbor.

SIX KNOWN DEAD, 21 INJURED, AT EMERGENCY HOSPITAL

Attack Made On Island's Defense Areas

By UNITED PRESS

WASHINGTON, Dec. 7.—Text of a White House announcement detailing the attack on the Hawaiian islands is:

"The Japanese attacked Pearl Harbor from the air and all naval and military activities on the island of Oahu, principal American base in the Hawaiian islands.

Oahu was attacked at 7:55 this morning by Japanese planes.

The Rising Sun, emblem of Japan, was seen on plane wing tips.

Wave after wave of bombers streamed through the clouded morning sky from the southwest and flung their missiles on a city resting in peaceful Sabbath calm.

According to an unconfirmed report received the governor's office

CIVILIANS ORDERED OFF STREETS

The army has ordered that all civilians stay off the streets and highways and not use telephones.

Evidence that the Japanese attack has registered some hits was shown by three billowing pillars of smoke in the Pearl Harbor and Hickam field areas.

All navy personnel and civilian defense workers, with the exception of women, have been ordered to duty at Pearl Harbor.

The Pearl Harbor highway was immediately a mess of racing cars.

A trickling stream of injured people began pouring into the city emergency hospital a few minutes after the bombardment started.

Thousands of telephone calls almost swamped the Mutual Telephone Co., which put extra operators on duty.

At The Star-Bulletin office the phone calls deluged the single operator and it was impossible for this newspaper, for sometime, to handle the flood of calls. Here also an emergency operator was called.

HOUR OF ATTACK—7:55 A. M.

An that Edouard L. Doty, ex-

ANTIAIRCRAFT GUNS IN ACTION

First indication of the raid came shortly before 8 this morning when antiaircraft guns around Pearl Harbor began sending up a thunderous barrage.

At the same time a vast cloud of black smoke arose from the naval base and also from Hickam field where flames could be seen.

BOMB NEAR GOVERNOR'S MANSION

Shortly before 9:30 a bomb fell near Washington Place, the residence of the governor. Governor Poindexter and Secretary Charles M. Hite were there.

It was reported that the bomb killed an unidentified Chinese man across the street in front of the Schuman Carriage Co. where windows were broken.

C. E. Daniels, a welder, found a fragment of shell or bomb at South and Queen Sts. which he brought into the City Hall. This fragment weighed about a pound.

At 10:05 a. m. today Governor Poindexter telephoned to The Star-Bulletin announcing he has declared a state of emergency for the entire territory.

Hundreds See City Bombed

Hundreds of Honolulans who hurried to the top of Punchbowl soon after bombs began to fall, saw spread out before them the whole panorama of surprise attack and defense.

Names of Dead and Injured

Schools Closed

All schools on Oahu, both public and private, will remain closed until further notice. Edward L. Doty, territorial director

BELOW: A small boat rescues a USS *West Virginia* crew member from the water in Pearl Harbor. Two men can be seen on the superstructure, upper left. The mast of USS *Tennessee* is visible beyond the burning *West Virginia*.

Early responded in the negative to a question whether Congress would be called into session tonight.

Little information was immediately available regarding the strength of the Japanese air attacks.

Dispatches from Honolulu said, however, that at least two Japanese bombers, their wings bearing the insignia of the Rising Sun, appeared over Honolulu at about 7:35 a.m. (Honolulu time) and dropped bombs.

The army's order affected not only the thousands of officers on duty in Washington, who have thus for performed their functions in civilian clothing to avoid a "militaristic" appearance, but all officers in every corps area, the United States' possessions and outlying bases.

Washington was expected to blossom tomorrow as a city of uniforms, because huge numbers of officers have been pouring into the city for months to perform the army's "overhead" functions.

Early said that so far as the president's information went, attacks were still in progress in Hawaii. In other words, he said, "we don't know that the Japanese have bombed and left."

Prepared Orders Involved

He went on to say: "As soon as the information of the attacks was received by the war and navy departments it was flashed immediately to the president at the White House. Thereupon and immediately the president directed the army and navy to execute all previously prepared orders looking to the defense of the United States. The president is now with the secretaries of navy and war. Steps are being taken to advise the congressional leaders."

Envoys at State Department

Kichisaburo Nomura, the Japanese ambassador, and Saburo Kurusu, the special Japanese envoy, were at the state department at the time of the White House's announcement of the attacks.

The two Japanese went to see Secretary of State Hull at 1:35 p.m. (E.S.T.) and remained about twenty minutes. They handed to the secretary Tokyo's reply to the statement of principles which he gave to them on November 26.

After their departure, the state department announced that Hull informed the Japanese that a document presented by them was "crowded with infamous falsehoods and distortions."

Hull Is Indignant

The department's statement said Hull read the Japanese reply and "immediately turned to the Japanese ambassador and with the greatest indignation said:

"I must say that in all my conversations with you (the Japanese ambassador) during the last nine months I have never uttered one word of untruth. This is borne out absolutely by the record.

"In all my fifty years of public service I have never seen a document that was more crowded with infamous falsehoods and distor-

tions—infamous falsehoods and distortions on a scale so huge that I never imagined until today that any government on this planet was capable of uttering them."

Beyond the tense White House announcement and the swift orders disclosed at the war and navy departments, there was no specific information on the military measures the United States was taking.

At the navy department, officials said that all inquiries as to operations were being referred to the White House, but officers informally reported that for several months all American warships in the Pacific had been in constant readiness for battle and that vigorous counter measures had long been planned for such incidents as the Japanese surprise attacks.

Aircraft Carrier in Action

Dispatches from Honolulu said a naval engagement was in progress off of Honolulu, with at least one enemy aircraft carrier in action against Pearl Harbor defenses.

The blunt language Hull used in addressing the Japanese envoys was reflected in their faces as they left the state department.

There was no trace of a smile.

Hull kept them waiting for fifteen minutes. Kurusu, neatly dressed in well-pressed blue, impatiently paced the floor, and engaged momentarily in whispered conferences with Nomura. The latter had taken a seat on a leather sofa in the waiting room.

Envoys Shun Reporters

When they left Hull's office, reporters at the state department, unaware that the announcement already had been made of the bombings, endeavored to question them again.

"Is this your last conference?" one reporter asked Nomura.

He received no reply whatsoever.

"Will the embassy issue a statement later?"

"I don't know."

Followed by a swarm of reporters and photographers, the two Japanese finally escaped into an elevator.

Hull had been at his desk since 9:45 a.m. At 10 o'clock Secretary of War Stimson and Secretary of the Navy Knox were closeted with him for three full hours.

Chinese Ambassador Shih

The Chinese ambassador, Dr. Hu Shih, was seen leaving the department in mid-afternoon before the Japanese arrived, but officials would not say with whom he had consulted or even confirm the fact that he had been in the building.

As news of the bombings spread, crowds collected before the White House gates. People milled about talking in anxious terms.

The White House itself became a bedlam of activity. Reporters, photographers and radio men besieged [the] president's offices, jamming the press room in capacity.

Fresno Bee, Fresno, CA, Sunday,
December 7, 1941

NIPPONESE HELD IN NAVAL CENTER

NORFOLK (Va.), Dec. 7 (AP)—Col. Charles B. Borland, Norfolk director of public safety, immediately ordered the arrest of all Japanese nationals in this strategic naval center today as soon as he learned of the Japanese attacks on the United States Pacific bases.

Borland said his orders were issued to Chief of Police John F. Woods and that every available officer was pressed into roundup work. The number of Japanese here is not large. Woods at once informed police officials of Portsmouth, where the great Norfolk Navy Yard is located; Newport News, where the Newport News Shipbuilding and Dry Dock Company is building nine aircraft carriers and three cruisers; and other nearby cities of the action Norfolk has taken. He suggested they take similar action.

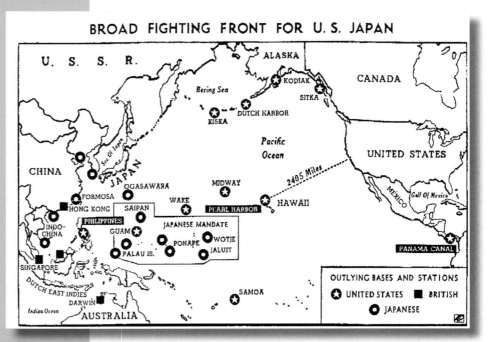

BROAD FIGHTING FRONT FOR U.S. JAPAN

An AP map published on Dec. 7, 1941, in the *Fresno Bee*, Fresno, California, illustrates Pearl Harbor's strategic location in the array of U.S., British, and Japanese naval bases and air stations in the Pacific.

A policeman frisks one of the Japanese American citizens arrested in a roundup that followed Japan's declaration of war on the United States, Norfolk, Virginia, Dec. 7, 1941.

CHURCHILL, U.S. ENVOY CONFER ON BRITISH ROLE

LONDON, Dec. 1 (AP)—A British statement, composed with the aid of United States Ambassador John G. Winant, was expected "fairly soon" tonight as London awaited fulfillment of Prime Minister Churchill's promise to declare war on Japan "within the hour" if she attacked the United States.

Churchill and Winant were closeted in conference quickly after President Roosevelt's announcement Japanese planes had attacked Hawaii and the Philippines and British sources said Britain's cabinet probably would be called for a rush meeting during the night.

The prime minister and ambassador were said reliably to be out of London but it was assumed that both were in closest communication with Washington.

The first hour after the Washington announcement was disclosed here passed without notice of a British war declaration.

Efforts to communicate with the Japanese embassy here by telephone were unsuccessful.

Preparations for any eventuality in the Pacific have long been underway by Britain and the empire.

★ ★ ★

Abilene Reporter-News, Abilene, TX, Monday, December 8, 1941

UNITED STATES DECLARES WAR

Britain, Allies Join Fight Before U.S. Officially Acts

WASHINGTON, Dec. 8. (AP)—The United States, through its Congress, declared war today on Japan.

Overwhelmingly, and with the greatest unity shown in many a day on Capitol Hill, the Senate and House backed up President Roosevelt's request for a war declaration with unprecedented speed; the Senate vote, first to be recorded, was 82 to 0. The officially announced loss of two warships and 3,000 men dead and wounded in Japan's raid on Hawaii was fresh in the minds of the legislators.

The Senate and House had assembled together to hear President Roosevelt ask the declaration. They cheered him enthusiastically and then pushed the resolution through with not a moment's waste of time. The single adverse House vote was that of Miss Jeannette Rankin, Democratic congresswoman from Montana, who was among the few who voted against the 1917 declaration of war on Germany. Roll call was 388–1.

WASHINGTON, Dec. 8. (AP)—President Roosevelt asked Congress today to declare war against Japan.

He made the solemn, historic request after disclosing to the nation that yesterday's sudden Japanese attack on Hawaii had cost the United States two warships and 3,000 dead and wounded.

"I ask," the chief executive declared, "that the Congress declare that since the unprovoked and dastardly attack by Japan on Sunday, December 7th, a state of war has existed between the United States and the Japanese empire."

The president said that yesterday was "a date which will live in infamy."

He recited the events since Japan's assault on America's Pacific bastions and said he had "directed that all measures be taken for our defense."

"Hostilities exist," Mr. Roosevelt asserted. "There is no blinking at the fact that our people, our territory and our interests are in grave danger.

"With confidence in our armed forces—with the unbounding determination of our people—we will gain the inevitable triumph—so help us God."

Mr. Roosevelt addressed the House and Senate, meeting in joint session for the second time within a generation to hear a president ask for a declaration of war. His words were solemn but brief.

He said Japan had undertaken a "surprise offensive" extending throughout the Pacific, noting that the Nipponese empire not only had attacked Hawaii and the Philippines but also Malaya, Hong Kong, Guam, Wake and Midway islands.

"Always we will remember the character of the onslaught against us," the president said.

"No matter how long it may take us to overcome this premeditated invasion, the American people in their righteous might will win through to absolute victory.

"I believe I interpret the will of the Congress and of the people when I assert that we will not only defend ourselves to the uttermost but will make very certain that this form of treachery shall never endanger us again."

Declaring Japan guilty of an "unprovoked and dastardly attack" on a "date which will live in infamy," President Franklin D. Roosevelt asks Congress to declare war, Dec. 8, 1941. Standing behind him are Vice President Henry A. Wallace, left, and House Speaker Sam Rayburn. Congress approved FDR's war declaration that day.

Nebraska State Journal, Lincoln, NE, Tuesday, December 23, 1941

100,000 JAP INVADERS OF LUZON HELD IN CHECK

Tanks and Artillery Meet Attack Along 20-Mile Front 150 Miles North of Manila

MANILA (Tuesday) (AP)—A heavy force of Japanese sea-borne troops, possibly as many as 100,000 and supported by airplanes, landed Monday at Santo Tomas on the gulf of Lingayen northwest of here, but Gen. Douglas MacArthur's headquarters announced that American defenders had the situation well in hand.

American tanks and artillery immediately went into action between Santo Tomas and Damortis, a town several miles south of the landing place. (Washington already had announced that the fighting centered in the 20-mile coastal stretch along the gulf northward to Agoo, which is just north of Santo Tomas.)

The army communiqué said: "The engagement Sunday occurred in the vicinity of Santo Tomas, in Union province. Latest reports indicate our troops are holding a position north of Damortis. The enemy was very active in the air Sunday. Numerous places were bombed and the ground attack was supported by aircraft."

Three Transports Sunk

One unconfirmed report from Dagupan on the gulf said that at least three Japanese transports out of the 80 which had been sighted outside were sunk in the gulf itself.

Reliable sources said it was possible that many more had been destroyed by the American forces, who were using artillery and tanks against the landing parties.

It still was not known whether the Japanese had been able to bring any considerable amount of equipment ashore.

Although American tanks already had gone into action, it also was not clear whether the Japanese intended to unload all of the 80 transports in Lingayen Gulf, or try to shove shock forces ashore elsewhere during the night.

No Reports from Davao

An army spokesman said no reports had been received from Davao on Mindanao Island about the progress of the hard fighting there.

The prolonged silence about the far southern theater indicated that communications may have been cut.

A score or more of Filipino army recruits under training at Camp Murphy were reported to have been killed by Japanese air bombs. Several score were injured, newspaper dispatches said.

Gen. MacArthur's communiqué late Monday said that the ground forces in the Lingayen area "more than held their own," and the general added "our troops are behaving well."

The assailant had appeared in heavy force in 80 transports (with a force which Washington estimated at 80,000 to 100,000 men), but not all of his marauders had even reached the shore, for in at least one area Japanese destroyers and troop ships were put to flight by the heavy American guns and that landing was thus prevented.

Rumors were heard at headquarters during the day of the sinking of Japanese transports in the gulf, but these had not been officially confirmed.

Expected Attack There

The struggle was joined in an area which MacArthur long had anticipated as the focal point of the major Japanese effort; for unofficially, the battle was reported as centered in the 20-mile coastal stretch along the gulf of Lingayen extending northward from the port of Lingayen to the town of Agoo. Lingayen itself is 110 miles northwest of Manila.

The Lingayen coastal area commands two approaches to Manila. One, a flat interior corridor averaging some 40 miles in width over which railroad and road communication runs down to Manila; the other, an indirect highway from Lingayen which loops around the northern end of the mountains of western Luzon, then turns southward toward Manila.

Whether United States air or naval forces had gone into action against the invasion armada was not stated either at Manila or Washington. Counting its naval escort and supply ships, the Japanese invasion fleet numbered perhaps 100 vessels.

Manila's official report said that heavy guns shattered one landing spearhead.

The armada was shielded from aloft by swarms of Japanese planes.

It was announced officially that tank combat figured in the new struggle but whether these included barge-landed Japanese tanks was not clear. . . .

A timely renewal of a pledge of allegiance to the United States came from the chief of the Moros of southern Mindanao, famed as the world's fiercest killers.

LEFT: The public market place at San Pablo, Laguna, on Luzon, teemed with local shoppers on Christmas Day, Dec. 25, 1941, when Japanese bombers hit the market and left this picture of stark devastation. In the litter of dead animals, wrecked buildings, and burned market wares, rescue workers found 25 dead and 60 injured, most of them women and children.

INSET: In one of the last pictures to leave the Philippines before Manila fell to the Japanese, Gen. Douglas MacArthur is shown pinning a Distinguished Service Cross on Capt. Jesús A. Villamor, of the Philippine Air Force, for heroism in the air, Dec. 22, 1941.

CHAPTER FOUR

1942

On New Year's Day 1942, 26 Allied nations signed the Declaration by United Nations, laying the foundation for the postwar United Nations. It was a profoundly forward-looking act of faith at a time when the Allies were suffering defeats throughout Asia and Europe.

Manila fell to the Japanese on Jan. 2, followed by Kuala Lumpur, Malaya (present-day Malaysia), on the eleventh. Japan invaded the Dutch East Indies (Indonesia) and menaced Singapore, where 80,000 British troops ignominiously surrendered on Feb. 15. These were headline events. But on Jan. 20, on an estate seized from a wealthy Jewish family in the Berlin suburb of Wannsee, members of the German military and government secretly gathered to plan in detail the extermination of Europe's Jews, the genocide known today as the Holocaust.

On Jan. 24, U.S. troops landed in Samoa, the first step of a campaign to arrest the Japanese advance in the Pacific. Two days later, the first American forces arrived in the European theater, disembarking in Belfast, Northern Ireland.

On Feb. 2, American general Joseph "Vinegar Joe" Stilwell was appointed commander of Allied forces in China, Burma, and India, and chief of staff to Generalissimo Chiang Kai-shek. Given virtually no support in the largely neglected China-Burma-India Theater, Stilwell became legendary for his brilliant improvisation against nearly impossible odds.

Back in America, President Roosevelt signed Executive Order 9066 on Feb. 19. Its neutral tone authorized the War Department to designate "military areas" and then exclude anyone from them whom it felt to be a danger. But it had a specific target: the more than 112,000 Japanese Americans living along the West Coast. They would be forced from their homes and moved into "internment" camps for the duration of the war. Three days after this, FDR ordered Gen. Douglas MacArthur to evacuate the Philippines and assume command in the Pacific from a headquarters in Australia. MacArthur left with his wife and son on March 11. Six days later he arrived in Australia, where he made a vow to the people of the Philippines: "I shall return."

Japanese forces continued to fan out through the Pacific, seizing one island after another and closing in on Port Moresby in New Guinea, with the intention of invading Australia. On March 9, Japanese troops entered Rangoon, Burma, while another Japanese force landed in the Solomon Islands on the fourteenth. Absent MacArthur, Bataan fell on April 9, making POWs of 78,000 U.S. Army and Filipino troops, who were sent on the infamous Bataan Death March to camps in the north.

Desperate to lift American public morale, FDR authorized the daring Doolittle Tokyo Raid of April 18. Lt Col. James "Jimmy" Doolittle led 16 twin-engine B-25 bombers from the flight deck of

USS *Hornet* in strikes against Tokyo, Kobe, Yokohama, Nagoya, and Yokosuka. The damage they inflicted was light, but the vengeance strike against the heart of Japan gave the American people a much-needed taste of victory.

During May 4–8, U.S. admiral Chester W. Nimitz faced off against Japanese admiral Isoroku Yamamoto, architect of the Pearl Harbor attack, in the Battle of the Coral Sea. Despite the loss of the aircraft carrier *Lexington*, Nimitz repelled an invasion force targeting New Guinea.

On Europe's Russian Front, the German armies scored a crushing defeat against the Red Army at Kharkov (Kharkiv) during May 12–28. Yet, in the Pacific, Nimitz prevailed at the Battle of Midway, fought during June 4–7, forcing Japan to break off its Pacific advance and offensive. Adm. Yamamoto had hoped to lure the surviving vessels of Pearl Harbor to destruction at Midway Atoll. Instead, he lost 3,057 men, four carriers, a cruiser, and more than 300 aircraft. U.S. losses were some 362 men, the carrier *Yorktown*, a destroyer, and 144 aircraft. In a diversionary attack coordinated with Midway, the Japanese invaded Attu and Kiska in the Aleutian Islands, Alaska Territory, on June 6–7. The first invasion of American soil in 128 years, it was successfully defeated by a combined army and navy counterstrike.

While Midway occupied all the headlines during this period, in deepest secrecy, the Manhattan Project was launched and began work on developing the nuclear weapons that would ultimately end the war against Japan.

Also claiming a large share of the news were the victories of Rommel and his vaunted Afrika Korps at Tobruk in June. Rommel then moved farther east to Egypt, where the First Battle of El Alamein began on July 1.

On the western front, Gen. Dwight D. Eisenhower arrived in London on June 24 as commander of American forces in Europe, while on the eastern front, Sevastopol fell to the Germans on July 4, ending Red Army resistance in Crimea. But it was the mounting British defeats in North Africa—plus those in Malaya and India—that most threatened to change the course of history. They triggered a House of Commons censure motion against Churchill, which was narrowly defeated on July 2. Soon after this, on July 11, Rommel ran short of ammunition, and El Alamein became a stalemate.

In the Pacific, U.S. land forces went on the offensive for the first time in the war, landing on Japanese-held Guadalcanal on Aug. 7. It was the start of six brutal months of fighting that halted Japanese expansion in the Solomon Islands.

The U.S. Army Air Forces scored its own breakthrough on Aug. 17 when it launched its first B-17 heavy bomber raid in Europe, targeting the Sotteville railroad yards at Rouen, France. Two days later, however, a premature attempt at a British-Canadian joint cross-channel raid, Operation Jubilee, ended in disaster at Dieppe, France. Most of the raiders were killed or captured. Autumn brought better news, when Gen. Bernard Law Montgomery led his Eighth Army to victory against Rommel in the Second Battle of El Alamein on Nov. 3. Five days later, the Allies launched Operation Torch, a major landing in North Africa, the first step in a planned assault on Italy, part of what Churchill called the "soft underbelly of Europe."

Amid the movement of great armies, fragmentary news began to leak out of Europe about the mass killing of Jews. On Nov. 24, Rabbi Stephen Wise, president of the World Jewish Congress, held a press conference appealing to Roosevelt to move against the genocidal plan. Two weeks later, the Polish government-in-exile also issued a report, *The Mass Extermination of Jews in German Occupied Poland*, which prompted an Allied pledge to punish those responsible. What did not leak to the public were the results of a bold experiment carried out on Dec. 2 at the University of Chicago by scientists under the direction of Italian refugee Enrico Fermi. It was the first self-sustaining, controlled nuclear fission chain reaction—proof that atomic weapons were feasible.

A coastal defense gun is fired from fortified American positions on Corregidor Island, at the entrance to Manila Bay in the Philippines, May 6, 1942.

★ ★ ★ INTERNMENT OF JAPANESE AMERICANS, FEBRUARY 19, 1942 ★ ★ ★

San Pedro News-Pilot, San Pedro, CA, Friday, February 20, 1942

STIMSON GIVEN NEW POWER BY ROOSEVELT

No Specific Areas Mentioned; Action Directed at Japs

WASHINGTON (AP)—President Roosevelt has authorized and directed Secretary of War Stimson to set up military areas in the country from which any persons, either alien or citizen, may be barred or removed.

The executive order of the president mentioned no specific areas, but it was no secret that his action was directed to a large extent toward citizens of Japanese extraction whose presence at certain strategic points might be deemed inimical to the war effort.

Officials said that the order did not constitute application of martial law, but it appeared to be only a step short of it.

The executive order would apply to citizens of German and Italian descent as well, and to native-born Americans of any ancestry.

The executive order, signed yesterday by the president, and withheld until today at the request of the war department, directs the secretary of war and military commanders he may designate to "prescribe military areas in such places and of such extent as he or the appropriate military commander may determine, from which any and all persons may be excluded, and with respect to which, the right of any person to enter, remain in, or lease shall be subject to whatever restrictions" the secretary or commander may impose.

Designed to curb both espionage and sabotage, the order was based on the authority vested in Mr. Roosevelt as president and as commander-in-chief of the army and navy.

It said that the "successful prosecution of the war required every possible protection against espionage and against sabotage to national defense material, national defense premises, and national defense utilities."

Not only aliens, but also American citizens could be removed, under the authority granted Secretary of War Stimson, from the vicinity of vital naval or army bases, defense installations of any kind, and even the factories turning out war equipment.

Certain proscribed areas had been set up along the West Coast some time ago, and aliens were barred from them. But the new order says the designation of new military areas shall supersede these.

The war secretary was authorized to supply necessary transportation, food, shelter and other accommodations for residents of any of the new military areas who might be excluded from them. This would be a temporary arrangement, until other plans were worked out.

Any necessary steps required to enforce compliance with the restrictions to be imposed may be taken by the secretary of war or his military commanders under the broad authority delegated by the chief executive. This includes the use of federal troops.

★ ★ ★

OPPOSITE: Japanese American citizens from San Pedro, California, arrive at an assembly center at the Santa Anita racetrack in nearby Arcadia before being moved inland to relocation centers, April 5, 1942.

ABOVE TOP: Japanese citizens wait in line for their assigned homes at an internment camp reception center in Manzanar, California, March 24, 1942.

ABOVE: Civilian Exclusion Order No. 5, posted at First and Front Streets in San Francisco, April 7, 1942, directed the removal of persons of Japanese ancestry from a large neighborhood in that city, the first area in San Francisco to be affected by evacuation.

Bakersfield Californian, Bakersfield, CA, Friday, February 20, 1942

OPPOSE REMOVAL OF JAPS TO KERN AREAS

WASHINGTON, Feb. 20. (AP)—President Roosevelt has authorized and directed the secretary of war to set up military areas in the country from which any persons, either alien or citizen, may be barred or removed.

Southland proposals to move unwanted Japanese to central California, including Kern County, met with sharp opposition by the Kern County defense council members last night at a meeting in the courthouse. The council's opposition was recorded in a unanimously approved motion requesting the federal government to remove from the state of California all Japanese (both citizens and aliens) and any alien deemed dangerous by the proper authorities.

Chairman L. A. Burtch of the council's agricultural committee submitted the motion after a similar stand was taken by the agricultural committee. He said the farm defense group had rejected inquiries from Los Angeles on "how many Japanese of southern California we could accommodate in Kern County."

A presidential order to move Germans, Italians and Japanese—including Nisei, American-born Japanese—from California and possibly other coastal areas is expected by Monday, it was said.

Although supporting the plan to have federal officials remove Japanese from the state, probably to concentration camps, Alfred Siemon, mayor of Bakersfield and vice-chairman of the defense council, termed the motion "absurd" because of its disregard of the constitutional rights of citizen-Japanese. Mr. Siemon's suggestion that the motion be phrased to recommend "appropriate measures" be taken for the removal of Japanese, was lost in the discussion.

"What about the Japanese boys who are wearing the uniform of the United States Army at Kern County Airport? Would you move them out of the state, too?" asked Mr. Siemon. The questions went unanswered.

Favor Axis Alien Ban

Growing demands were voiced in Kern County and California today for the internment of German and Italian aliens, as well as any second-generation members of those nationalities considered dangerous. It was pointed out that Japanese are easily recognized where Germans and Italians are not. Several thousand Axis aliens and their families reside in Kern, of which about 800 are Japanese.

Perched high upon a pile of baggage and with a military policeman watching, a Japanese American boy in San Francisco awaits the return of his parents before they are deported to a concentration camp in the California desert, April 6, 1942.

Spokesman Review, Spokane, WA, Saturday, February 21, 1942

NISEI PROTEST FORCED EXODUS

By The Associated Press

LOS ANGELES, Feb. 20.—Fifteen hundred Nisei—second-generation Japanese-Americans—organized the United Citizens' league last night preparatory to a fight to prevent evacuation of loyal aliens and citizens of Japanese descent from being evacuated inland from the Pacific Coast.

"We need action and need it now," declared Larry Tajiri, former Washington, D.C., correspondent for a Japanese news service. "We are loyal to the American flag, but race hatreds are being stirred up now in the Fascist pattern."

Kay Sugahara, produce merchant, said: "If the army and navy say we are a menace, let's get out. But if it's merely a question of fighting politicians that would gain favor by hopping on 'those defenseless Japs' we should fight them to the last ditch."

Joseph Shinoda, florist and former member of the anti-Axis committee, demanded that authorities give Japanese-Americans a part in the war effort.

Nearly 1,000 Japanese aliens recently have been taken into custody in California and many official and civic groups have demanded that every Japanese be moved inland at least 200 miles.

An aerial photograph from June 21, 1943, of the housing barracks at the Granada War Relocation Center, built by the U.S. Army Corps of Engineers in Amache, Colorado.

News-Palladium, Benton Harbor, MI, Thursday, April 9, 1942

JAPS TAKE BATAAN; DEFENDERS IN TRAP

36,853 Face Death or Capture; Escape to Corregidor Cut

By The Associated Press

WASHINGTON, April 9—Secretary of War Stimson indicated today that 36,853 gallant American and Filipino soldiers faced death or capture as the result of the apparent collapse of the stubborn defense of Bataan Peninsula in the Philippines.

Secretary Stimson said that Lieutenant General Jonathan M. Wainwright yesterday had 36,853 effectives on Bataan when the Japanese succeeded in enveloping the east flank of the defense lines despite a heroic counterattack attempt by physically exhausted troops.

A war department communiqué earlier had announced that Japanese successes indicated "the probability that the defense of Bataan had been overcome" and Stimson discussed the situation at his press conference.

Surrender Authorized

President Roosevelt has authorized the Philippine commander to make any decision he deemed necessary in the light of events, Stimson said. Stimson told reporters that latest reports from the Philippines indicated that Corregidor and the other fortifications guarding the entrance to Manila Bay still stood, but declined to make predictions as to how long they could hold out.

"This is only a temporary loss," Stimson said. "We shall not stop until we drive out the invaders from the islands."

Stimson said the figure of 36,853 effectives was in the report received yesterday from General Wainwright. He stressed that this figure included only the men fighting on Bataan at that time.

Excluded were American and Filipino troops guarding the defenses of Corregidor and the other islands, the wounded, nearly 20,000 civilian refugees, and some 6,000 Filipino laborers who were non-combatant.

Reinforcements Failed

Stimson disclosed that under the direction of Brigadier General Patrick J. Hurley, former secretary of war who is now minister to New Zealand, urgent efforts were made beginning last January 11 to reinforce the besieged Philippine forces. From a base in

The front pages of newspapers outside of a corner drugstore in Hayward, California, report the fall of Bataan on April 9, 1942. By this time, the forced removal of Japanese Americans was already underway in that state as well as in Oregon; by the end of the month, it was happening in Washington and Alaska as well.

American soldiers are marched away by their Japanese captors in Bataan, Philippines, early April 1942. Approximately 78,000 U.S. and Filipino troops were forced to walk approximately 60 miles north to Camp O'Donnell in Capas, on what would be known as the Bataan Death March. An estimated 7,000 to 10,000 POWs lost their lives during the brutal trek.

Australia several shiploads of supplies were sent to the Philippines, and part of these supplies reached Corregidor and Bataan.

"But for every ship that arrived, we lost nearly two ships," Stimson said.

Because of these supplies, the defenders were never short of ammunition, the secretary said, but had been on short rations. Stimson said he saw no reason why resistance by isolated, relatively small forces should not continue in northern Luzon, on the island of Mindanao and elsewhere blows have been struck, aside from further defense of Corregidor. . . .

"Our troops, outnumbered and worn down by successive attacks by fresh troops, exhausted by insufficient rations and the disease prevalent in that peninsula, finally had their lines broken and enveloped by the enemy," the secretary said. "We do not know the details of what has happened since that communiqué, but it is evident as stated therein that the defenses on Bataan have been overcome.

Praises Officers, Men

"A long and gallant defense has been worn down and overthrown. We have nothing but praise and admiration for the commanders and the men who have conducted this epic chapter in American history."

Stimson explained also that both General Wainwright and General Douglas MacArthur, his predecessor, had nothing but praise for the Filipino soldiers who had been fighting side by side with the Americans.

President Roosevelt's message to General Wainwright, he said, was sent yesterday. In the message, Stimson said the chief executive expressed his "full appreciation of the enormous difficulties confronting General Wainwright and told him he had nothing but praise for his method of conducting the defense and for his soldierly conduct throughout." Stimson said the president told Wainwright that "any decision he reached now would be in the interests of the country and the splendid troops he commanded."

The war secretary said he disclosed the exact figures for the effectives in the final stage of the struggle because he anticipated there would be "great exaggeration by the Japanese of the number of men who have gone down."

Stimson declined to estimate the numerical odds against which the defenders fought. Earlier reports had indicated the invaders had at least six divisions on the peninsula. The total enemy strength on Luzon Island has been estimated at from 200,000 to 300,000.

The defenders had no air support of any substantial size recently, Stimson said, adding, "that is what made the outcome practically a foregone conclusion."

Santa Cruz Sentinel, Santa Cruz, CA, Saturday, April 18, 1942

TOKYO BOMBED, SAYS RADIO

By The Associated Press

The long-awaited bombing of Tokyo, first installment of repayment for Pearl Harbor and the start of offensive warfare directly against the heart of Imperial Japan, apparently got under way at noon today (Saturday) for the Tokyo radio announced that enemy planes had raided the city for the first time.

There was no immediate confirmation from the United States War and Navy Departments in Washington.

The Tokyo shortwave carried the indignant declaration of the Japanese agency that schools and hospitals were damaged, although the casualties were "as yet unknown."

"Invading planes failed to cause any damage on military establishments," said the announcement, which was recorded by the CBS listening post in San Francisco.

How the raid may have been executed was not immediately brought out. It suggested methods similar to the attack March 4 by a naval air task force on Marcus Island, within a thousand miles of the Japanese homelands, or the 13-bomber forays against the Philippine invasion bases this week.

According to the Japanese broadcast picked up the CBS listening station in San Francisco, "the raiders came from several directions." Interceptor planes went into action, anti-aircraft gins roared, and according to the Japanese military authorities, nine of the raiding planes were shot down. Most of the bombs, it was claimed by the Tokyo broadcast, fell on the outskirts of the city and did not strike any military establishments.

ABOVE: Lt. Col. James H. Doolittle, USAAF (front), leader of the raiding force, wires Japanese medals to a 500-pound bomb during ceremonies on the flight deck of USS *Hornet* shortly before his force of 16 B-25 bombers took off for Japan, April 18, 1942. (As a gesture of defiance, Doolittle wired several friendship and goodwill medals the U.S. had earlier received from Japanese diplomats to the tails of his bombs.)

LEFT: A B-25 Mitchell bomber about to take off from USS *Hornet's* flight deck for the initial air raid on Tokyo, April 18, 1942.

Extra   # THE HIGH POINT ENTERPRISE   **Extra**

VOL. 58—NO. 108   ASSOCIATED PRESS—NEA SERVICE   HIGH POINT, N. C., SATURDAY MORNING, APRIL 18, 1942   WIDE WORLD FEATURE SERVICE   PRICE FIVE CENTS

U. S. BOMBS TOKYO

Big Airmada Wreaks Havoc On Continent

Vast Fleet of British Bombers Pounds Axis-Held Territory; Nazis Strike Back

(By The Associated Press)

LONDON, April 17.—Clearing weather unleashed wave upon wave of RAF planes today for the virtually ceaseless offensive against the German-dominated continent, and Nazi bombers struck back savagely at a south coast town which they said was Southampton.

A great force swept Northern France and returned across the strait, preceded by the angry sound of German anti-aircraft barrages on the occupied mainland coast. Spitfires blanketed a great area as they continued the shuttles of destructions across the

FOUR REASONS WHY U. S. BOMBED JAPAN YESTERDAY — These are four of the several reasons why United Nations bombers appeared over Japan yesterday or last night.

First Time In History Japan Has Been Bombed; Say 9 Planes Shot Down

Tokyo and Yokohama Feel Weight of United States' Retribution; Other Important Japanese Points Raided; Japs Claim Little Damage Inflicted

TOKYO (from Japanese broadcasts), April 18—(AP)—Allied warplanes laden with fire bombs and explosives struck today by daylight at the

PLANES WERE AMERICAN

SAN FRANCISCO, April 18.—(AP)—The Tokyo radio, in a Chinese-language broadcast picked up here by CBS today, identified the planes which bombed Tokyo as American.

"American planes raided Tokyo for the first time, bombing hospitals," the announcer said.

"On the afternoon of the eighteenth, American airplanes flew over the sky of Tokyo for the first time, dropping bombs on where there are no military

BELOW: Two sizeable Japanese naval vessels, (visible at the bottom, center left) at Yokosuka Naval Base, near Yokohama, lay directly in the path of bombs from the Doolittle raid, April 18, 1942. This photo was taken from the window of a raiding B-25 plane.

The Evening Independent, Massillon, OH, Wednesday, May 6, 1942

EXHAUSTED DEFENDERS OF CORREGIDOR SURRENDER TO OVERWHELMING JAP ARMY

FALL OF MADAGASCAR NAVAL BASE TO BRITISH IMMINENT

Midnight Landing on Fortress Ends Siege of 28 Days

By ROGER D. GREENE
Associated Press War Editor

Overwhelmingly outnumbered, hungry and exhausted, Lieut.-Gen. Jonathan Wainwright's forces surrendered to the Japanese today after 28 days of fiery siege in the battle of Manila Bay.

A war department bulletin issued at 4:15 a.m. Eastern War Time—more than 16 hours after the Japanese launched a midnight landing assault on Corregidor Island fortress—announced briefly:

"Resistance of our troops has been overcome. Fighting has ceased, and terms are being arranged covering the capitulation of the island forts in Manila Bay."

A war department communiqué said one of the last messages received from Gen. Wainwright reported that casualties among the defenders were heavy during the last few days.

In addition to the regular garrison, about 3,500 U.S. Marines had been sheltered on Corregidor after withdrawing from Bataan Peninsula. The communiqué said military installations on the tiny "Gibraltar of the Philippines" had also been severely damaged by constant Japanese shelling and aerial bombing.

Gen. Wainwright reported that for the fourth consecutive day there were 13 separate air attacks on Corregidor on May 5, and that the final shelling by Japanese 240-millimeter siege guns had destroyed barbed wire entanglements and other defenses.

Japanese shock troops he said crossed the narrow stretch of waterfront from Bataan to Corregidor in a large fleet of steel barges for the direct assault. About 7,000 American and Filipino men and women were believed involved in the surrender of the four mid-bay forts after holding out for nearly a month against Japanese forces which overran the Bataan Peninsula on April 9.

Other Forts Succumb

Besides Fort Mills on Corregidor, Forts Drum, Frank and Hughes on three other smaller islands guarding the entrance to Manila Bay succumbed to the tempestuous Japanese attack.

Corregidor alone had undergone more than 300 air raids and in the final day before the Japanese landing attack had been dive-bombed 13 times and shelled incessantly for five hours.

Most of Corregidor's shores defenses—pillboxes, barbed wire entanglements and other obstructions—were believed to have been blasted away.

Running desperately low on food and ammunition, the tiny American-Filipino garrisons had received a heartening message from President Roosevelt shortly before the end.

"You have given the world a shining example of patriotic fortitude and self-sacrifice," the president said. "The American people ask no finer example of tenacity, resourcefulness and steadfast courage. . . . You have become the living symbols of our war aims and the guarantee of victory."

The fall of Corregidor, giving Japan's invasion armies control of the best harbor in the Orient, catapulted a series of other Japanese conquests, including: Hongkong, Dec. 25; Manila, Jan. 2; Singapore, Feb. 15; Batavia, March 5; Rangoon, March 8, and Bataan, April 9.

The victory which the Japanese won at great cost gave them control of the best harbor in the Orient and strengthened the long communications lines they have thrust toward Australia and India. American-Filipino troops continued to plague the enemy with guerilla warfare in various parts of Cebu Mindanao and Panay Islands. It was believed here, although there was no official word, that General Wainwright remained with his troops to the end. . . .

Just how many survived the long ordeal of air raid and artillery bombardments was not known, but it was generally estimated there were about 7,000 men and women altogether on the fortified islands.

After defending Corregidor Island in the Philippines for nearly a month, American and Filipino soldiers were forced to surrender to the Japanese on May 6, 1942. Revise last sentence as follows: This photograph, captured from the Japanese—made as a propaganda piece for the Japanese press—depicts a forced restaging of the surrender in front of the U.S. Army Malinta Tunnel complex.

North Adams Transcript, North Adams, MA, Friday, June 5, 1942

AMERICAN AND JAPANESE FLEETS REPORTED IN MAJOR ENCOUNTER

FALL OF MADAGASCAR NAVAL BASE TO BRITISH IMMINENT

Several Warships Hit

HONOLULU, June 5 (AP)—American defenders, spurred by initial successes, closed battle today with a strong Japanese sea-air task force in what may be a finish fight for possession of Midway Island.

Already the island garrison had scored hits on an enemy battleship, an aircraft carrier and possibly other war vessels. Raiding planes were brought down in great number.

By JOHN M. HIGHTOWER

WASHINGTON, June 5 (AP)—American and Japanese fleet units apparently were engaged today in one of the greatest battles of the Pacific as a result of the enemy's attempt yesterday to raid the strongly garrisoned United States outpost on Midway Island.

Commenting on a communiqué issued at Pearl Harbor early today by Admiral Chester W. Nimitz, commander in chief of the Pacific fleet, naval experts emphasized that Nimitz said "attacks on the enemy are continuing."

Torpedo Squadron Six TBD-1 aircraft are prepared for launching on USS *Enterprise* the morning of June 4, 1942. USS *Pensacola* is in the right distance and a destroyer is in plane guard position at left.

A Douglas SBD-3 Dauntless scout bomber of USS *Enterprise*'s Bombing Squadron Six is parked on board USS *Yorktown* after landing on June 4, 1942. This plane, damaged during an attack on the Japanese aircraft carrier *Kaga* that morning, landed on the *Yorktown* because it was low on fuel. It was later lost with the *Yorktown*.

This seemed to indicate, it was said, that the fight which started at Midway yesterday morning had continued for many hours with both American and enemy units maneuvering for advantage in what may be a crucial engagement determining the enemy's ability to strike at more vital points, including Pearl Harbor, the United States West Coast, Alaska and even the Panama Canal.

The action off Midway involved not only Japanese aircraft carriers but battleships and heavy cruisers. As great as this force appeared to be, however, there remained a possibility that it was engaged in a diversionary operation and that a main force was developing an attack elsewhere. It was the first time that Japanese battleships have been reported east of home waters.

There is no immediate indication whether a major portion of the enemy fleet was involved, but observers agreed that the presence of a large force more than 2,000 miles from Yokohama indicated the Japanese were bent on reducing America's growing offensive power in the Pacific and possibly bringing the war within threatening distance of the West Coast.

The Japs' grand strategy was still to be disclosed, and Washington authorities could at best only cite the possibilities based on what has been announced to date. The Midway and Dutch Harbor assaults, however, were viewed as evidence of a carefully conceived plan which may have any one of these ultimate actions in view:

1. An effort preliminary to an attack on Russia, to destroy or conquer Alaskan bases and thereby cut a route over which aerial reinforcements might be moved to the Soviet armies in Siberia.

2. Clear the way for a new and powerful attack on Pearl Harbor, or even the western U.S. coast and Panama, by trying to knock out aerial reconnaissance and interception forces which may be based on Midway and Alaska.

3. A new attempt to cut U.S. supply lines into the Southwest Pacific by forceful attacks on the Guardian Islands south of Hawaii, after, the Japanese would hope, having diverted American forces into the North Pacific.

4. A knockout try against the bases from which Japan may be or may have been attacked, including past and future air raids on the Japanese homeland and submarine operations against Japanese shipping. . . .

If the enemy's plan is to try to wipe out Midway's preliminary to attacks farther east—in which case the Dutch Harbor attack would have been chiefly diversionary—he may anticipate that he is in for trouble. Yet, just as at Wake and at Baatan and Corregidor in the Philippines, if the Japanese went to take Midway at any cost—and the fact that battleships, aircraft carriers and cruisers took part in yesterday's raids indicates that may be their intention—they may possibly succeed.

An attempt to drive the United States out of Hawaii unquestionably would produce one of the greatest battles of history, but aside from the Hawaiian Islands there are many much less strongly held outposts in the Pacific which probably could be taken.

What use the enemy could make of them once he was in possession is another matter. Wake Island, so far as is known, has cost the Japs more than they have profited by it. They expended seven warships, many planes and hundreds of men to capture it. They installed various equipment to make it into a plane base. Then a U.S. task force went over on February 24 and bombed their equipment out of existence.

★ ★ ★

Logan Daily News, Logan, OH, Saturday, June 6, 1942

JAP FLEET SUFFERS HEAVILY NEAR MIDWAY

U.S. VICTORY MAY BE COMPARABLE TO CORAL SEA

Enemy Force Appears to Be Limping Away in Retreat

HONOLULU, June 6 (AP)—Crushing defeat of a big Japanese fleet which attempted to seize Midway Island in a desperate bid for control of the mid-Pacific grew in proportions today as the United States pressed home new attacks on an enemy which appeared to be limping away.

Possibly presaging a victory even greater than that of the Coral Sea, Admiral Chester W. Nimitz said Japanese aircraft carriers, battleships, cruisers and transports were dealt damaging blows by the alert and fully prepared Midway defenders.

"While it is too early to claim a major Japanese disaster, it may be conservatively stated that United States control remains firm in the Midway area," the Pacific fleet's commander-in-chief announced last night. "The enemy appears to be withdrawing, but we are continuing the battle." . . .

If Japan hoped to catch by surprise the Midway defenders who have beaten off five weaker assaults, dating back to December 7, the surprise worked in reverse. Preparations for just such a major blow, carrying with it a threat to Hawaii and even the United States mainland, have gone forward swiftly since the war opened. They have been so exhaustive that Admiral Nimitz, returning a month ago from a visit to Midway, voiced praise for the effective coordination he had witnessed there.

He said the Midway fliers in the present battle "have added another shining page to their record of achievements" and "on every occasion when we have met the enemy. Our officers and men have been superlative in their offensive spirit."

The fight for Midway is for the last island outpost west of Hawaii still in United States hands. Guam and Wake Island fell to the Japanese, the latter after an epic struggle by the marines. . . .

Midway's outpost is poised like a dagger over Japan's Marshall Islands to the southwest and the enemy's big gamble, its first with such heavy and costly armament in all the battle it has waged at sea to date, was indicative of its determination to knock out the possible stepping stone to a westward resurgence of the United States in the Pacific.

In this June 4, 1942 photo, crewmen aboard USS *Yorktown* are seen trying to put out a fire after the carrier was hit by Japanese bombs during the Battle of Midway.

Richmond Times-Dispatch, Richmond, VA, June 6, 1942

RUMOR LAID TO AXIS

NEW YORK (AP)—Competent observers expressed the belief yesterday that rumors of a new Japanese attack on Pearl Harbor were started by German radio broadcasts which have been recorded in New York and London since shortly before 8 a.m. (E.W.T.).

All these broadcasts were sent out as "news items" under Oslo, Stockholm or Shanghai dates by Nazi radio stations in Berlin or in other parts of German-occupied Europe, and all of them were patently garbled versions of Thursday's Japanese aerial raid on Midway Island. . . . The only authority specifically cited for the information in any of the broadcasts was "an American news service." Persons familiar with Axis broadcasts said this was a typical example of Nazi "war of nerves."

OPPOSITE PAGE: During the Battle of Midway, a Japanese heavy cruiser of the Mogami class lies low in the water after being bombed by U.S. naval aircraft, May 1942.

ABOVE: Scene on board USS *Yorktown* shortly after she was hit by three Japanese bombs during the Battle of Midway, June 4, 1942. The man with the hammer at right is likely covering a bomb entry hole in the forward elevator. Later the vessel had to be abandoned and was sunk by a Japanese submarine torpedo hit.

71

Rocky Mount Telegram, Rocky Mount, NC, Monday, August 31, 1942

NAVY RELEASES REPORT ON RAID

Guadalcanal Action Sees Many Heroes

U.S. Marines climb ashore Guadalcanal Island, August 1942.

WASHINGTON Aug. 31 (AP)—The navy today released the following report of the Guadalcanal action, dated Aug. 14, from Sgt. James W. Hurlbut of Arlington, Va., a marine corps combat correspondent:

"This is no parade ground bunch of marines on Guadalcanal. The pretty blue uniforms are all back home and the green dungaree field uniforms are torn and dirty. The boys are rough, tough and nasty, and they are plenty mad. They don't need any entertainment to keep their morale up. A little chow, a lot of ammunition and an enemy to use it on and the boys will take the situation in stride.

"To a man, the marines in the Solomon Islands pay tribute to the gallantry of the naval units that took part in the attack. During the torpedo bombing attack launched by the Japanese on Aug. 8, gunners of those units manned their guns with devastating effect, scoring hit after hit on the low-flying enemy planes.

"Only meager details of the naval engagement which took place during the night of Aug. 8–9 have been received at Guadalcanal. We know, however, that no enemy ship slipped through to aid the beleaguered Japanese land forces.

"Enemy losses in the South Pacific are also measured in millions of dollars' worth of equipment and thousands of man hours of construction work taken over by the marines on Guadalcanal. The surprise attack was made so swiftly that the Japs had no time to sabotage their own material and construction. They headed for the hills so fast that breakfast was left unfinished on many camp tables. . . .

"Enemy action at present is mainly of a harassing nature. Snipers operate at night, but they are few in number and have done almost no damage. Almost every day at noon enemy bombers have flown high over the island, but about all they do is indicate the time. Yesterday seven bombs were dropped, ruining a flock of coconuts and nothing else. Several enemy submarines are operating off Guadalcanal. Early this morning they surfaced and peppered our area with five-inch shells, but without effect. Just after noon they tried the same trick with the same result.

"Heroism is taken as a matter of course. There have been countless examples of gallantry beyond the call of duty, but it seems that every man has surpassed himself in whatever effort he has faced."

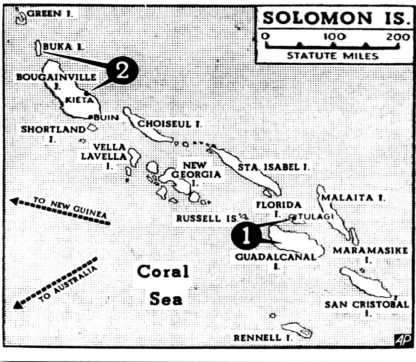

ABOVE, TOP: Three U.S. Marines point menacing Springfields toward enemy territory from a sand-bagged foxhole out beyond the front lines on Guadalcanal, Oct. 14, 1942.

ABOVE: Two U.S. Marines display a captured Japanese flag on Guadalcanal, Aug. 30, 1942.

RIGHT: Map from the *Morning Call*, Allentown, Pennsylvania, Aug. 11, 1942. The U.S. Navy announced the attack on the Japanese-occupied Solomon Islands was continuing and meeting with "considerable enemy resistance" after U.S. and Australian troops had landed in the Tulagi area (1). The Japanese first landed at Kieta on Jan. 25 and another base was established at Buka (2).

San Bernardino County Sun, San Bernardino, CA, Sunday, November 8, 1942

AMERICAN ARMY INVADES FRENCH AFRICAN COLONIES

Second Front Opened with Large Landings on Atlantic and Mediterranean Coasts

By The Associated Press

WASHINGTON, Nov. 7.—Powerful American expeditionary forces are landing on the Atlantic and Mediterranean coasts of the French colonies in Africa in the first big-scale offensive of the war under the Star-Spangled Banner.

An announcement of the action, obviously aimed at winning complete domination [of the continent] and reopening the Mediterranean Sea for the united nations in conjunction with the victorious British drive westward from Egypt, was made in a simultaneous announcement tonight by President Roosevelt and a communiqué from the war department.

The White House statement said the purpose of the move was twofold:

1. To forestall an Axis invasion there which "would constitute a direct threat to America across the comparatively narrow sea from Western Africa."

2. To provide "an effective second front assistance to our heroic allies in Russia."

Thus the Axis had an emphatic answer to its attempts to "fish for information" by broadcasting accounts of heavy Allied troop convoys escorted by warships mustering at the rock of Gibraltar in recent days.

The troops apparently were some of those which have been concentrated in the British Isles for some time, itching for action as they went through the final stages of their battle training, for they were commanded by Lieut.-Gen. Dwight D. Eisenhower, commander-in-chief in the European theater whose headquarters had been in Britain.

Gen. Eisenhower broadcast a message to the people of French North Africa on behalf of the president assuring them that "we come among you solely to destroy your enemies and not to harm you" and issued a proclamation instructing them how to

Douglas SBD-3 Dauntless scout-bombers and Grumman F4F-4 Wildcat fighters on the flight deck of USS *Santee* during Operation Torch, the November 1942 Allied invasion of North Africa. Note the yellow Operation Torch markings visible around the fuselage stars of some of the planes. Also note the distance and target information temporarily marked on the carrier's flight deck.

cooperate. To signify cooperation, the general directed that they fly the French tricolor and the American flag, one above the other, or two tricolors by day and shine a searchlight vertically into the sky by night. He also directed French naval and aviation units to remain idle.

Eisenhower's message indicated that the troops were pouring ashore in Morocco, which has both Atlantic and Mediterranean shores, and the remainder of French North Africa which comprises Algeria and Tunis on the Mediterranean. Landings also presumably were being made in the French West African colonies, including Senegal, whose capital of Dakar lies only 1,870 miles across the South Atlantic from the bulge of Brazil.

The announcement gave no details of the composition of the troops and their equipment, for obvious military reasons, but said that they were equipped with "adequate weapons of warfare" and that they would "in the immediate future, be reinforced by a considerable number of divisions of the British army."

Announcement of the landings was timed to coincide with the actual debarkation of the troops on their destinations at 9 p.m. Eastern War Time (3 a.m. Sunday, West African Time), and was made only after a reassuring message from Mr. Roosevelt's own lips had been broadcast to the French people, asking for their aid to rout their own enemies. The landing, the announcement said, was being assisted by the British navy and air forces.

BRITISH BREAK SECOND STAND BY AXIS ARMY

By Associated Press

CAIRO, Nov. 7—Approximately 100,000 men of Marshal Rommel's Axis army of 140,000 were reported captured or pinned down in pockets far behind the swiftly moving African front today as the British Eighth Army swept on toward the Libyan border after smashing the German armor in its second attempted stand.

Disregarding the thousands of foot soldiers left in the dusty backwash of the battlefront, Lieut.-Gen. Bernard L. Montgomery's British and American tanks tore into the disorganized flanks of their main prize—the battered remnants of the German armored divisions—west of Matruh, in an effort to eliminate them entirely. They already had caught up with this fleeing force once and sent it into headlong, harassed retreat a second time.

British and U.S. troops disembark from a convoy ship—a former transatlantic cruise liner, the *Duchess of Richmond*—Algiers, in November 1942. Operation Torch was launched on Nov. 8, 1942, with numerous successful landings along the Algerian coast.

Capital Times, Madison, WI, Wednesday, November 25, 1942

NAZIS PLAN TO KILL ALL JEWS IN SEIZED AREAS—DR. WISE

2 Million Were Already Slaughtered by Extinction Order, Claim

By The Associated Press

WASHINGTON—Details of a campaign which Dr. Stephen S. Wise said was planned to exterminate all Jews in Nazi-occupied Europe by the end of the year are to be laid before a committee of leading Jewish organizations today in New York.

The story—which Dr. Wise said was confirmed by the state department and a personal representative of President Roosevelt—deals with how more than 2,000,000 Jews already have been slaughtered in accordance with a race extinction order by Adolf Hitler.

Before leaving for New York to address the committee this afternoon, Dr. Wise, chairman of the World Jewish Congress and

This iconic photograph, taken between April 19 and May 16, 1943, depicts Jews captured by Nazi SS and SD troops during the suppression of the Warsaw Ghetto Uprising being marched to the Umschlagplatz (collection point) for deportation. The SD trooper Josef Blösche (second from right with the submachine gun pointed at the boy) was tried for war crimes by an East German court in 1969, sentenced to death, and executed in July of that year.

president of the American Jewish Congress, said he carried official documentary proof that "Hitler has ordered the extermination of all Jews in Nazi-ruled Europe in 1942."

After a consultation with state department officials, he announced they had termed authentic certain sources which revealed that approximately half of the estimated 4,000,000 Jews in Nazi-occupied Europe already had been killed and that Hitler was wrathful at "failure to complete the extermination immediately."

To speed the slaughter of the other half during the remaining month before the edict's deadline, Dr. Wise said the Nazis were moving some four-fifths of the Jews in Hitler-ruled European countries to Poland. There, he said, Nazi doctors were killing them at the rate of "more than 100 men an hour, per doctor," by injecting air bubbles into their veins—"the simplest and cheapest method" they could find.

Dr. Wise, who heads the committee, asserted that already the Jewish population of Warsaw had been reduced from 500,000 to about 100,000.

(The Polish government-in-exile reported in London Tuesday that Heinrich Himmler, Nazi Gestapo chief, had ordered the extermination of one-half of the Jewish population of Poland by the end of this year and that 250,000 had been killed through September under the program.)

Dutch Jews at Camp Westerbork—a deportation center established by the Nazis in northeastern Netherlands—board a freight train that will take them to Auschwitz, 1942 or 1943. The German Jewish photographer who took the photograph, Rudolf Breslauer, was killed in Auschwitz in February 1945.

Wilkes-Barre Record, Wilkes-Barre, PA, Monday, June 1, 1942

JEWS MUST WEAR STARS

VICHY, UNOCCUPIED FRANCE, May 31 (AP)—All Jews over six years of age in occupied France were ordered by the Germans in Paris today to display the Star of David as big as the palm of the hand everywhere in public.

The order, which becomes effective June 7, said the insignia "must be worn fully visible on the left breast, solidly stitched onto the clothing." Police will distribute the stars, for which the Jews must surrender one point of their clothing ration card.

A yellow Star of David, once worn by a Jew in Nazi Germany, in the collection of Museum Otto Weidt's Workshop for the Blind in Berlin. Weidt, who owned a brush-making company during World War II, employed and hid many Jews throughout the war.

CHAPTER FIVE

1943

The joint Australian–U.S. recapture of Buna, New Guinea, on Jan. 2 portended a year in which the tide would at last turn in favor of the Allies. From Jan. 14 to 24, Roosevelt and Churchill defiantly met in embattled North Africa at the Casablanca Conference, emerging with an agreement to accept nothing short of unconditional surrender from the enemy.

On Jan. 18, a small number of those confined to Warsaw's Jewish ghetto resisted German troops who attempted to round up ghetto inmates for "deportation" to the Majdanek and Treblinka death camps. This modest uprising was a prelude to the mass Warsaw Ghetto Uprising of April 19 to May 16. The uprising, the first armed revolt of civilians in German-occupied Europe, was crushed but inspired heightened resistance activity from the Polish underground.

In North Africa, British forces captured Tripoli on Jan. 23, and, in Europe, the U.S. Eighth Army Air Force launched the first all-American raid against Germany on the twenty-seventh, hitting the naval base at Wilhelmshaven. In Russia, Georgy Zhukov was elevated to marshal on Jan. 18, and 13 days later, Field Marshal Friedrich Paulus surrendered to him at Stalingrad; 91,000 surviving soldiers of the German Sixth Army became POWs. This battle was the turning point of the eastern front war.

In the Pacific, Guadalcanal was secured on Feb. 9, the first milestone in what, after Midway, had become an American offensive. This American high point was somewhat blunted by Rommel's counterattack in western Tunisia, which sent the green U.S. II Corps into disorganized retreat at Kasserine Pass during Feb. 19–24. Gen. George S. Patton Jr. was rushed in to take over II Corps and rehabilitate it. On March 23, he led it to victory at El Guettar, Tunisia.

On April 18, American fliers reaped rare personal vengeance against Adm. Isoroku Yamamoto, when, acting on radio intercepts, a flight of P-38 fighters was dispatched to intercept and shoot down the aircraft carrying him on an inspection tour over Bougainville, New Guinea. The battlefield assassination of the architect of the Pearl Harbor attack made for jubilant headlines in the States. In Japan, it created despair. Yamamoto was the nation's most popular and revered military leader.

On May 13, Axis forces surrendered in Tunisia, yielding control of North Africa to the Allies. On May 19, Churchill addressed an enthusiastic joint session of the U.S. Congress. The U.S.–U.K. alliance was at its zenith, and on May 26, in Paris, the French resistance became a mass movement as disparate groups banded together as the CNR (Conseil National de la Résistance).

On June 8, the bitter year-long Aleutian Islands Campaign wound down after Japanese forces began evacuating Kiska Island, their last tenuous toehold on U.S. territory. In the Mediterranean, on the eleventh, British forces took the Italian island of Pantelleria, halfway between Tunisia and Sicily. Lampedusa fell the next day, putting the Allies in position to invade Sicily.

On the eastern front, the Red Army counteroffensive continued with the Battle of Kursk. Begun on July 5, it was the largest tank battle in history. Not only was Germany's "invincible" armor defeated by Russia's legendary T-34 tanks, its "invincible" Luftwaffe was shot out of the skies.

Hitler called off the Battle of Kursk on July 13, having also to contend with Operation Husky, the Allied invasion of Sicily, which had commenced on July 10. On Aug. 17, Sicily fell. Yet the Führer found encouragement in a July 7 meeting with Gen. Walter Dornberger, head of development of Germany's rocket program. Seizing on what he considered a *Wunderwaffe* ("wonder weapon"), Hitler gave Dornberger's V-2, then under development as the world's first ballistic missile, top funding priority. It would soon take a toll on London and other cities.

On July 25, Italy's Fascist Grand Council voted to oust Mussolini. Il Duce was arrested, removed from office, and replaced by Marshal Pietro Badoglio, who secretly asked the Allies for surrender terms. Hitler, however, dispatched an SS rescue mission under commando leader Otto Skorzeny, which freed Mussolini on Sept. 12. After meeting with Hitler, Mussolini was installed in northern Italy as the puppet ruler of the "Italian Social Republic." Badoglio had already signed a secret armistice on Sept. 3, and the Allies landed at Salerno on the ninth. On Sept. 28, citizens of Naples rose up against their German occupiers in anticipation of the Allies' arrival.

American Pacific forces launched Operation Cartwheel on Oct. 12 with the purpose of capturing the Japanese airbase at Rabaul, linchpin of Japan's control of New Guinea. The next month, on Nov. 20, U.S. Marines landed on Tarawa and the army attacked the Makin Atoll, both in the Gilbert Islands. Rabaul, Tarawa, and Makin all eventually fell to U.S. forces, but at a cost in American lives that profoundly shocked the home front. Such heartbreakingly bloody victories would prove typical of the rest of the Pacific War.

Two days later, on the western front, U.S. Eighth Air Force B-17s targeted Schweinfurt, home of the German ball bearing industry. Since ball bearings are essential to everything that moves or has moving parts, Allied strategists believed a successful raid would critically cripple Germany's war effort. Sixty of the 292 bombers sent on the mission were lost, together with 600 crewmembers, and Oct. 14 became infamous as "Black Thursday."

That same day, inmates of the Sobibor (Poland) death camp stealthily killed 11 SS officers and several camp guards. Although they had planned to kill all the guards and walk out of the main gate of the camp, the initial killings were discovered, and the inmates ran for their lives under heavy fire. About half of the 600 prisoners in the camp dispersed into the forest, where 100 were eventually recaptured and executed.

Despite the heavy losses in Schweinfurt, American and British aircrews launched continuous heavy bombing of Berlin beginning on Nov. 23, an event reported globally via CBS Radio on Dec. 3 by Edward R. Murrow in a broadcast titled "Orchestrated Hell." The next month, Christmas Eve brought news that Gen. Eisenhower had been elevated to Supreme Allied Commander of the Allied forces in Europe. Back on Dec. 7, though, he had been named—secretly—to command Operation Overlord, the Allied liberation of Europe via amphibious landings at Normandy.

Allied Forces, troops, guns and transport are rushed ashore, ready for action, at the opening of the Allied invasion of Sicily, July 10, 1943.

Pomona Progress Bulletin, Pomona, CA, Tuesday, January 26, 1943

FDR, CHURCHILL MEET IN NORTH AFRICA FOR 10 DAYS TO DRAFT PEACE DEMANDS

President's Round Trip Made by Air; Complete Victory Only "Terms"

By WES GALLAGHER

CASABLANCA, FRENCH MOROCCO, Jan. 26 (AP)—President Roosevelt and Prime Minister Churchill, in the most unprecedented and momentous meeting of the century, have reached complete agreement on war plans for 1943 designed to bring about the "unconditional surrender" of Germany, Italy and Japan, it was disclosed today.

Defying every tradition, the president of the United States flew across 5,000 miles of the Atlantic Ocean for a 10-day meeting with Winston Churchill which saw the leaders of the two nations bring Gen. Charles de Gaulle and Gen. Henri Honoré Giraud together

Franklin D. Roosevelt talks with Winston Churchill on the lawn of the President Roosevelt's villa during the Casablanca Conference, Morocco, Jan. 17, 1943.

for the first time in a little villa just outside this city. Virtually the entire war staffs of both nations participated in day and night discussions which ended Sunday afternoon with a press conference before a group of war correspondents flown secretly from Allied headquarters halfway across North America.

These are the high spots of the of conference, which Roosevelt and Churchill agreed was unprecedented in history and may decide the fate of the world for generations to come:

ONE—The leaders of America and Britain, both military and civil, have agreed on a war plan for 1943 designed to maintain the initiative in every theater of the war.

TWO—Churchill and Roosevelt agreed that peace can come only through unconditional surrender of Germany, Italy, and Japan.

THREE—Generals Giraud and de Gaulle, meeting for the first time under sponsorship of the president and prime minister, are negotiating for a united French movement designed to put French armies, a navy and an air force again into the field against the Axis.

FOUR—Premier Joseph Stalin of Russia was kept informed of the results of the conferences. In fact, Churchill and Roosevelt offered to meet Stalin very much farther to the east, but the Russian chief was unable to leave the USSR, due to the need of his directing the present Red Army offensives.

The president and prime minister also have been in communication with Generalissimo Chiang Kai-shek and "have apprised him of the measures which they are taking to assist him in China's magnificent and unrelaxing struggle for the common cause."

FIVE—Maximum material aid to Russia and China will be one of the prime aims of the U.S. and Britain.

SIX—Roosevelt visited American troops in the field in North Africa, the first American president to visit an active war theater since Abraham Lincoln.

The meetings were held in a closely guarded, barbed wire–surrounded enclosure at a hotel in Casablanca under the greatest secrecy. . . .

The president said the unconditional surrender of Germany, Italy, and Japan did not mean destruction of the populations but destruction of the philosophy of these countries based on conquest and reigns of terror. All resources of the United Nations have been pooled and will be administered according to one central plan decided upon at the conference, the president said, but he gave no hint of when or where the military strength of the United Nations would smash against the Axis. . . . Churchill declared that despite the fact that there may be some delay at times, there is a design and purpose and unconquerable will to enforce unconditional surrender upon the criminals who plunged the world into war.

Decatur Daily Review, Decatur, IL, Tuesday, January 12, 1943

FIVE BROTHERS ENLIST TO AVENGE PAL; MISSING

WATERLOO, IOWA (AP)—The five Sullivan brothers, who enlisted in the navy together shortly after Pearl Harbor intent on avenging a pal killed in the sneak attack, are missing in action, the Navy informed their parents today.

The brothers served on the cruiser *Juneau*, which a navy communiqué last night disclosed was lost in battle around the Solomon Islands during November.

The brothers were George T., 29; Francis H., 26; Joseph E., 23; Madison A., 22; and Albert L., 20.

The five Sullivan brothers, from left to right: Joseph, Francis, Albert, Madison, and George, are shown in this Jan. 12, 1942, photo taken aboard USS *Juneau* at the time of her commissioning ceremonies at the New York Navy Yard. The sons of Thomas and Alleta Sullivan of Waterloo, Iowa, all five brothers died after the *Juneau* was sunk by a Japanese submarine on Nov. 13, 1942. The brothers had enlisted in the navy on the condition they be allowed to serve together.

Rhinelander Daily News, Rhinelander, WI, Monday, February 1, 1943

REDS CRUSH SIEGE FORCE OF 330,000; CAPTURE OFFICERS

Berlin Admits Loss of Sixth Army at Stalingrad

By The Associated Press

The German high command announced today that its southern group of the Sixth Army commanded by Field Marshal Friedrich Paulus, long encircled in the Stalingrad area, had been "overwhelmed after more than two months of heroic defense against superior forces."

Its communiqué, broadcast from Berlin and recorded by the Associated Press, said another German group in the northern part of Stalingrad still was holding out.

On other sectors of the Russian front the communiqué asserted, "fighting continues with undiminished violence."

Another Berlin broadcast said it was announced authoritatively that Paulus was severely wounded.

Soviet soldiers fire on trapped German forces from a snow-covered hill in Stalingrad, Jan. 9, 1943, at the start of the final Soviet offensive during the Battle of Stalingrad, one of history's bloodiest battles.

Germany's Field Marshal Friedrich Paulus, who was captured in Stalingrad by the Soviets on Jan. 31, shown at Red Army Headquarters in Stalingrad during interrogation, March 1, 1943. Paulus—who, contrary to the reports from Berlin, was not wounded—infuriated Hitler by surrendering instead of fighting to the death.

The German propaganda machine, forced at last to acknowledge that the trapped Nazi forces at Stalingrad have been virtually wiped out, is struggling desperately to soften the effect of this catastrophe on the German people.

Berlin broadcasts, recorded by the Associated Press, sang the praises of "the army of the dead" and maintained that its sacrificial stand had frustrated a great Russian breakthrough by tying up Soviet divisions needed elsewhere on the front.

Adolf Hitler himself promoted Paulus to the rank of field marshal and raised Artillery Gen. Heitz of the Second Army Corps to colonel general.

The German radio declared that the defeated German forces had offered "inconceivable resistance" to overwhelming odds of men and machines, with "plain soldiers and generals fighting shoulder to shoulder with bayonets and sabers if no other weapon was still good."

News of the Paulus promotion was coupled with the announcement of the promotion of three other Nazi generals to the rank of field marshal. They were listed as Col. Gen. Ewald von Kleist, Col. Gen. Baron Maximilian von Weichs and Col. Gen. Busch.

News-Review, Roseburg, OR, Wednesday, February 17, 1943

JOE DIMAGGIO GOES INTO U.S. ARMY

SAN FRANCISCO, Feb. 17. (AP)—Joe DiMaggio reported for induction into the U.S. Army today expecting to become a $50-a-month private before nightfall.

The New York Yankees' $43,750-a-year star, 28, married and classified 3-A, applied to his local draft board for voluntary induction.

"When I get in that khaki I'll have my first peace of mind in over a year," said the two-time American league batting champion, holder of the consecutive game hitting streak (56) and twice acclaimed the most valuable player of his league.

"So will Dorothy (his wife). It's been kind of rugged for us, but it's all turned out as I prayed it would, and I'll be happy when Joe DiMaggio, the baseball player, becomes just another Joe in Uncle Sam's army."

The possibility that DiMaggio intended swapping uniforms cropped up several weeks ago after he effected a reconciliation in Reno, Nev., with his wife, former Dorothy Arnold, one-time radio and night club singer.

Joe DiMaggio, center, front row, is sworn into the U.S. Army by Capt. M. A. Branson along with other inductees in San Francisco, Feb. 17, 1943.

Daily Pantagraph, Bloomington, IL, Tuesday, April 6, 1943

LAUNCHES DESTROYER NAMED FOR HERO SONS

AP Telemat

Mrs. Thomas Sullivan of Waterloo, Ia, gives a mighty whack with the champagne bottle, launching the destroyer USS *The Sullivans* at the Bethlehem shipyards at San Francisco. Lt. Mel Venter, at left, gets a bath for being too close to the action. Between is the Sullivans' sixth child, Genevieve, 26, who is awaiting induction into the WAVES. The destroyer is named in honor of the Sullivans' five sons, lost when the cruiser on which they served went down in the South Pacific.

Salt Lake Tribune, Salt Lake City, UT, Wednesday, April 14. 1943

DIVE BOMBERS BEAR NAMES OF SULLIVANS

EL SEGUNDO, Cal., April 13 (AP)—Five sleek dive bombers, right off the assembly line, were dedicated Tuesday to the five Sullivan brothers of Waterloo, Iowa, who lost their lives in the sinking of the cruiser *Juneau* in the battle of Savo Island. The parents, Mr. and Mrs. Thomas F. Sullivan, and their daughter, Genevieve, a new WAVE recruit, were present as small engraved plaques, bearing the name of each boy, respectively—George, Francis, Joseph, Madison and Albert Sullivan—were placed in the planes' cockpits.

Lt. Cmdr. C. D. Tripolitis, inspector of naval aircraft, officiated at brief ceremonies at the Douglas plant, where Sullivan, in a plea to workers, asked them to "pitch in and make these planes of yours the Waterloo of the Japs and Nazis."

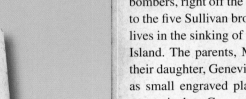

USS *The Sullivans* on Oct. 29, 1962, below. The destroyer, named after the Sullivan brothers, was launched on April 4, 1943, as shown in the photo of the launch ceremony in San Francisco, left.

St. Louis Globe-Democrat, St. Louis, MO, Saturday, May 22, 1943

YAMAMOTO, ARCH HATER OF U.S., SLAIN IN BATTLE

By The Associated Press

Admiral Isoroku Yamamoto, the Japanese Navy's commander in chief, author of the Pearl Harbor attack and the man who once boasted he would dictate peace terms in the White House, was killed last month in air combat on some far southern front, Tokyo announced yesterday.

Emperor Hirohito ordered a state funeral and raised him posthumously to the rank of Admiral of the Fleet. The Imperial Diet (Parliament) was called into session for today to pay its respects. Tokyo broadcasts told of nationwide mourning.

Despite the defeats suffered by his command in the Coral Sea, off Midway and in the Solomons, Yamamoto was this war's greatest idol of the Japanese people, to whom the defeats were reported as victories.

He probably was the No. 1 enemy of the United States, both in the bitterness of his hate and the damage he inflicted on American armed forces. He was rated Japan's ablest sea fighter. If he died in action, as Tokyo says, he was the highest-ranking officer of any of the belligerents to meet such a death in this war. He was 59.

A voice choked with emotion read this imperial headquarters communiqué to the nation:

"Admiral Isoroku Yamamoto, commander in chief of the combined fleet, gallantly met death aboard a warplane which engaged in an encounter with the enemy while directing general strategic operations during April this year."

"Admiral Mineichi Koga, who has been appointed Yamamoto's successor, is now commanding the combined fleet."

A subsequent broadcast said Yamamoto died "on the very front lines of the south," indicating a locale somewhere over the long arc of islands north of Australia, from Timor to the Solomons. There were heavy air combats over the Solomons early in April, others over New Guinea in the middle of the month. . . .

An undated file photo of Adm. Isoroku Yamamoto, commander in chief of the Japanese combined fleet and mastermind of the attack on Pearl Harbor. Yamamoto died after his plane was intercepted by U.S. Army Air Forces aircraft on April 18, 1943, over Bougainville Island in Papua New Guinea, and shot down.

Some American naval men in Washington expressed skepticism concerning the Tokyo version of Yamamoto's end. They said his forces had met so many reverses in recent months that he might have committed hara-kiri; it also was possible that he died a natural death.

In either case, it was pointed out, the high command almost certainly would have dressed up his demise with heroic trappings to keep alive the legend of his success as a factor for national morale. Other observers were doubtful of the hara-kiri theory; reports that other Japanese commanders killed themselves have lacked confirmation and have drawn Japanese denials.

Yamamoto was Japan's foremost advocate of the union of air and sea power and was one of the first commanders of any nationality to develop this combination to its maximum effectiveness. . . .

Yamamoto held a hatred for the United States which surpassed that of any other Japanese of high station, at least in vigor of its expression. Ten days after Pearl Harbor a Tokyo broadcast, apparently trying to build him up as a hero, quoted him as having written the following to a friend several months previously: "Any time war breaks out between Japan and the United States I shall not be content merely to capture Guam and the Philippines and occupy Hawaii and San Francisco. I am looking forward to dictating peace to the United States in the White House at Washington."

His hatred of America, according to popular Japanese accounts, was instilled by his father, who told him that the "barbarians came in their black ships," broke down the doors of Japan, threatened the Son of Heaven and trampled on Nippon's ancient customs. This referred to the voyages of the American commodore Matthew G. Perry in 1853 and 1854 to open Japan to intercourse with the rest of the world. Yamamoto joined the navy, he once said, so he could "return Commodore Perry's visit."

Oakland Tribune, Oakland, CA, Wednesday, May 12, 1943

VAST SURRENDER IS CONTINUING

Only One Fighting Center Remains on Peninsula! Air Bombing by Allies Halted to Protect Own Ground Forces

ALLIED HEADQUARTERS IN NORTH AFRICA, May 12 (AP)— Col. Gen. Jurgen von Arnim, Axis commander in Tunisia, was captured by the British, it was announced today.

By EDWARD KENNEDY

May 12 (AP)—A rough circle nine miles in diameter in the gaunt Tunisian hills north of Enfidaville is all that is left to the Axis in North Africa tonight, and it is crumbling rapidly under Allied assault from all sides. German resistance already has dissolved on Cap Bon to the north, where British armor made a complete tour of the peninsula and then cut inland and began rounding up tens of thousands of unnerved Germans.

The Germans had made no real attempt to hold the cape, but threw up their arms and raised white flags in ready token of surrender without even attempting an Axis Dunkerque when a single squadron of British armored cars reached Cap Bon Lighthouse at 3 p.m. yesterday.

Germans of the 15th Panzer Division, captured by the British Eighth Army near El Guettar in Tunisia, await transportation to a prison camp, May 5, 1943.

Air Bombing Halted

So thoroughly have the patrols of Lieut. Gen. K. A. N. Anderson infiltrated into Cap Bon Peninsula that Allied air bombing of the bomb-riddled area was called off late yesterday because of the danger of hitting friendly troops.

The Germans and Italians are offering considerable resistance in the mountains west of Bou Ficha and north of Enfidaville. Bou Ficha is just north of Enfidaville in the British Eighth Army's sector. Hemmed in against the Gulf of Hammamet by the British above and below them, the encircled Axis army faces a third spearhead aimed by the French 19th Corps which dashed toward the coast after crushing a German army into complete and unqualified surrender on the slopes east of Zaghouan yesterday.

Much Booty Taken

The communiqué said the prisoners taken by the Second U.S. Army Corps and their French allies in Northern Tunisia now total 37,998. In addition, huge Axis booty was taken, including large numbers of 88-millimeter guns and tanks, much of which will be turned over to the French units.

A wirephoto depicting one of the trucks in a convoy carrying thousands of unguarded German soldiers driving themselves to Allied prisons near Tunis, after the Allied victory in Tunisia, May 12, 1943.

HITLER'S "INVINCIBLES" MEEKLY DRIVE OWN CARS—TO PRISON

By DANIEL DE LUCE

MEDJEZ-EL-BAB, Tunisia, May 12 (AP)—Africa's strangest procession moved in the pre-dawn darkness today from the tip of Cap Bon Peninsula to the bomb-scarred hamlet of Medjez-el-Bab, 34 miles west of captured Tunis.

Adolf Hitler's invincibles were driving themselves, unescorted, to Allied prison pens.

German and Italian soldiers, crowded into every kind of vehicle in their armies except tanks, streamed in a dust-choked file almost bumper to bumper through the battle zone in which the North African campaign was fought for six months and concluded with a six-day Allied attack.

Mile after mile, the beaten Axis survivors drove without any sort of British guard along a route where military police were 10 miles or more apart.

Like uncertain tourists, the surrendered enemy kept inquiring the correct way to their ultimate destination, and at every hail from curious Allied service troops far behind the erstwhile front the Axis vehicles came to a full halt. French native-born Italians and Arabs stared openmouthed at this parade which seemed endless and continued all night. The procession swung through Tunis itself along streets where every house proudly flew the tri-color.

Some Axis prisoners played accordions and mandolins, but mostly these truckloads of defeated men were grimly, wearily silent.

There was not a single report of any prisoners trying to escape into the countryside, although it would have been easy.

Attempting to bring back a dispatch to a plane far inland, I got caught in the traffic jam of enemy transport and my British chauffeur observed: "The Jerries (Germans) look more fed up with the war than the Italians. I never thought I'd see rags of Jerries trying to get to a barbed wire cage ahead of me."

No ignominy the Poles suffered in 1939 or the French in 1940 surpasses the spectacle of able-bodied veteran German soldiers driving hundreds of German vehicles, to captivity.

And not a Britisher visible around for miles.

Arizona Republic, Phoenix, AZ, Thursday, July 8, 1943

REDS TAKE TERRIFIC NAZI TOLL

Huns Stopped Cold Except in Belgorod Area

By LYNN HEINZERLING

LONDON, July 8 (AP)—A grinding German tank and infantry assault against savage Russian resistance drove into an additional "few villages" Wednesday near Belgorod at the southern end of a raging 200-mile front, where the Nazis had captured two towns Tuesday, but the Germans still were unable to achieve a major breakthrough, the Russians announced today.

The German advance was made in great battle fury during which lines and trenches and even entire villages changed hands time and again.

The Russians said their troops were counterattacking late last night and "are now fighting to restore the position." The Russians said that elsewhere along the fiery front the Germans were stopped cold.

The loss of the "few villages" was acknowledged in the Soviet midnight communiqué recorded here by the Soviet monitor. Earlier, a special communiqué had told of the Germans' rushing up vast reserves and listed huge new Nazi tank and plane losses which stagger the imagination. During Wednesday alone, the Russians said, the Germans lost 520 tanks and 229 planes, making a three-day total of 1,681 tanks and 649 planes. The number of Germans killed, which the Russians are not attempting to total, is more than 13,000 listed in scattered sectors.

Wednesday's Nazi tank toll included 40 of the crack 60-ton "Tiger" tanks, the Germans' latest land battleships.

This was Germany's supreme effort to crush the Red Army—Hitler's third and perhaps final fling before an Allied invasion hits him from the west. Dispatches from both Berlin and Moscow made it clear that the Germans were making a major attempt, drawing up their air reserves from the remainder of Europe. . . .

Moscow Attack Indicated

"The battle of Kursk is on," said this commentator at another point, perhaps indicating the Nazis' first objectives for a possible wheeling movement toward Moscow itself.

The Russians admitted that the German troops had "made some little progress" today in the Belgorod sector. . . . But along the remainder of the front, particularly in the Kursk and Orel sectors to the north, the Russians said "all enemy attacks failed."

The Germans, however, asserted their troops had made "deep penetrations" in the Orel sector as well as at Belgorod despite the resistance of "400,000 crack Soviet troops supported by very strong tank and artillery forces."

RIGHT: Soviet troops follow their tanks in a counterattack during the Battle of Kursk, the largest tank battle in history, July 1943.

OPPOSITE PAGE: German troops, following the advance of German tank columns between Belgorod and Orel, Russia, take full cover during a barrage from a Soviet artillery shell, July 28, 1943.

Corsicana Daily Sun, Corsicana, TX, Saturday, July 10, 1943

POWERFUL ALLIED INVASION FORCE LANDED SICILY TODAY

Warplanes, Warships Supported Land Forces in Attack Upon Sicily

By DANIEL DE LUCE

ALLIED HEADQUARTERS IN NORTH AFRICA, July 10 (AP)—Allied armies invaded Sicily today and, with warplanes and warships in support, battled through coastal mine fields, barbed wire and gun emplacements in an effort to consolidate bridgeheads for the second European front.

American, British and Canadian forces of Gen. Dwight Eisenhower's command struck from landing barges by night, opening the big push they had awaited since they cleared North Africa of the Axis two months ago. Swarms of Allied bombers, fighter-bombers and fighters—engaged only yesterday in the final massive blows of an aerial offensive that had rocked Sicilian targets for weeks—roared across the Mediterranean narrows at dawn and formed an aerial umbrella for the fighting men aground.

(Axis broadcasts said the Allies, spearheaded by parachute units and strongly supported by sea and air, landed on both the southern and eastern coasts of the bomb-battered island which is a segment of Metropolitan Italy. The Italian high command said "Axis armed forces are decisively counterattacking." . . .

Battle for Europe

The long-heralded Battle of Europe was under way. Naval bombardments covered the snub-nosed, shallow draft landing vessels as they slipped from convoys a mile or more offshore and headed for the rocky, precipitous coast.

Through wire and hot machine-gun fire the Allied forces cut out their bridgeheads and then, with hardly a moment's pause, began battering their way toward the interior of the island. Official details of the first phase of the invasion were expected to be issued later.

Liberators of the U.S. Ninth Air Force, striking from Middle East bases by daylight yesterday, smashed the general headquarters and "nerve center of Axis Sicilian defense forces" at Taormina, a Cairo communiqué announced. Taormina lies on the Messina Strait, which narrows northward to separate Italy and Sicily by only two miles. The target area was declared "reduced to rubble and left in smoke and flame." . . .

Ten major air bases of Sicily are among the military prizes immediately at stake in the Allied invasion. As many as 300 enemy aircraft once rose from these fields in a single day to dispute the Allied challenge for air domination, but continued raids trimmed that number considerably. . . .

Every Allied soldier who embarked for Sicily last night did so with the belief that the opening of the second front in Europe is the most important action in store for Allied arms. Once Sicily could be occupied, the whole course of the war in the west might be altered to hasten the defeat of both Italy and Germany.

The Italians, for the first time since the First World War, have been forced to fight on the soil of their native land. Whether this would stiffen their courage and induce them to surpass their record in Africa was a question that only further combat could answer.

British troops wade ashore from landing craft, July 10, 1943, at the opening of the Allied invasion of Sicily.

LEFT: Transport pilots and paratroopers receive a final briefing in North Africa before starting on their invasion mission to Sicily, July 10, 1943. Even their dog, "Little Spotty," listens intently.

RIGHT: A map from the *Harrisburg Telegraph*, Harrisburg, Pennsylvania, July 25, 1943—Allied drives cut Sicily in two: A U.S. drive from the Enna region captured Palermo, Sicily's capital on the north shore, and cut off Axis troops in the western part of the isle. Meanwhile, heavy fighting still raged around Catania in the east. Heavy lines indicate approximate battle lines (July 23) after the successful Palermo drive, and arrows show principal moves.

91

Harrisburg Telegraph, Harrisburg, PA, Sunday, July 25, 1943

MUSSOLINI QUITS

King Accepts Resignation; Badoglio Heads All Forces

A jovial Mussolini and Hitler on their way to a meeting that would conclude the Munich Agreement (see pages viii and xviii), Sept. 28, 1938. As a gesture of friendship, Hitler met Mussolini with his car at the Italo-German border.

By The Associated Press

LONDON, July 25—Dictator Benito Mussolini resigned as premier of Italy and King Vittorio Emanuele, in a possible bid for peace with onrushing Allied armies, assumed command of Italian forces for "a stand against those who have wounded the sacred soil of Italy."

Marshal Pietro Badoglio, former chief of staff and never an admirer of Fascism, came out of retirement to succeed Mussolini as head of a military government accorded "full powers" by the King to do what is best for a war-shattered and weary country. The broken Mussolini went into the shadows after twenty-one years of dictatorship in which he had tried to recreate the ancient glories of Rome on a basis of Fascism and military alliances with Germany and Japan.

Shattering Blow to Hitler

This dramatic turn in Italy's fortunes was a shattering blow to Germany and Japan, Mussolini's Axis partners. No immediate comment was forthcoming from Berlin and Tokyo.

Badoglio, the 71-year-old new premier, had been dismissed as chief of staff by Mussolini on December 6, 1940. He issued a proclamation tonight telling Italians: "On orders of His Majesty the King, I am taking over the military government of the country with full powers." He called on all Italians to rally around the King. "The war continues," he added. "Italy, grievously stricken in her invaded provinces and in her ruined towns maintains her faith in her given word, jealous of her ancient traditions."

The King in his proclamation said Italy, "By the valor of its armed forces and the determination of all its citizens, will find again a way of recovery."

These sensational announcements, recorded by the Associated Press, may be the opening Italian peace moves. They came as Allied troops were sweeping across Sicily off the southern Italian mainland, less than a week after the 500-plane American air attack on the Fascist capital of Rome, and amid reports that widespread peace demonstrations had occurred in Italy's main cities.

An official British statement was expected tonight on this startling political and military turn in the war.

"No consideration must stand in our way and no recrimination must be made," said the King's proclamation. "We must stand against those who have wounded the sacred soil of Italy."

Boastful Career Ended

The "resignation" of the bald, squat, boastful Mussolini ended a career that began with the Fascist march on Rome in 1922. The international and domestic standing of Mussolini, however, has steadily deteriorated since he led his country into war in the summer of 1940.

Mussolini was conferring with Adolf Hitler last Monday when the huge American air attack was delivered on rail and airport installations at Rome. Mussolini apparently appealed to Hitler for aid in resisting the Allied onslaughts which clearly are aimed at knocking Italy out of the war as quickly as possible. . . .

If that was his plea he undoubtedly failed in his mission. The King's proclamation, which in effect dismissed the originator of Fascism, followed.

Oakland Tribune, Oakland, CA, Monday, September 13, 1943

"RESCUED" DUCE THANKS HITLER

LONDON, Sept. 13 (AP)—The German radio, expanding bit by bit in its gleeful reporting of the release of Benito Mussolini, declared today that the former Italian premier's family as well had been freed from internment by "SS (Elite Guard) commandos."

A German news agency broadcast, declaring "it is difficult to express in words the feelings which animated Hitler and Il Duce during the historic conversation," said one of the first acts of the former dictator upon his "liberation" had been to talk by telephone with the German Führer.

Twelve hours after his release was announced by Berlin, broadcasts recorded by the Associated Press began a full-blast exploitation of the incident, hailing it as a masterstroke and "an audacious venture."

The German broadcasts attempted to spread intriguing mystery over the incident, by declaring official quarters were tight-lipped over the whole occurrence.

(A United Press dispatch from Madrid quoted reliable sources there to the effect German armored speedboats and Nazi paratroops "rescued" Mussolini from La Maddalena Island, off the northeastern tip of Sardinia.)

Benito Mussolini is shown in front of a hotel on the Gran Sasso massif in Italy, where he was being imprisoned by the Italian government, Sept. 12, 1943. Gathered around the overthrown Italian dictator are some of the German paratroopers who raided the hotel in a daring rescue mission.

Bakersfield Californian, Bakersfield, CA, Friday, September 3, 1943

ALLIES SMASH INTO ITALY IN FIRST INVASION OF EUROPE!

EIGHTH ARMY LANDS IN BLOW AT HITLER'S FORT AS YANKS SCREEN PUSH

British, Canadians Win Foothold in South Italy After Pre-Dawn Crossing from Sicily Under Cover of Land, Sea, Air Bombardment

By EDWARD KENNEDY

ALLIED HEADQUARTERS IN NORTH AFRICA, Sept. 3. (AP)—British and Canadian troops, spearheading the first of several expected invasions of Hitler's Europe, won a foothold in southern Italy today after a pre-dawn crossing from Sicily under cover of a terrific land, air and sea bombardment.

A Berlin broadcast acknowledged that the invasion forces quickly captured Reggio Calabria across the Strait of Messina from Sicily, and Scilla, a small seaport 12 miles to the northeast.

The broadcast, recorded by the Associated Press in London, said one invasion column headed by many tanks already was pushing eastward beyond Reggio Calabria after a stiff fight in which, it was claimed, many landing barges were sunk and considerable losses suffered by attacking forces.

The United Nations radio at Algiers, in a broadcast heard by United States government monitors, said the British stormed through the wreckage of pillboxes, costal batteries and road blocks under the first impact of the attack and were pushing through lemon and olive groves (crisscrossed with ditches and mine fields towards the 6,000-foot Aspromonte—"bitter mountain.") . . .

Steel Canopy

The seasoned warriors of General Sir Bernard L. Montgomery's Eighth Army under the overall command of General Dwight D. Eisenhower, stormed across the choppy straits in close-packed little boats before dawn under a screaming canopy of steel from land batteries and a sea force of cruisers, destroyers, monitors and gunboats. Overhead flew dark formations of hundreds of planes which smashed a path through the beach defenses and scrambled the enemy's network of communications throughout the Italian toe.

Brenner Blocked

In crippling pre-invasion assaults, Flying Fortresses knocked out at least temporarily the vital railroad feeding German troops through the Brenner Pass into Italy, and United States Mitchell bombers wrecked kingpins of railway defense lines in the Naples area.

The Fortresses, winging 1,500 miles round trip in their deepest strike yet into Italy, destroyed the railroad bridge at Bolzano, 35 miles below Brenner Pass, and cut the railroad at Trento, 30 miles farther south with four direct hits. Freight yards at Bologna, 170 miles south of the page also were wrecked. . . .

First Landing

The first of the invaders, British and Canadian contingents of General Montgomery's famed command, set foot on the Calabrian coast opposite eastern Sicily at 4:30 a.m. (7:30 p.m. P.W.T.). . . . American planes and warships played a prominent role in the preparation and support of the landings.

The invasion, the first Allied land attack on the European mainland since the Dieppe raid in August 1942, came just 19 days after the final cleanup of Sicily on August 18 in a campaign that lasted 38 days. . . .

Canadian Move

Even before the close of the victorious Sicilian campaign, the hard-hitting Canadians were withdrawn from the front and it was understood they were drilling for a new assignment. Today's attack presumably was "it." As they did in the Sicilian campaign for the first time, the Canadians teamed up with units of General Sir Bernard L. Montgomery's famous Eighth Army, toughened and battle-scarred from their long series of triumphs over the Axis across the northern edge of Africa.

The enemy apparently knew the attack was coming, for yesterday German and some Italian planes made several attacks on points along the Sicilian side of the straits, including Augusta. They lost at least four planes in these attacks. . . .

First Blow

The first blow from land was struck at the mainland at 11:33 a.m. August 16, when a 155-millimeter "long tom" of the United States Seventh Army artillery fired the first shell from a vineyard in the Sicilian hills.

The brief announcement that the invasion had begun was made at Allied headquarters shortly after dawn. War correspondents, knowing an important announcement was likely, had risen at 4:30 a.m., and waited anxiously as the sky reddened in the east.

BELOW: Allied troops board an invasion craft in Italy, Sept. 3, 1943.

RIGHT: A U.S. Army poster depicting a B-17 Flying Fortress dropping two bombs, 1943.

U. S. ARMY

FLYING FORTRESS

Deadly Queen of the Skies_ pride of the Army Air Forces

NAZIS LOSE 104 PLANES, YANKS LOSE 60 IN RAID

WASHINGTON, Oct. 15 (AP)—General Henry H. Arnold, chief of the United States air forces, reported officially today 60 Flying Fortresses and 593 crew members were lost in yesterday's raid on Schweinfurt, but "at least half" of the crew members "are believed to be alive as prisoners of war on the basis of past experience."

The American bombers, Arnold said, encountered the "most intense fighter opposition" so far met over Europe.

"That," he declared in a formal statement, "is the payoff on the importance which the Nazi attached to his ball bearing industry at Schweinfurt. The more important the target the more fiercely he fights to protect it."

By *HENRY B. JAMESON*

LONDON, Oct. 15 (AP)—Photographs revealed today the giant Nazi ball bearing factory at Schweinfurt was obliterated by the terrific American heavy bomber assault that cost the Eighth Air Force 60 bombers and precipitated perhaps the greatest battle in aerial warfare.

At least 104 German fighters were downed by the Fortress sharpshooters and their Thunderbolt escorts in the attack yesterday. Two U.S. fighters failed also to return from the two-hour battle that raged all the way from Europe's coast to the target and back again.

The reconnaissance photographs revealed Schweinfurt's plants, where probably 50 percent of the Nazis' war-vital roller bearings are produced, were wiped out by the precision-pattern crews who were told in advance a successful blasting of the target might shorten the war by six months.

The fact the Germans threw up "everything in the book" in defense of that vital industrial center indicated they, too, considered the factories of the highest importance to the war effort.

"Without the slightest hesitation, I would say our boys encountered the stiffest and fiercest fighter opposition in the history of aerial warfare," an Eighth Air Force spokesman said.

"What we did to the Germans yesterday will be felt severely—and soon."

The number of Fortresses that participated in the raid was not disclosed, but it was described officially as "large."

ABOVE: A U.S. Flying Fortress is seen shortly after raiding a vital ball bearing manufacturing center in

Despite the opposition, the American bombers planted their bombs over all of the 72 acres of factory buildings housing one of Germany's most important centers for producing bearings—an essential for virtually every piece of mechanized war equipment.

"There ought to be ball bearings rolling all over Germany," said one crewman who watched hundreds of bombs pour into the target area. The 60 heavy bombers announced officially as missing constituted the greatest loss ever inflicted upon the Allied air forces by the Nazis in a single raid.

It exceeded by one the 50 lost by the Americans Aug. 17 in the prolonged raid on Schweinfurt and Regensburg when formations hitting the latter target made their celebrated shuttle trip to Africa. The RAF lost its greatest number, 58, in a night attack on Berlin Aug. 23.

The minimum of 104 Nazi fighters knocked down yesterday fell far short of previous American achievements. The record of 307 destroyed on the Schweinfurt-Regensburg attack Aug. 17 still stands. The second highest number of enemy fighters destroyed, 142, was claimed in the American raid on Bremen and Vegesack a week ago today when the German rocket device made one of its first reported appearances.

Rocket-carrying German fighters were observed yesterday by several Fortress men, one of whom—Lt. Perry D. Row, of Wichita, Kan.—said a projectile that whizzed over his wing from a long way off "looked like a big red brick."

The German overseas radio, in a broadcast recorded by the Ministry of Information, admitted that considerable damage was done to Schweinfurt's residential section yesterday.

Other German broadcasts, declaring "flying commanders which set out early this morning are constantly finding more wreckage," said 123 American aircraft were shot down. Fourteen German fighters were lost, it was said.

BELOW: Ground crew members at a bomber station in England watch anxiously as a U.S. Flying Fortress, returning from a raid on ball bearing plants at Schweinfurt, Germany, bursts into flame after crash landing, Oct. 14, 1943.

ABOVE: This U.S. Flying Fortress returned safely to Britain after the attack on ball bearing plants at Schweinfurt, but cast off a propeller in landing and ripped a hole in its own fuselage, Oct. 14, 1943.

CHAPTER SIX

1944

The year opened promisingly for the Allies. On Jan. 22, American and British troops landed at Anzio, Italy, which put them in position to march against Rome. And just five days after the Anzio landings in Italy, the horrific Siege of Leningrad in Russia was finally broken. During 872 days of horror, more than 1 million of the city's civilian residents had died of starvation and disease.

Operations at Anzio soon bogged down, and it was May 23 before U.S. general Mark Clark took the offensive. Still, by spring, it was clear that the momentum had swung in favor of the Allies. Many believed victory would come before Christmas—at least in Europe. As for the war against Japan, that nation had been put on the defensive since the 1942 Battle of Midway, yet American casualties only became heavier on land as well as at sea.

From Russia, Joseph Stalin continued badgering both Winston Churchill and Franklin D. Roosevelt to open up a western front by invading France. At last, on April 22, 1944, the western Allies launched Exercise Tiger, a rehearsal for the Normandy invasion, or Operation Overlord. Soon after this, U.S. general Dwight Eisenhower, Supreme Allied Commander, Europe, oversaw the assembly of some 160,000 Allied troops in more than 5,000 ships and landing craft for the initial landing. Troops were to land along a 50-mile-wide swath of Norman beaches. The naval component of the force was led by British admiral Sir Bertram Ramsay, who swept English Channel invasion routes clear of mines and prepared to set up engineering marvels dubbed Mulberry harbors. These portable dock facilities would facilitate the rapid off-loading of men and equipment on the French coast to sustain the invasion in the aftermath of the landings. To this was added Operation Pluto, the construction of dual oil pipelines from England and across the Channel to France. These would fuel victory in Europe.

The invasion was precisely timed to coincide with a full moon—needed for visibility—and half tide, necessary to accommodate the landing craft. These conditions were available only between June 5 to June 7, but only June 6 provided a narrow window of passable weather. Eisenhower seized on it as D-Day.

At 5:50 a.m., the battleships bombarded Nazi shore defenses, even as the first landing ships closed in on the beaches. At 6:30, the bombardment ceased, and the landings began. Thanks to an elaborate deception campaign in the run-up to the invasion, resistance was lighter than expected along the landing zone—except at the beach code-named Omaha. Here, German artillery and machine guns took a ghastly toll on the Americans, who nevertheless prevailed at the cost of some 2,500 left dead on the beach.

In a bizarre incident on June 3, three days before the landings, the AP teletyped a flash across news wires, announcing that the Allies had landed in France. The cause of this blunder? A young British teletype operator practicing her typing skills. The very next day,

June 4, Lt. Gen. Mark Clark's forces—for real—began the liberation of Rome, which on June 5 became the first of the Axis capitals to fall to the Allies. News of this victory was overshadowed by D-Day.

The summer brought more triumphs. At the invasion's center, the breakthrough out of Normandy came at last on July 27, when U.S. general Omar Bradley's First Army opened a gap in the German lines. On the southern wing, George S. Patton's Third Army began its head-long westward advance that, by war's end, captured or killed more enemy soldiers and liberated more towns and villages than any other military operation in the war.

In the meantime, on July 20, Adolf Hitler was wounded in an assassination attempt that was part of an abortive military coup d'etat. Ten days before this, in the Pacific, Saipan—on the threshold of Japan itself—had been declared "secured" after nearly a month of fighting in which some 5,000 Americans and at least 23,000 Japanese troops were killed—along with some 22,000 civilians. Many of these Saipan residents, refusing to surrender, leapt off Marpi Point, a high plateau on the island's northern tip.

As the Allied forces pressed westward across Europe, Eisenhower briefly detoured to liberate Paris on Aug. 25, after more than four years under Nazi occupation. The next month, on Sept. 11, advance elements of the First Army, a recon platoon belonging to the 5th Armored Division, crossed the Our River into Germany. The enemy homeland had been penetrated.

British field marshal Bernard Law Montgomery, anxious for a major breakthrough into Germany, commenced Operation Market Garden on Sept. 17. The largest Allied airborne operation in the war, Market Garden ended in disaster, with the loss of 17,000 Allied troops (killed, wounded, or captured)—more casualties than D-Day had cost.

In the Pacific, Gen. Douglas MacArthur, who had been forced to flee the Philippines on March 11, 1942, redeemed his celebrated pledge—"I shall return"—when he led an Allied amphibious landing at the Philippine island of Leyte on Oct. 20. Notwithstanding the Market Garden setback, this, along with the overall Allied west-ward advance in Europe, created what Eisenhower called "victory fever."

By December, it seemed obvious that the German armies were defeated. And yet, on Dec. 16, a quarter-million troops of the "defeated" Wehrmacht and Waffen-SS stormed through the Ardennes in the northern sector of the Allied front and surrounded American positions, beginning the six-week Battle of the Bulge. On Dec. 22, Brig. Gen. Anthony McAuliffe, acting commander of the beleaguered 101st Airborne, received a German surrender demand. His heroically colloquial reply was quickly transmitted worldwide: *"Nuts!"*

On Christmas, elements of Patton's Third Army stopped the German advance and, the next day, broke through the enemy lines to link up with McAuliffe's troops in Bastogne, Belgium.

Troops and crewmen aboard a Coast Guard–manned landing craft as it approaches a Normandy beach on D-Day, June 6, 1944.

Decatur Daily, Decatur, AL, Thursday, January 27, 1944

GERMAN SIEGE OF LENINGRAD FULLY BROKEN

Nazis Are Forced to Yield Large Area to Russians

LONDON, Jan. 27 (AP)—Russian general Leonid A. Govorov announced today that Leningrad had been completely liberated by the two-week Red offensive, with the Nazis driven 40 to 60 miles from the city and more than 700 nearby towns and villages freed. The exceptional honor of 24 salvoes from 324 guns reserved for the greatest victories was ordered fired by the guns of Leningrad for the armies, the people of Leningrad and the Red fleet.

"As a result of the fighting a task of historic importance has been solved—the city of Leningrad has been completely liberated from the enemy blockade and from barbaric enemy shelling," said a special bulletin recorded from a Moscow broadcast by the Soviet monitor.

By EDDY GILMORE

MOSCOW, Jan. 27 (AP)—The Russians have reached the bank of the Luga River west of Novgorod, a *Pravda* dispatch reported today as the Leningrad army of Gen. Leonid A. Govorov and the Volkhov army of Gen. K. A. Meretskov continued to smash from opposite directions into the Germans' Baltic salient. The Luga is only about 10 miles east of the Leningrad-Vitebsk railway, one of the two remaining railways radiating southward from Leningrad that remain available for German use.

The *Pravda* dispatch said three German regiments were defeated in a clash on the Luga.

This photo, taken in Leningrad during the frigid winter months of 1942, shows citizens of that city collecting water from a broken main during the 872-day siege by German invaders. The military blockade was one of the longest and deadliest in history—some historians estimate that more than 1 million died of starvation and disease.

Bradford Evening Star, Bradford, PA, Thursday, January 27, 1944

CAPT. JIMMY STEWART REFUSES PROMOTION TO MAJOR—WANTS HIS JUNIOR OFFICERS RECOGNIZED FIRST

A U.S. LIBERATOR BOMBER BASE, ENGLAND, Jan. 27 (AP)—Capt. Jimmy Stewart, formerly of Hollywood and now leader of a Liberator bomber squadron, is the talk of his airmates at this base because he startled a superior office by turning down a promotion to major. Friends of the actor, who won his wings the hard way, quoted him as explaining his refusal by saying that he didn't want to be raised to a higher rank "until my junior officers get promoted from lieutenant."

Stewart has piloted his bomber on three raids—as a squadron commander he flies only occasionally and fellow fliers say he did a "swell job." On the ground he puts in long hours at executive work. Friends say Stewart has avoided social gatherings, except for occasional appearances at the officer's club, where he usually is the life of the party and the group's favorite pianist.

The best testimonial to his career in the Army was given a few days ago when some visiting G.I.'s from another Liberator base made some remarks anent his rapid rise to rank within hearing of Stewart's crew. The remarks precipitated a verbal blast from Stewart's men that left no doubt around the Eighth Air Force that there's nothing Hollywoodish about the new story "Mr. Smith Goes to Berlin."

Maj. James Stewart, center, talks over the final details of a mission with fliers before they take off from England in January 1944. Stewart, who flew bombing missions over Europe as a squadron commander, had been promoted to operations officer of a bomber group in England.

Freakish Thaw

A sudden, freakish, warm thaw has turned the Russian-German front below Leningrad into quagmires, muddy roads, unlocked swamps and flooded rivers, front dispatches reported, but the Red Armies kept up their great northern offensive.

In weather the like of which seldom has been seen in the Leningrad area, Russian troops strove mightily to clear the last remaining 35 miles of the Leningrad-Moscow trunk railway still in German hands and make possible the resumption of direct rail traffic between Russia's two largest cities.

The big junction towns of Tosno, Luban and Chudovo are in hourly peril from the advancing Soviet forces, dispatches said, and it was difficult to see how all of them will be able to remain in German hands for another 24 hours. . . .

The great Russian offensive which lifted the siege of Leningrad was now in its fourteenth day, and was rolling through the German lines with apparently unabated momentum. In its first 12 days it had brought death to more than 40,000 Nazis and had routed 10 enemy divisions—normally 150,000 men—on the Leningrad front alone, the Russian communiqué declared.

On June 26, 1944, a man contemplates a mound of German helmets and weapons—trophies seized by the Red Army from the Germans after the Siege of Leningrad ended—in the Museum of the Defense and Siege of Leningrad.

Brownsville Herald, Brownsville, TX, Tuesday, May 23, 1944

PICO, HITLER LINE STRONGHOLD TAKEN

Gen. Clark Establishes Headquarters at Anzio; Nazis Rushing Reserves

ALGIERS (AP)—The Fifth Army has launched an offensive on the Anzio beachhead with the Mediterranean Tactical Airforces providing the aerial spearhead for the assault.

ON THE ANZIO BEACHHEAD (AP)—Lt. Gen. Mark W. Clark established a Fifth Army advanced command post on the beachhead after inspecting American troops here yesterday. . . .

USS *LST-77* off-loads M4 Sherman tanks at Anzio, Italy, May 1944.

ALLIED HEADQUARTERS, NAPLES (AP)—Allied troops, fighting against German reinforcements hastily flung into battle, have struck deeper into the Germans' mountain barrier only 22 miles from the Anzio beachhead, seizing more mountain heights northeast of Terracina, it was announced today.

The German high command declared—without confirmation here—that the Fifth Army on the beachhead had launched a strong infantry and tank assault, supported by planes, at the center of that front and "fighting is in full swing." Berlin broadcast said the beachhead Fifth Army attacked after intensive artillery fire, hitting southwest and west of Aprilia, and in the Cisterna-Littoria sector.

Headquarters declared the Germans have thrown their full reserve strength south of Rome in the Hitler line battle, and the Allied main and beachhead armies are engaging 17 Nazi divisions, some of them already badly mauled. . . .

In the town of Piedimonte, four miles west of Cassino, the enemy still was clinging to strong points while Eighth Army troops, including Poles, were on three sides of this strong natural position. (Last night the Morocco radio said Eighth Army forces had captured Piedimonte). . . .

The Allied beachhead force observed the start of its fifth month at Anzio by inflicting heavy casualties on the Germans with artillery fire which broke up a German counterattack on raiding forces which the Allies had sent out. Some prisoners were taken.

Between 500 and 750 Flying Fortresses and Liberators, together with many hundreds of medium, light and fighter-bombers, were thrown into a great aerial onslaught against enemy concentrations, communications and positions in night and day support of the ground forces.

Clovis News Journal, Clovis, NM, Tuesday, May 23, 1944

CASSINO AND MONASTERY FREE OF NAZIS AT LAST

By LYNN HEINZERLING

WITH THE EIGHTH ARMY ON MONASTERY HILL ABOVE CASSINO, ITALY, May 19 (AP)—The great bastion of Cassino, and this stately hill hallowed by the works of St. Benedict, were free of Germans today for the first time in more than six months, but furious battles still swept on up the Liri Valley toward the Adolf Hitler line.

Polish troops, fighting through the stark hills north of Cassino while the British Eighth Army swarmed across the Rapido River to cut highway No. 6 behind the town, forced German Gen. Richard Heidrich's crack parachute troops out of their pillboxes and rubble heaps and sent them north in swift retreat.

From this hill where St. Benedict founded the Benedictine order in 529 A.D. and laid out the foundations for the monastery which until three months ago was a glistening gem against the sky, I looked down on what remains of Cassino, free at last of street fighting and the chatter of machine guns. . . . Nowhere in the world is the devastating power of aerial bombardment more evident than on the crest of this ancient hill.

View of the destroyed Italian town of Cassino, May 26, 1944, several days after the city's capture by the Allies. Hangman's Hill, the scene of bitter fighting during the long and bitter siege of the stronghold, is shown in the background. The nearby Monte Cassino fourteenth-century monastery—believed to be a German fortress—was controversially bombed by the Allies on Feb. 15 and reduced to rubble.

Richmond Times-Dispatch, Richmond, VA, Monday, June 5, 1944

FIFTH ARMY CAPTURES ROME

SOME INSTALLATIONS WITHIN ETERNAL CITY DESTROYED BY NAZIS

Allies Pursue Germans Northward After Mopping Up Center of Capital

By EDWARD KENNEDY

NAPLES (AP)—Fifth Army troops captured ancient Rome last night, smashing German resistance in the heart of the Eternal City and sweeping on northward in pursuit of battered German forces which had dynamited some installations.

The mop-up of the center of Rome—the first Axis European capital to fall to Allied troops—was completed at 9:15 p.m. (3:15 p.m., E.W.T.) by Americans and Canadians under Lt. Gen. Mark W. Clark.

How much of the city was razed by the beaten German garrison was not immediately learned, but most of the bitter all-day fighting occurred in the suburban areas. The last German rearguard unit was crushed by Allied gunners in front of the Bank of Italy, almost within the shadow of Trajan's Column.

A smoke pall hung over parts of the city, where the Germans began their demolitions shortly after 3:30 p.m. (The BBC in a broadcast recorded by NBC said this indicated the Germans had "probably destroyed the bridges over the Tiber River" which runs southward through the city and then southwest to the Tyrrhenian Sea. Across the Tiber lies Vatican City.) . . .

(A Madrid dispatch to the *London Daily Mail* said Pope Pius XII had held urgent consultations Sunday with the papal secretary of state, Luigi Cardinal Maglione, and had prayed in his private chapel. Vatican City itself was reported sealed off from Rome behind a double Swiss guard. The pope declared in a speech last

Romans crowd the streets to cheer soldiers of the Fifth Army as they make their way through the Italian capital, June 5, 1944.

Friday that "whoever would dare lift a hand against Rome would be guilty of matricide." The pope and his administrative seat of the Roman Catholic Church had been ringed by German troops ever since the Allied offensive got under way in Southern Italy in September 1943.)

Front dispatches from Edward Kennedy and Daniel De Luce, Associated Press correspondents who entered Rome with the Allied troops, said the final drive from the suburbs began after General Clark appeared in the fighting area, where bullets whizzed about his head. The Germans had thrown up roadblocks of wrecked vehicles and other material, and shelled important road intersections with 88-mm. self-propelled guns. This slowed the Allied drive by troops of the old Anzio beachhead, and fighting continued to the edge of the ancient Forum in the center of Rome. . . .

Hysterical with joy, Roman citizens at the city's outskirts amid kisses and tears waved on United States and Canadian tanks and infantrymen dashing up the Via Casilina and then battering into German defenders holding up the suburbs, a front dispatch from Associated Press correspondent Daniel De Luce said. . . .

Every Precaution Taken to Spare City

While the Fifth fought the enemy at the gates of Rome, the British Eighth Army to the southeast continued its advance after its function with other American and French troops below Valmontone.

With Rome's capture so imminent, the Allied command called on Romans to save the historic metropolis from destruction, and to keep highways open so the Allies could push on through "without delay in order to continue the destruction of the German armies farther north."

This followed headquarter's pledge to take every precaution to spare the city, coupled with the warnings that the enemy would be thrown out by force if he made a stand in the city.

BELOW: U.S. soldiers march past the Colosseum in Rome in pursuit of retreating Axis troops, June 5, 1944.

MORE THAN 9,600 YANKS KILLED IN ROME DRIVE

WASHINGTON (AP)—The battle for Rome, from the time the Allies swept across the Messina Straits onto the Italian Peninsula last Sept. 3, cost the lives of more than 9,600 Americans.

Secretary of War Stimson reported last Thursday that the Italian campaign from the date of the landing to May 28 totaled 55,150, including 9,686 killed, 36,910 wounded and 8,554 missing.

Many others have been killed, wounded or lost in battle since then. Thousands died in North Africa and in Sicily to pave the way for the direct attack on Italy.

★ ★ ★ D-DAY, June 6, 1944 ★ ★ ★

Evening Independent, Massillon, OH, Tuesday, June 6, 1944

ALLIES INVADE FRANCE

LAUNCH DRIVE TO LIBERATE EUROPE

Montgomery Leads Troops in Plunge Across Channel

BULLETIN LONDON, June 6 (AP)—The German news agency DNB said in a broadcast shortly before 10 a.m. (4 a.m. E.W.T.) that Anglo-American troops had been reinforced at dawn at the mouth of the Seine river in the Le Havre area.

By WES GALLAGHER

SUPREME HEADQUARTERS, ALLIED EXPEDITIONARY FORCE, June 6 (AP)—American, British and Canadian troops landed in northern France this morning, launching the greatest overseas military operation in history with word from their supreme commander, Gen. Dwight D. Eisenhower, that "we will accept nothing except full victory" over the German masters of the continent.

One of the most famous images of the war, this photo was taken around 8:30 p.m. on the eve of D-Day, June 5, 1944. Supreme Allied Commander Dwight D. Eisenhower speaks with paratroopers of the 101st Airborne Division at RAF Greenham Common airfield in England. They would be among the first Allies to land in France the next day. Eisenhower recalled one of the soldiers yelling out, "Now quit worrying General, we'll take care of this thing for you!"

The invasion, which Eisenhower called "a great crusade," was announced at 7:32 a.m. Greenwich Mean Time (3:32 a.m., E.W.T.) in this one-sentence communiqué No. 1:

"Under the command of General Eisenhower, Allied naval forces supported by strong air forces began landing Allied armies this morning on the northern coast of France."

It was announced moments later that Britain's Gen. Sir Bernard L. Montgomery, hero of the African desert, was in charge of the assault.

The locations of the landings were not announced.

Eisenhower himself wished godspeed to the parachutists who were the first to land on the enemy-held soil of France.

For three hours previous to the Allied announcement the German radio had been pouring forth a series of flashes reporting that the Allies were landing between Le Havre and Cherbourg along the south side of the bay of the Seine and along the north coast of Normandy.

This would be across the channel and almost due south of such British ports as Hastings, Brighton, Portsmouth and Bournemouth.

The Germans also said parachutists had descended in Normandy and were being engaged by Nazi shock troops.

The landings had been in progress several hours before the Allied communiqué was issued.

Allied soldiers leaped onto the shores which the Germans have spent nearly four years in fortifying, while Allied planes and ships hurled into those defense barrages which the Nazis admitted were terrific. The fleet included several battleships, which the Germans said set the whole Seine bay area ablaze with their fire.

The Germans announced also that American reinforcements began landing at dawn, aided by artificial fog, and that in some places dummy parachutists were dropped to confuse the defense.

French patriots previously had been warned by Allied radio broadcasts to get out of areas within 35 kilometers (22 miles) north of the coast to escape the shock of battle and the gigantic aerial bombardment.

The Germans said the bombers ranged as far north as Dunkerque, the unhappy port from which the beaten British army escaped almost exactly four years ago. All England resounded with the thunder of their coming and going.

An Associated Press correspondent flying over the French coast in a B-26 Marauder reported seeing the fields inland strewn with hundreds of parachutes and dotted with gliders, while great naval forces fired into the coast fortifications.

On several occasions thousands of troops, even with correspondents aboard, sailed out in great fleets to almost within shell range of German defenses in Europe as though they were going to attack while Nazi reconnaissance planes closely checked convoys.

These feints have been carried out on widely separated points.

The supreme command made no bones about its intention to attack, but the surprise was that the Germans did not know where the main blow was coming.

Gen. Eisenhower speaking with a 101st paratrooper at Greenham Common, June 5, 1944.

In four previous big amphibious landings to date the Allies obtained tactical surprise three times—at Anzio, Sicily and in North Africa. At Salerno the Germans guessed the landing spot and were waiting.

During the 48 fours previous to the landings RAF and American bomber fleets dropped a stupendous tonnage of bombs on the West Wall's defenders.

A canopy of American and British bombers and fighters turned the Todt fortifications on which Hitler had pinned his hopes into a jumping, jagged mass of flames.

On the fringes of the attack big gray battlewagons of the sea slipped through the channel waters, awaiting any challenge from the battered Nazi fleet.

The western front opening climaxed years of patient preparation by the top military minds of America and Britain, and in hard work in factories and munitions plants by millions of Americans and Briton.

The plan of attack was the same which General Eisenhower had when he came to England in June 1942, but which was shelved during the improvised North African operation.

This morning the sweat and toil of the factory worker of American and Britain, and the cool planning of the military men of both countries, bore fruit.

Every weapon that has proved its worth since Pearl Harbor was in the hands of the fighting men of the United Nations.

What success they would meet no one could say with certainty.

U.S. paratroopers fix their static lines before preparing to jump before dawn over Normandy on D-Day, June 6, 1944.

By HOWARD COHAN

WITH UNITED STATES PARACHUTE TROOPS, June 6 (AP)—American paratroopers—studded with battle-hardened veterans of the Sicilian and Italian campaigns—landed behind Hitler's Atlantic wall today to plant the first blow of the long-awaited western front squarely in the enemy's vitals.

The Allies' toughest, wiriest men of war cascaded from faintly sunlit skies in an awesome operation.

Twin-engined C-47s—sisters of America's standard airline landships—bore the human cargo across the skies, simultaneously towing troop-laden CG-4A gliders—to merge in a single sledge-hammer blow paving the way for frontal assault forces.

Armed with weapons from the most primitive to the most modern, the paratroopers' mission was to disrupt and demoralize the Germans' communications inside the Nazis' own lines.

There was no immediate indication that their dynamite and flashing steel and well-aimed fire was not succeeding in the execution of plans rehearsed for months in preparation for the liberation of occupied Europe.

The steel-helmeted, ankle-booted warriors wore a red, white and blue American flag insignia on the sleeve and camouflaged green-splotched battle dress.

★ ★ ★

The Delta Democrat-Times

48th Year   (NEA)   GREENVILLE, MISSISSIPPI Tuesday, June 6, 1944   Associated Press (AP)   No. 235

EXTRA!   EXTRA!   EXTRA!

INVASION!

The Invasion Coast Lies Close to Supplies

Nazis have expected invasion of northern France even before Allied troops landed in North Africa. Extensive defenses have been erected along the coast from the Spanish border to Denmark. But the Maginot line was not invincible and it was built more strongly and with greater thoroughness than the Nazi forts on the invasion coast.

Allied Troops Land In Northern France

SUPREME HEADQUARTERS, ALLIED EX-PEDITIONARY FORCE, (AP) – American, British and Canadian troops landed inNorthern France, this morning, launching the greatest overseas military operation in history with word from their supreme commander, Gen. Dwight D. Eisenhower, that "we will accept nothing except full victory" over the German masters of the continent.

The invasion, which Eisenhower called "a great crusade," was announced at 7:32 a. m. Greenwich Mean Time (3:32 a. m., Eastern War Time) in this one-sentence communique No. 1:

"Under the command of General Eisen-hower, Allied naval forces supported by strong air forces began landing Alliedarmies this morning on the Northern coast of France."

It was announced moments later that Britain's Gen. Sir Bernard L. Montgomery hero of the African desert, was in charge of the assault

The locations of the landings were not announced.

Eisenhower himself wish land on the enemy-held soil

For three hours previous been pouring forth a series tween Le Havre and Cherbo along the north coast of Nor

This would be across the Hastings, Brighton, Portsmo

The Germans also said pa engaged by Nazi shock tro

The landings had been in progress
Allied soldiers leaped onto the she
lied planes and ships hurled into those
The fleet included several battlesh
The Germans announced also that
that in some places dummy parachutes
French patriots previously had bee
(32 miles) of the coast to escape the sh
The Germans said the bombers ran
ish army escaped almost exactly four
All England resounded with the th
An Associated Press correspondent
inland strewn with hundreds of parach
fortifications.
In a special order of the day issued
"We will accept nothing except full
Eisenhower told his men they wer
months," and warned them that they w
Berlin said the "center of gravity"
miles southeast of Cherbourg.
Caen is 10 miles inland from the se
Heavy fighting also was reported
One of Belin's first claims was that
Montgomery, hero of the
commander

Nazis Report Allies Swarm Ashore In Area Between Cherbourg-LeHarve

LONDON (AP)—The Berlin radio said today that "combined British-American landing operations against the western coast of Europe from the sea and air are stretching over the entire area between Cherbourg and Le Havre."

The broadcast declared that grand scale amphibious operations are under way on a broad front between the mouth of the Seine and the Estuary of the river Vire.

"A large number of Allied landing boats of various types and light Allied Naval forces in considerable strength are taking part," Berlin added.

"Six heavy Allied warships and 20 destroyers are off the mouth of the Seine."

The river Vire empties into the Atlantic 30 miles southeast of Cherbourg, indicating that the reported invasion was occurring all along the northern side of the Normandy peninsula stretching along the Bay of the Seine between Cherbourg and Le Havre.

"Fierce fighting against Allied forces in the Caen area," 10 miles inland from the Normandy coast and 30 air line miles southwest of Le Havre, was reported by the Germans.

Caen is near the h

GEN. DWIGHT D. EISEN-HOWER . . . supreme Allied commander . . . raised Kansan who knit together American, British and French forces in North Africa into unified command . . . "Ike"...eft West Point, 1915, was lieutenant colonel, 1940 . . . after the war went through Infantry Tank School, Command and General Staff School, War and Army Industrial colleges . . . 1935 to Philippines as MacArthur's chief of staff...

THE AP INTER-OFFICE

JUNE–JULY 1944

A Staff News Bulletin   AP Bureaus Around the World

INVASION ISSUE

RIGHT: Cover of the June–July 1944 issue of The *AP Inter-Office: A Staff News Bulletin for AP Bureaus Around the World*, which highlighted The Associated Press's coverage of D-Day. The cover features Henry P. "Hank" Jameson, AP's first casualty of the June 6 invasion and the first war correspondent to be injured on D-Day out of the entire press corps. According to the cover story, he was accompanying the Ninth Air Force Engineers when an 88mm shell hit their landing craft. Jameson suffered a dislocated shoulder and a wrenched leg.

Salt Lake Telegraph, Salt Lake City, UT, Tuesday, June 6, 1944

D-Day Chronology Traces Early Steps of Landing

By The Associated Press

12:37 a.m. (Eastern War Time)—German news agency transoceanic broadcasts that the Allied invasion has begun.

1 a.m.—German DNB agency broadcasts Le Havre being bombarded violently and German naval craft fighting Allied landing craft off coast.

1:56 a.m.—Calais radio says: "This is D-Day."

2:31 a.m.—Spokesman from Gen. Eisenhower in broadcast from London warns people of European invasion coast that "a new phase of the Allied air offensive has begun" and orders them to move 22 miles inland.

3:29 a.m.—Berlin radio says: "First center of gravity is Caen," big city at base of Normandy peninsula.

3:32 a.m.—Supreme Headquarters, Allied Expeditionary Force, announces that Allied armies began landing on northern coast of France.

3:40 a.m.—SHAEF announces Gen. Sir Bernard L. Montgomery is in command of assault army, comprising Americans, British, Canadians.

3:42 a.m.—Berlin says heavy Allied warships were shelling Le Havre and parachute troops are floating down on Normandy.

4 a.m.—Supreme Headquarters say a number of feints preceded invasion.

4:07 a.m.—Germans say Allies were reinforced at dawn at the mouth of the Seine near Le Havre.

4:47 a.m.—French patriots warned to evacuate areas 22 miles bordering coasts to escape aerial bombardment.

5:35 a.m.—Berlin reports strong air attacks on Dieppe; says cruiser and landing boat have been sunk off Cherbourg.

5:49 a.m.—Enemy says four British parachute divisions landed between Le Havre and Cherbourg.

5:50 a.m.—U.S. battleships and marines participating.

6:24 a.m.—Prime Minister Churchill says 4,000 ships and several thousand lesser craft formed probably world's greatest invasion armada: "Everything is proceeding according to plan."

7:03 a.m.—German destroyers and E-boats rushing into operational area and "no doubt are being dealt with," headquarters say. H-hour announced as between 6 and 8 a.m. British time (midnight and 2 a.m. E.W.T.).

7:08 a.m.—Allied landing forces establish beachheads and are advancing inland, aerial pictures show. RAF bombers attacked Osnabrück, Germany, air ministry announces.

7:24 a.m.—Swedish reporters in Berlin report dozen landings with main attack toward Caen.

7:32 a.m.—Supreme Headquarters announces beachhead secured and dug in.

8:01 a.m.—Germans announce landing on Channel Islands of Guernsey and Jersey; say Allied tanks land at Arromanches midway between Cherbourg and Le Havre; Allies incessantly employing assault boats off Ouistreham.

8:10 a.m.—Paris radio says battle in Normandy "seems to be gaining in depth."

The 15-inch guns of HMS *Warspite* shell German positions on the Normandy coast, June 6, 1944.

LEFT: A first-wave battalion on the beach of Normandy on D-Day, June 6, 1944. One soldier operates a walkie-talkie radio directing other landing craft to the safest spots for unloading their parties of fighting men.

ABOVE: An LCVP (Landing Craft, Vehicle, Personnel) from the U.S. Coast Guard–manned USS *Samuel Chase* disembarks troops of Company E, 16th Infantry, 1st Infantry Division, who wade through churning water—and German machine-gun, artillery, and rifle fire—onto Omaha Beach on the morning of June 6, 1944.

LEFT: An aerial view of Allied soldiers and assault vehicles storming Normandy's Utah Beach on D-Day, June 6, 1944.

LEFT BOTTOM: Landing supply ships putting cargo ashore on Omaha Beach, Normandy, mid-June 1944. Note the Army half-track convoy forming up on the beach and the barrage balloons overhead raised by the African American 320th Barrage Balloon Battalion.

BELOW: Men of the American assault troops of the 16th Infantry Regiment, wounded while storming Omaha Beach during the Allied invasion of Normandy, wait by the chalk cliffs at Colleville-sur-Mer for evacuation to a field hospital for further treatment, June 6, 1944.

8:34 a.m.—Berlin reports "fierce fighting going on everywhere," with Nazi counterthrusts in progress.

9:10 a.m.—Big channel guns on French coast fire on Dover.

9.15 a.m.—11,000 Allied planes bomb and strafe miles of Norway coast.

9:20 a.m.—Marshal Petain broadcasts to Frenchmen to avoid reprisals.

9:34 a.m.—Germans report Nazi counterattacks knock out 35 Allied tanks in Seine bay area and making progress east of Cherbourg.

9:40 a.m.—Supreme Headquarters receives information beachheads established in Normandy with troops striking inland.

10:40 a.m.—Unconfirmed reports says Hitler en route to France. Germans identity four American and two British airborne divisions operating in Normandy and Seine bay areas.

11:15 a.m.—Allies reported several miles inland in Normandy. Germans report penetration between Caen and Isigny.

Monroe News-Star, Monroe, LA, Monday, July 10, 1944

CONQUEST OF SAIPAN FINISHED

WAR 1,000 MILES NEARER JAPAN

Vast New Possibilities of Sea And Air Smashes Opened

RESISTANCE COSTLY

U.S. PACIFIC FLEET HEADQUARTERS, PEARL HARBOR, July 10 (AP)—Vast new possibilities of sea and air smashes toward Japan and the Philippines surged into view today with the conquest of Saipan and Noemfoor Islands in the western Pacific.

Onrushing American forces wrested Saipan Saturday from a terrified Japanese garrison trapped on the island's northern tip. It fell 24 hours after Allied forces under Gen. Douglas MacArthur completely took over Noemfoor near New Guinea's northwest end.

Associated Press war correspondent Rembert James representing the combined Allied press, came through with the first details of the savage bitter-end struggle the trapped Japanese offered on Saipan.

"Organized Japanese resistance ended just before dusk yesterday," he wrote. "Civilians were surrendering by the hundred. In 25 days of battle American forces had battered the first great hole in Japan's inner defense armor and carried the war more than 1,000 miles westward. From Saipan, American planes can fly across Japan's sea and air routes southward from the empire and even Japanese home islands will be in reach of long-range planes."

Marines take cover behind a sand dune on the beach at Saipan during the Marianas invasion, July 1944.

LEFT: Flak fills the sky as anti-aircraft guns of the U.S. Navy task force, covering the amphibious landing operations at Saipan, Mariana Islands, fight off a Japanese attack, June 1944.

BELOW: Machine gunners turn up the heat as they cover advancing marines in the final cleanup on northern Saipan. In the background a 37-mm gun crew stands ready to beat off any counterattacks that the Japanese can muster.

James said probably 95 percent of the Japanese garrison, estimated at more than 20,000 when the invasion began June 14, had been destroyed.

"The finale yesterday was an ugly spectacle of senseless dying," he continued.

Enemy troops, weakened to a point of exhaustion by two days of futile counterattack, were pushed steadily backward. The desperation and panic behind the enemy lines helped to crumble Japanese defenses.

"American airmen flying over the trapped foe saw signs of bewilderment and terror among the troops and civilians there. At one place scores of Japanese swam out into the sea as the battle drew nearer. . . . There was nowhere to swim to and they had to swim back or drown."

The strategic value of Saipan was immense.

"Saipan offers the best possibilities for airfield development of any of the islands captured from the Japanese in the central Pacific campaign," said Vice-Adm. John H. Hoover, commander of the central Pacific forward area. "Its main airstrip is far the best that we have taken and the island's size offers additional advantages of wide dispersal."

BELOW: The forward patrol of a U.S. Marine unit advances through a grassy ravine in Saipan as they follow Japanese communication lines in an effort to locate enemy positions, July 8, 1944.

ABOVE: A U.S. Marine discovers a Japanese family—a mother, her four children, and their dog—hiding in a hillside cave, June 21, 1944, on Saipan. In the battle's final days, some 4,000 terrified Japanese civilians, mostly women and children, fled to the north of the island, a high plateau called Marpi Point. The Japanese military had convinced many of them that it was their duty to kill themselves rather than fall into the hands of the cruel Americans. More than a thousand either were killed by Japanese troops or chose suicide, many jumping off Marpi Point.

U.S. Marine reinforcements move through the shattered Japanese-held village of Garapan, capital of Saipan, June 1944.

Super fortresses could operate from Saipan with devastating power against Tokyo, 1,450 miles north, or the Philippines, 1,500 miles west. The island also has great potentialities as a naval supply point and submarine staging base. It is less than 150 miles north of Guam, first United States territory taken by Japan after the outbreak of war.

Organized resistance of Saipan collapsed rather suddenly, Adm. Chester W. Nimitz announced, following a day of suicidal counterattacks that penetrated the American lines in some places as much as 2,000 yards but cost the enemy 1,500 dead.

At least 11,500 Japanese—probably thousands more—were killed and more than 7,000 enemy civilians were imprisoned. American casualties to June 28 were 1,474 dead and 8,278 wounded.

Associated Press correspondent William L. Worden said a series of wheeling movements chopped off whole sections of the line in the prelude to the final battle. The complicated flanking movements of three divisions swung the American line like the cracking of a whip. This left the Japanese on the extreme northern point of the island separated from those facing the army's 27th Division on the northwest.

He said dozens of pockets of civilians cowering in ruins or caves came into the American lines. A prisoner of war camp for the first time in this war has many unwounded Japanese soldiers in it. Civilian internment camps for Koreans, Chamorro and Japanese workers are overflowing with thousands of reunited families.

Japan's frantic defense of Saipan cost her at least 58 ships and more than 900 airplanes. The Americans lost 172 planes, and had four ships damaged. . . .

Col. Albert L. Waner, of the army's bureau of public relations, estimated that 60,000 Japanese have been killed in the central and southwest Pacific in the last seven months, 40,000 in Burma and India, and thousands more in China.

★ ★ ★

Washington C. H. Record-Herald, Washington Court House, OH, Thursday, July 20, 1944

HITLER REPORTED INJURED IN ASSASSINATION ATTEMPT

LONDON, July 20 (AP)—Berlin announced that Adolf Hitler was burned and bruised in an unsuccessful bombing attempt on his life today.

Three of Hitler's military leaders were seriously injured, while his chief military advisor, Col. Gen. Alfred Jodl, was less seriously hurt along with five other generals and two admirals.

A source in London with close European connections said the incident probably occurred at Breda, Holland, reported to be the headquarters of Field Marshal Erwin Rommel. . . .

(The British radio said Hitler also suffered a brain concussion, and said this explained a 14-hour break overnight in telephone communications between Berlin and Stockholm.)

The broadcast announcement did not give the scene of the attack, but it obviously took place while Hitler was surrounded by high members of the military staff—perhaps at Hitler's headquarters.

The announcement came 16 hours after Tokyo's announcement of the fall of Premier Hideki Tojo, and Berlin said Hitler, after the attack, received Benito Mussolini, third member of the ill-starred trio who led the Axis into war.

Among the seriously injured, Berlin said, was Lt. Gen. Schmundt, chief of the German army's personnel department and chief military aide de camp to Hitler for several years. Two lieutenant colonels named Brandt and Borgmann, and a "collaborator" named Berger also were listed as seriously injured. Slightly injured were these: Generals Jodi, Hitler's personal military aide; Karl Bodenschatz, aide to Hitler; Günther Korten, chief of staff of the German air force, Buhle, Heusinger and Walter Scherff; Admirals Voss and von Putkammer.

Reichsmarshal Herman Göring at once went to Hitler upon learning of what had happened, the Berlin broadcast added.

"The Führer himself, besides light burns and bruises, sustained no injuries," the announcement from Berlin said. "He had immediately taken up his routine work afterwards and, as it had been planned, received the Duce (Mussolini) for a lengthy discussion."

Only yesterday, the Russian press published a statement by the captured commander of the 41st German Army Tank Corps, Lt. Gen. Edmund Hoffmeister, saying there was grave dissent in ranks of the German high command, with old generals dissatisfied with Hitler's strategy in refusing to retreat.

It was the second time, at least, during the war that Hitler narrowly missed death. The first time was November 8, 1939, when a bomb exploded in the Munich Beer Hall after the Führer had left a celebration marking his ill-fated putsch of 1923.

The Berlin broadcasts did not immediately name the time or place of the bombing attempt. Hitler has been reported spending a great deal of his time on his mountaintop at Berchtesgaden. The captured Gen. Hoffmeister said it was there that Hitler recently held a conference of 150 generals and admirals to outline his strategy. The Hoffmeister statement, as published in Moscow, described Hitler then as of swollen face, of low and jumbled voice.

For a dictator, however, Hitler's life has been singularly free of recorded attempts to assassinate him. The most notable episode developing from internal opposition to Hitler was in June 1934, shortly after he had taken power in Germany, when he led the ruthless "blood purge" of Capt. Ernst Roehm and his associates. Roehm's movement was described as a "rebellious riot" in the Reichstag session which Hitler summoned to hear his accounting.

Adolf Hitler and Benito Mussolini inspect the ruined briefing room at Hitler's "Wolf's Lair" headquarters near Rastenburg, East Prussia, July 20, 1944. It had been destroyed by a bomb in an attempt by German officer Claus von Stauffenberg and other conspirators to assassinate Hitler. Mussolini had arrived on a previously planned visit earlier in the day.

Helmut Hirsch, a 21-year-old Jew, was arrested December 20, 1936, however, on what informed persons in Berlin at the time said were charges of carrying explosives for the purpose of making an attempt on the life of a high German personage. Berlin dispatches at the time said his intended victim may have been Hitler.

Hirsch was executed despite intercession on his behalf by the United States government. Hirsch was a naturalized U.S. citizen who was arrested at Berlin upon his arrival from Prague, Czechoslovakia.

In the Munich beer hall bombing, Hitler left the hall just minutes before a time bomb exploded in a pillar of the hall near the rostrum where he had spoken to his party followers. Six persons were killed and more than 60 injured in the blast.

An arrest was made for the bombing, but Berlin authorities never announced the outcome of their investigation. At the time the Gestapo attempted to pin responsibility on British agents.

Weather Forecast
FAIR AND COOLER.
Sunrise, 5:33. Sunset, 8:10.

VOL. LXXV NUMBER 154
WHOLE NO. 23,322

THE INDIANAPOLIS NEWS

LAST EDITION

THURSDAY EVENING, JULY 20, 1944.

34 PAGES   Entered as Second-Class Matter at Postoffice, Indianapolis 6, Ind. Issued daily except Sunday   FOUR CENTS

HITLER INJURED BY BOMB

F. D. R. on Air Tonight After He Wins Renomination

NEW JAP CABINET TERMED RUSE

Ballot This Afternoon on Running Mate

Wallace, Truman Main Contenders; Jackson Flays G.O.P.

By MARK THISTLEWAITE
The News Staff Correspondent

CHICAGO, July 20.—Strife was uppermost as the Democratic national convention met at noon Thursday in second-day and perhaps final session to adopt a platform, nominate President Roosevelt for a fourth term and select his running mate.

In an effort to discount the G. O. P. record of three days, which has been attributed to "Dewey efficiency," the party managers decided to cram into the second day all the things that the convention came here to do even though it might take all night.

But harmony moves which had

Other convention stories, Pages 7, 8, 9, 10 and 11, Part 1.

been designed to restore unity and expedite business had failed after numerous conferences, some of which lasted until sun up. As sleepy-eyed delegates and laymen assembled to witness final organization of the convention by the induction of Senator Samuel D. Jackson, Indiana, into the post of permanent chairman, dissension was in the air more than ever before and was spreading.

New Dealers and anti-New Dealers were still fighting over social and economic reforms. Southerners and northerners were fighting over Negro equality versus white supremacy. Liberals and Conservatives were clashing over the vice-presidency. Delegates from the farm states and rural areas were protesting domination of the convention by city bosses. The cleavage in labor had been widened by opposing stands taken by the A. F. L. and the C. I. O. on Vice-President Wallace's renomination.

A floor fight over the platform was threatened unless the planks concerning minority segments of the population were modified at the final session of the resolutions committee, which, without mentioning anti-poll tax, anti-lynching or fair employment practices, had squinted at northern Negroes rather than at southern Negroes. Incensed, Tennessee, which had voted in caucus to vote for President Roosevelt, threatened its action and announced no decision on a fourth-term nomination would be attempted until after the platform had been adopted.

Floor Fight Predicted.

More important was a floor fight

HOOSIERS AT CONVENTION—E. Curtis White (right), former state senator from Marion county, chats with Mayor Jess T. Pavey (left) of South Bend, at the opening of the Chicago national Democratic convention.
—A. P. Wirephoto

Don't Make American Ballot Hitler's Secret Weapon, Sen. Jackson Appeals

By a STAFF CORRESPONDENT

CHICAGO, July 20.—Senator Samuel D. Jackson told a cheering Democratic national convention Thursday that "America will win this war "finally and completely" no matter who is elected

President of the United States next November.

But a change in national administration is "dangerous" to contemplate, he warned. It might well prove to be the "tragedy of this generation."

"How many battleships would a

Democratic defeat be worth to Tojo?" he asked. "How many Nazi legions would it be worth to Hitler? Could Goebbels, himself, do better to bolster Axis morale than the word that the American people had upset this administration?"

He continued: "America can not afford to take a chance. We must not allow the American ballot box to be made Hitler's secret

The full text of Senator Jackson's speech is on Page 8, Part 1.

weapon. Change means interruption. Interruption means delay. The American people will not vote for change, interruption and delay."

A committee composed of Governor Schricker and Mrs. Samuel M. Ralston, of Indiana, and Governor J. W. Broughton, North Carolina; Herbert O'Conner, of Maryland, and Prentice Cooper, of Tennessee, was named to escort Jackson to the platform.

Schricker was given a great hand when he was introduced and Jackson received still a greater hand, as the convention stood and applauded while the band played

Indiana Delegates Split; Most Are for Wallace

By WILLIAM L. TOMS
The News Staff Correspondent

CHICAGO, July 20.—With the self-styled liberal element apparently taking things in hand at the Democratic national convention, the Indiana delegation found itself definitely split over the matter of a choice for a 1944 running mate for President Roosevelt. Delegation leaders took a poll of the Hoosier contingent and ascertained that an even dozen were for the renomination of Vice-President Wallace, despite the fact that

power director, a count which included McNutt's own vote.

Five others were listed as favoring Judge Sherman Minton.

Other convention stories, Pages 7, 8, 9, 10 and 11, Part 1.

former United States senator from Indiana, although Judge Minton was expending little energy in his own behalf.

A stray half vote was recorded as for Senator Harry Truman, of Missouri, and that fractional favor was accredited to Daniel J. Tobin.

Russians Storm Lwow, Gateway to Mid-Europe

Reds Breach Bug River Defenses; Latvian Drive Shoves Germans Back

MOSCOW, July 20 (AP).—Germany's mutilated armies retreated Thursday to the outskirts of Lwow, pawn of two world wars, while approximately fifty miles to the north Soviet troops smashed through the Bug river defense line which from 1939 to 1941 was the frontier between Poland and Russia.

The gains at the south end of the flaming battlefront were matched with a new offensive along the north Latvian border, in which Red army troops shoved the Nazis back twenty-six miles on a forty-five-mile front in two days. Front dispatches said that Red army tanks and riflemen, after

capturing Sokal, forty-five miles north of Lwow and bridging the Bug, had reached for the first time Polish territory which had been the victim of Nazi overlordship for nearly five years.

[The German radio said that Russian troops had reached Augustow at the base of the Suwalki triangle, eight miles from the boundary of pre-war Poland. The Germans consider the Suwalki triangle between East Prussia and Lithuania a part of the Reich, annexed in the fourth partition of Poland in 1939. Augustow is just south of the Suwalki border.]

Last reports said that barely eight miles northeast of Lwow the Red army had four to five German divisions completely pocketed in the rear at Brody.

Premier Stalin's high command reported gains in many sectors of the 600-mile front, along which the prized objectives of Kaunas, Daugavpils (Dvinsk) and Brest-Litovsk were nearly within the Red army's grasp.

Battle-scarred Lwow, hub of six important rail lines and in Soviet hands the last time in 1941, appeared certain to be lost by the reeling German defenders, who fell

Map, Page 3.

Continued on Page 12, Column 3

Judges Chosen for Two More Gaming Trials

Ranking Aids Badly Hurt

ADOLF HITLER

LONDON, July 20 (AP).—Berlin announced that Adolf Hitler was burned and bruised in an unsuccessful attempt on his life Thursday.

Three of Hitler's military leaders were seriously injured, while his chief military advisor, Colonel General Alfred Jodl, was less seriously hurt, along with five other generals and two admirals.

[The British radio said that Hitler also suffered a brain concussion, and said this explained a fourteen-hour break overnight in telephone communications between Berlin and Stockholm.]

The broadcast announcement did not give the scene of the attack, but it obviously took place while Hitler was surrounded by high members of the military staff—probably at Hitler's headquarters.

Among the seriously injured, Berlin said, was Lieutenant General Schmundt, chief of the German army's personnel department and

chief military aide de camp to Hitler for several years.

Two lieutenant colonels named

Continued on Page 12, Column 6

2 Officers Will Succeed Tojo in Tokyo Shift

U. S. Won't Be Fooled by "Window Dressing," Says Sec. Patterson

WASHINGTON, July 20 (UP)—Acting Secretary of War Robert B. Patterson, warning that the change in Japanese leaders may be just "window dressing," predicted Thursday that those in control in Japan would install "the toughest and most ruthless commanders" for the army and navy posts.

The Japanese need not think that because they change their leaders we will forget what happened at Pearl Harbor and thereafter," Mr. Patterson told a press conference.

Commenting on the fall of Premier Hideki Tojo, Patterson said that the United States would not be fooled by any move in Japan to install leaders who pretend to be friendly to the United States.

Tojo's fall, however, is proof that the Japanese people are beginning to be aware of the serious character of Japanese defeats, he said.

By the United Press

Emperor Hirohito Thursday commissioned General Kuniaki Koiso and former Premier Admiral Mitsumasa Yonai, both known to be friendly toward the United States before Pearl Harbor, to form a new Japanese cabinet in succession to that of General Hideki Tojo, which resigned en bloc after confessing it could not win the war.

Announcement by the official Japanese Domei news agency that two political "moderates" had been intrusted with the organization of a new government confirmed that the extremist military clique which put Tojo in power and engineered the sneak attack on Pearl Harbor had lost control of Japan.

The move was regarded by some observers as the first step toward an ultimate Japanese attempt to win a negotiated peace, though no immediate peace bid is anticipated.

Sources familiar with the Japanese political situation suggested that the new cabinet would attempt to intensify the Japanese war effort,

British Take 8 More Towns on Paris Road

SUPREME HEADQUARTERS, British armored for

San Bernardino County Sun, San Bernardino, CA, Thursday, July 27, 1944

YANKS SMASH INTO REAR NAZI POSITIONS

Five-Mile Gains Scored in Wide Gap Near St. Lo

SUPREME HEADQUARTERS, ALLIED EXPEDITIONARY FORCE, July 27 (Thursday) (AP)—A great combined American tank and infantry assault smashed through the German first and second defense lines and into the rear artillery positions west of St. Lo Wednesday, scoring gains up to five miles deep through a four mile-wide breach in the Nazi positions.

At least 14 towns, including two important road junctions, fell in the drive, which outflanked the stubborn Nazi line running northwestward to the coast.

On the eastern flank of the Allies' Normandy beachhead, the British-Canadian offensive bumped to a standstill against the toughest defense belt yet encountered, and press dispatches reaching London early today reported a serious setback in the Orne-Odon wedge where the British were said to have been hurled from the town of Esquay and strategic hill 112. This dispatch remained without headquarters confirmation.

New High in Precision

The new American push in its second day was "marked by a precision and cooperation among armored infantry, artillery and air units not reached by any American army thus far in the war," Associated Press Correspondent Wes Gallagher wrote from the front late last night.

The Americans cut the highway from St. Lo to Coutances near St. Lo and made their deepest inland penetration of the invasion, leaving in their wake uncounted dead and captured of the Nazi 353rd Infantry and Third Parachute Divisions.

The assault, with doughboys riding tanks into battle like cowboys on steel ponies, breached the enemy line between St. Lo and Périers, badly mauling two enemy divisions in a hailstorm of tank fire, bullets, artillery shells, and bombs from the sky.

Marigny Captured

It threatened to force withdrawal of the Nazis fighting desperately to hold the line to the northwest from Périers to Lessay, near the coast. The American First Army was attacking all along a 20-mile front from Lessay inland—in its biggest blow since Cherbourg and possibly since D-Day—and the breadth and force indicated at least a corps was in action. (An Army corps is at least two divisions and probably more.)

The U.S. armored fist crashed through the outer crust of German defenses, and in flaming street battle against Nazi panzers, including giant 52-ton tanks, captured Marigny, a road-junction town seven miles west of St. Lo. . . .

"Cowboy Infantry"

In their breakthrough, hard-hitting American Sherman tanks and their "cowboy infantry" who leaped from the armored vehicles and knocked out Nazi gunposts, captured at least a dozen other villages, and sent back battle-stunned prisoners in uncounted procession.

A front dispatch said some of the first prisoners were parachutists, Hitler's picked troops so unnerved by the bomb and artillery fire that they surrendered sobbing and screaming, "This is not war—it is criminal." But German hedgerows, armored and field gun defenses, took their toll of the doughboy thrust. . . .

Rommel Pinned Down

The British Second Army was reported holding its ground—but no more than that. Latest reports indicated the British-Canadians had beaten off attacks against St. Martin-de-Fontenay and Verrières, towns five miles below Caen, but had not been able yet to take May-sur-Orne or Tilly-la-Campagne.

The German command again was committing large forces to this battle area, and one dispatch said reinforcements were being shifted from as far as the Caumont sector, 20 miles to the west.

A high British staff officer declared: "Rommel is definitely pinned down in Normandy and can't retreat. He's got to stay here and fight to the bitter end. If Rommel once starts to go back he's really in trouble. With our great aerial superiority, we could slaughter his transport. That's why he's now fighting madly to the end."

**A view from the hilltop overlooking the road leading into the town of Saint-Lô in Normandy, France, July 1944.
Two French children in the foreground watch convoys and trucks of equipment go through
their almost completely destroyed city en route to the front.**

Decatur Daily Review, Decatur, IL, Friday, August 25, 1944

NAZIS IN PARIS SURRENDER TO FRENCH TROOPS AFTER BATTLE THROUGH STREETS

Armored Force Routs Enemy in Final Stand

BULLETIN

NEW YORK (AP)—The German commander of Paris has surrendered to Brig. Gen. Jacques Leclerc and the commander of the French Forces of the Interior, Paris radio reported today in a broadcast recorded by Columbia broadcasting system.

Under terms of the surrender, German commanders were ordered to cease firing immediately and hoist the white flag.

"The weapons will be collected and the men gathered without weapons in a determined place, until new orders are given," the terms stipulated. "The weapons will be surrendered intact."

Captured German officers were led from the Hotel de Ville today and police had to keep the crowd from lynching them, said Radio Paris as heard by NBC.

LONDON (AP)—The Free French radio announced that Gen. Charles de Gaulle entered Paris at 7 p.m. (1 p.m. E.W.T.) today.

LONDON (AP)—Paris appeared to be in Allied hands tonight with the French Second Armored Division operating in the city. Fighting, however, still was going on in and around the French capital.

Gen. Eisenhower's supreme command declared that Brig. Gen. Jacques Leclerc's armor was operating in the capital and a broadcast from a reporter with American forces in France spoke of the liberation of Paris as "a fact."

As fighting continued, the French Forces of the Interior appealed by radio for Parisians to come "to the barricades."

Broadcasts from the city said the joyous citizenry already were celebrating their freedom. Other radio dispatches said American troops had entered the city in support of the French.

Nazis Barricaded for Stand

Lt. Gen. Joseph Pierre Koenig, commander of the French Forces of the Interior, announced at 6:02 p.m. that Leclerc's tanks were operating in the very heart of Paris and that the Patriots were holding all the main official buildings and most of the highways.

Koenig said the Germans had barricaded themselves for a stand-off fight in several places. He declared that First French armored patrols reached FFI headquarters in the Hotel de Ville (city hall) just off the Rue de Rivoli at 10 p.m. last night and that the bulk of the French armored division entered Paris this morning.

Both FFI and German broadcasts said heavy fighting was raging inside the city and that an American tank column had driven into the Paris outskirts from Versailles in the west and along the Paris-Étampes road leading south. The Germans said the heaviest clashes with tanks and patriots were near the Arc de Triomphe and the Palais du Luxembourg.

De Gaulle Awaits Entry

Gen. Charles de Gaulle was said to be at Bagneux, a southwestern suburb six miles from the center of Paris, waiting to be conducted into the capital.

The old revolutionary war cry of the Parisians, "To the barricades," was sounded in appeals to the populace to rally to the final fight for liberation, which was said to center at the École Militaire, the Palais du Luxembourg and the district of Clichy in north Paris. But fighting was said to be dying down in the old tapestry manufactory, the Gobelins, and the French were mostly in control of the suburbs—the Red Belt. The FFI was ordered to hold its positions at any price until relief arrived in strength.

"A great part of the capital has been liberated," a Col. Rolle, identified as an FFI commander, broadcast.

American forces stationed at Bourg-la-Reine and Bagneux started moving into the city at 8:15 a.m.

★ ★ ★

New York Stock Exchange and Curb Markets in This Edition

Pittsburgh
Sun-Telegraph

7 STAR FINAL NIGHT EXTRA

International News Service
International Soundphoto

VOL. 35—NO. 24   TWO SECTIONS   FRIDAY, AUGUST 25, 1944   ★ FOUR CENTS

Nazis Fleeing to Marne

FAMED ARC DE TRIOMPHE IN PARIS

YANKS, FRENCH ENTER PARIS

Nelson Expected To Quit

By WILLIAM S. NEAL
International News Service
WASHINGTON, Aug. 25.

U.S. Forces Capture Cannes

BULLETINS
WITH THE CANADIAN FIRST ARMY, France, Aug. 25.—(AP.)—Canadians late today established contact with Amer...

Kluge Quitting Channel

BULLETIN

How Americans Took City Told By Eyewitness

Paris Nazi Commander Surrenders

NEW YORK, Aug. 25.

Troops Fighting In Streets Get Wild Welcome

BELOW: Supreme Allied Commander Eisenhower surrounded by photographers and soldiers as he makes his way to his car during the liberation of Paris, August 1944. Directly behind Eisenhower is Free French general Marie-Pierre Koening.

St. Joseph News-Press, St. Joseph, MO, Friday, August 25, 1944

YANK ENTRY INTO PARIS DESCRIBED

By DON WHITEHEAD

PARIS, Aug. 25 (AP)—Street fighting raged through the heart of Paris today as American and French columns drove into the city from the south amid a tumultuous welcome from hundreds of thousands of Parisians.

The first French column to enter the city reached the Palais du Luxembourg at 10:20 a.m. The Germans, the collaborationist militia and the French Gestapo organization opened fire and the battle was on.

An American infantry column drove to Notre Dame at 11 a.m. in a spectacular ground attack. (This dispatch was filed at 12:28 p.m.—5:28 a.m. Central War Time.)

Rifles Crack

The columns fought toward the center of the city, where 5,000 French Forces of the Interior and city police have held out for the past week. Machine guns and rifles cracked on all sides as the column I was with drove to within a block of the Luxembourg.

Joyous, happy throngs who greeted the entrance of the tanks and infantry with a thundering welcome fled to the safety of buildings and within a few minutes the streets that were choked with humanity, laughing and crying over the liberation, were bare battlegrounds.

As I write this story the Germans are still holding out in the area on both sides of the Seine halfway along the Champs-Élysées, Place de la Concorde, Quai d'Orsay, Tuileries, gardens of the Louvre, the Madeleine, the Chamber of Deputies, the Senate and the Hôtel de Crillon.

French Fight French

French patriots have a grip on the Île de la Cité, the Palais de Justice, the prefecture of police, the prefecture of the Seine, and the factory district. But Frenchmen are fighting Frenchmen as well as Germans in liberating a city wild with happiness over the freedom which they waited for four years.

There was so much confusion and excitement over the entrance into the city that it is difficult to give a coherent account of the events that moved so swiftly, once the French armored column began rolling through the heavy morning fog that made vehicles look like prehistoric monsters appearing out of the swamps of creation.

But when the last enemy resistance crumbled at the gate to Paris, then this heart of France went mad—wildly, violently mad with happiness.

All the emotions suppressed by four years of German domination surged through the people. The streets of the city as we entered were like a combined Mardi Gras, Fourth of July celebration, American Legion convention and New Year's Eve in Times Square all packed into one.

Our column began to roll at 7 a.m. from Longjumeau, six miles south of Paris. A French captain stopped all correspondents one mile from town and insisted he had orders that no one without a written permit could enter the city. He told three British correspondents they would be shot if they drove by without a pass. An American colonel heard the story and said the captain was acting without proper authority. I drove to the blockade and suddenly my jeep lurched forward into the column (of troops). . . . At 9:57 a.m. my jeep rolled into Paris.

Never again do I expect to see such scenes as I saw on the streets of Paris. There was only a narrow lane through which the armor could roll. Men and women cried with joy. They grabbed the arms and hands of soldiers and cheered until their voices were hoarse.

Smothered by Kisses

When the column stopped I was smothered, but pleasantly, with soft arms and lips giving not one kiss, but the usual French double one. They hugged men and my jeep driver, and pinned French tricolors on us, and left us exhausted, with our bosoms covered with emblems and ribbons. An old man came up, saluted, and said, with tears in his eyes: "God bless America, you have saved France."

Men and women, old and young, and children stormed the jeep every time the column stopped and they were wild with emotion. Crowds were banked from the center of the streets in a cheering throng stretched for miles; there seemed to be no end and apparently everyone in Paris, except the Germans and collaborationists, was standing there to cheer, shout, cry, and leave themselves exhausted with happiness.

Our column moved to a point one block from the Luxembourg. Then from all sides burst machine fire. From housetops and windows guns rattled. Machine guns of tanks opened in reply. We leaped from the jeep and took cover behind a tank. Jerry Beatson of Rockford, Ill., was beside me and leveled his carbine at the top of the building. The gun cracked in my ear. "There's one—up there," he cried, and kept firing at the rooftop.

Bullets rattled on the streets and glanced off with ugly whines. The crowds, which a few minutes before lined the streets, melted as if a blast from a furnace had hit a snowbank. Then the streets were terribly lonely and barren except for armor with guns clattering. . . .

CONTINUED ON PAGE 127

LEFT: French civilians waving American and French flags sing "The Star-Spangled Banner" as they greet U.S. and Free French troops entering Paris, Aug. 25, 1944.

BELOW: Crowds of French citizens line the Champs-Élysées to cheer Free French Force tanks and half-tracks driving through the Arc du Triomphe, Aug. 26, 1944.

VIVE DE GAULLE

St. Louis Globe Democrat, St. Louis, MO, Saturday, August 26, 1944

TEXT OF DE GAULLE'S ADDRESS PROCLAIMING FREEDOM OF FRANCE

BELOW: Gen. Charles de Gaulle and his entourage set off from the Arc de Triomphe down the Champs-Élysées to Notre Dame for a service of thanksgiving for the liberation of Paris, Aug. 26 1944.

By The Associated Press

LONDON, August 25—Speaking to cheering crowds in front of the Prefecture in Paris, Gen. Charles de Gaulle proclaimed tonight the liberation of Paris and declared, "We will not rest until we march into enemy territory as conquerors."

The president of the French Committee of National Liberation, back in the capital after four years of fighting from exile, told his exultant listeners, "France will take her place among the great nations which will organize the peace. . . . She has the right to insist that she never again be invaded by the enemy who so often has invaded her. . . .

"Men and women, we are here in a Paris which stood erect and rose in order to free herself—a Paris oppressed, downtrodden and martyred, but still Paris. Paris is free now—freed by the hands of Frenchmen—the capital of Fighting France, of France the great eternal. It is not enough that with the aid of our dear and splendid Allies we should drive the enemies from our soil. After what happened to France, we will not rest or be satisfied until we enter—as is only right—upon the enemy's own soil as conquerors. We are going to fight on to the last day—to a day of total and complete victory."

Move Forward in Lurches

The drive on Paris began at 7 a.m. yesterday under sullen, drizzling skies. The French and American columns had moved into position on Wednesday afternoon facing the enemy's position west of Paris. . . .

In small towns people crowded along the streets despite the rain to wave tricolors and to cheer each vehicle that passed. Never have I seen more joyous faces than those along the road to Paris. It was a triumphal, exciting and colorful march. Pretty girls stood on the roadside and tossed flowers at the vehicles. As the columns would stop, they would deck the tanks and armored trucks with flowers until they seemed to be camouflaged as mobile flowerpots. Farmers tossed fresh tomatoes and apples to the troops.

Sgt. Bob Fraley of Des Moines, Iowa, Private Ray Rooney of Glen Ellyn, Ill., and Pvt. Harry Grand of Hamburg, Ark., sat in a jeep watching this outburst of emotion at the edge of the war.

"This is the first real holiday I've had in weeks," Fraley said. "We've been doing reconnaissance up where the fights really were tough. But this is like a circus."

RIGHT: Chaos—Parisians celebrating on the Place de la Concorde during a parade for Gen. Charles de Gaulle dive for cover as a hidden German sniper opens fire on the crowd, Aug. 26, 1944. Although the Germans surrendered the French capital, small bands of snipers still remained in the city.

American troops of the 28th Infantry Division march down the Champs-Élysées in a victory parade held in Paris on Aug. 29, 1944.

St. Louis Globe Democrat, St. Louis, MO, Tuesday, September 12, 1944

U.S. ARMY INVADES GERMANY

Part of Maginot Line Taken in 5-Mile Gain; 175 Planes Bagged

By The Associated Press

SUPREME HEADQUARTERS ALLIED EXPEDITIONARY FORCE, September 12 (Tuesday)—The rampaging First United States Army burst into Hitler's inner fortress of Germany yesterday and plowed ahead for five miles into the Reich, meeting the enemy on his home soil north of the frontier town of Trier— 55 miles from the Rhine and the great industrial city of Koblenz.

An artillery barrage first chewed up the German positions and then in "reasonable strength"—that was the official language—the doughboys crossed over to strike the blow for which the United Nations long had waited.

RIGHT: This AP map reproduced in the *St. Louis Globe Democrat* on Sept. 12, 1944, depicts, via arrows, the movements of the American First Army troops who entered Germany near Trier (large arrow in center) on Sept. 11, and, slightly farther north, troops who drove east of Liège to Limbourg. The U.S. Third and Seventh Armies joined forces to the south, near Sombernon, and the British Second Army drove toward Holland. Shaded areas represent the Siegfried Line.

BELOW: Gen. Courtney Hodge's First Army troops made history when they crossed the German frontier near Aachen and Trier, to battle for the first time on German soil. Here, American infantrymen cross the border from Belgium into the Aachen Forest, Germany, on Sept. 13, 1944.

YANKS INVADE GERMANY!

U.S. ARMIES JOINED

52 JAPANESE SHIPS SUNK BY U. S. NAVY OFF PHILIPPINES

WEATHER
Eastern Pennsylvania: Tuesday Rain Southeast Portion In Early Morning, and Northwestward To Border By Afternoon, Moderate Temperature.

Intelligencer Daily Journal.

The Leading Newspaper in the Garden Spot of America, Home Owned for Home Folks Since 1794 — 150th Anniversary Year

VOLUME LXXX.—NO. 314.   Entered as second class matter August 9, 1944 at the Post Office at Lancaster, Pa., under the Act of March 3, 1879. Reg. U. S. Pat. Off.   LANCASTER, PA., TUESDAY MORNING, SEPTEMBER 12, 1944   FINAL EDITION   SIXTEEN PAGES.   20c PER WEEK—4c Per Copy

Huge Task Force Bags Nip Convoy Off Mindanao

PILOT, SOLDIER DEAD; LIST 2 OUT OF ACTION

Lieut. Vogel Lost Year

Bulletins

REPUBLICANS WIN IN MAINE

Portland, Me.—(AP)—Republican candidates for Governor and three Congressional seats swept the field in Maine's State election Monday.

As unofficial tabulation of the vote neared completion, Hildreth, GOP candi-

MAN IS JAILED IN "ROOFING RACKET" HERE

L. W. Swartz Given 6-Month Te...

1st Army Plows Five Miles Into Reich Near Trier

The Americans probably were penetrating well into the Siegfried Line defense system at this point. The exact location of the Siegfried Line, also known as the West Wall, never has been disclosed officially.

It was a black day for German arms, for the Third United States Army seized a great part of the old French Maginot line intact and was breaking the last German line of defense on French soil—the Moselle River positions.

The British Second Army broke across the frontier of Holland and was bound for the weakest link in the 400 miles of the West Wall—the thin line of pillboxes, tank traps and forts stretching south from the German city of Kleve across the shortest route to Berlin.

Other elements of the First Army already were fighting through the minefields of the Siegfried Line south of the key city of Aachen, little more than eight miles from Germany's frontier, and were blasting fortifications inside the Reich with heavy artillery.

Not since the days of Napoleon has Germany been entered in strength and the doughboys who accomplished this modern feat had fought clear across the little duchy of Luxembourg in one day, freeing its capital of the same name en route.

Since this was no mere patrol entry into Germany, such as the tentative thrusts of the French in 1939 and the American raid of last week, it may well be the opening wedge in a series of full-scale attacks against Hitler's last prepared line of defense. . . .

Overrun Fortifications

In the drive to Aumetz the Third Army overran much of the old French fortifications and is in a position to strike northeastward toward Germany and the Saar in concert with the First Army.

With the junction of Third Army patrols and advance elements of the United States Seventh Army—driving from Southern France—in the vicinity of Sombernon, the sprawling lines of the Allies for more than 300 miles were joined almost solidly—from Holland south through Belgium, into Luxembourg and on into France—since the First Army earlier met the British in Northern Belgium. There remains only the small gap between the United States First and Third Armies, probably no more than 15 miles. . . .

Americans striking on Aachen's ancient route of European invasion were slowed by the densest mine fields seen since the beachhead fighting and before them were the concrete dragon teeth of the West Wall's tank barriers.

Sunday Times-Signal, Zanesville, OH, Sunday, September 17, 1944

YANKS ONLY 26 MILES FROM COLOGNE

U.S. Troops Reach Open Country After Piercing West Wall Beyond Aachen

SUPREME HEADQUARTERS ALLIED EXPEDITIONARY FORCE, Sept. 16 (AP)—The U.S. First Army, driving through the famed Siegfried Line in 24 hours, fought out into the open today on one of Hitler's super-highways within 26 miles of Cologne as six Allied armies pounded forward on a 500-mile front. The hard-hitting U.S. Third Army freed the western half of the town of Thionville, only 15 miles from the rich German industrial Saar basin, and in a lightning move sent tanks cutting in behind Metz, the most important French fortress city still in enemy hands.

The approach to Cologne was reported in a front dispatch which said Lt. Gen. Courtney H. Hodges' infantry had moved on 12 miles past of the surrounded German frontier fortress of Aachen and asserted the West Wall breach south of the city was so wide the whole German defense system was in peril. . . .

The Saar basin, with its wealth of coal, iron and industry, was imperiled by Lt. Gen. George S. Patton's Third Army fighting inside Thionville, only 15 miles away. Here the Third seized a section of the Maginot Line, which had been remodeled to form outworks for the Siegfried Line, and turned its German-installed 105-mm guns on the enemy holding the half of Thionville on the east bank of the Moselle. . . .

On the northern reaches of the front, the Germans threw in numerous counterattacks in an attempt to check an American push from the captured Dutch city of Maastricht eastward toward the thinner line of Siegfried defenses stretching north from Aachen. . . . The Germans also launched counterattacks against the British north of the Albert Canal near the Dutch border, but to the west they were giving away along the coast and the Poles of the

An American tank passing by rows of concrete dragon's teeth rides through the breach in the Siegfried Line torn by the First Army near Aachen, Sept. 16, 1944.

Salt Lake Tribune, Salt Lake City, UT, Sunday,September 17, 1944

DOUGHBOYS ORDERED TO TREAT GERMAN CIVILIANS AS ENEMIES

By ROBERT N. COOL

WITH THE U. S. FIRST ARMY IN GERMANY, Sept. 16 (AP)—Troops of the U.S. First Army will not be permitted to fraternize with German civilians and are expected to remember that they must treat them as enemies. For the first time, American troops are going into a country where the civilian population can be expected to be hostile and the army does not want the men to expose themselves to unnecessary danger, nor permit any leaks in security through the natural friendliness of doughboys.

In the drive across France, Belgium and Holland the troops were among friendly, sympathetic populations which were eager to assist. These conditions change at the border.

There is no doubt many of the Germans will be happy to see the arrival of the Americans because it means the end of the war for them, an end of the dreaded Gestapo and the finish of Nazi domination. But who will be a friend and who an enemy no soldier can say.

No longer can a doughboy stop along the road and chat even casually with the people and only those on official business will be able to leave bivouac areas to mingle with civilians. . . . Neither can soldiers wander about the country in small groups or singly on sightseeing expeditions, for there always is the danger of ambush by some of Hitler's fanatics or SS (elite) troops who have donned civilian clothes.

American soldiers will not be allowed to forget that for four years the Germans have been waging war against American allies and much of that time against America herself, and that the Germans individually, and collectively, are soldiers of the army.

Troops will be expected to conduct themselves in a reserved soldierly manner to dispute enemy propaganda, which has terrified the average German of the arrival of the American army. The German has been told for months that if an American army invades Germany there will be rape, pillage and mass murders.

Canadian First Army were 2½ miles into Holland. The main interest in the fighting centered, however, on the struggle around Aachen and it was on this sector that Supreme Headquarters said the Siegfried Line had been "completely penetrated." SHAEF emphasized that this did not imply a breakthrough, although suggesting strongly that one was likely, since a breakthrough is accompanied only when a breach is exploited to the extent that troops can pour through freely.

The drive put Lt. Gen Hodges' First Army infantry on Hitler's autobahn—a super highway on the road to Cologne and Berlin. It was considered likely there still were some fixed obstacles between them and the Rhine.

Aachen itself, once the capital of Charlemagne's empire of the West, appeared to be toppling, with patrols darting into the city and doughboys surrounding it. . . .

Patton's forces were setting the stage for a drive on the Saar and the Rhine from the south. Near Thionville they seized Fort Gendringen, which was built in 1870, remodeled as a part of the Maginot Line and given new guns by the Germans in 1940.

They found plenty of ammunition for the Krupp guns, and although they could not read the German instructions, they swung them east anyway and fired salvo after salvo on the Germans across the Moselle.

U.S. troops resting in Aachen Forest raise the Stars and Stripes after crossing the border into Germany, Sept. 17, 1944.

Arizona Republic, Phoenix, AZ, Monday, September 18, 1944

HUGE AIRBORNE INVASION ARMY TAKES BRIDGEHEAD IN HOLLAND

By HOWARD COWAN

LONDON, Sept. 17 (AP)—Gen. Dwight D. Eisenhower unleashed the powerful First Allied Airborne Army today, sending more than 1,000 air transport and glider loads into Holland at the northern tip of the Siegfried Line in a bold attempt to skirt it and drive for Berlin.

That clearly was the assignment of the sky soldiers—already reported in field dispatches to have driven the Germans from several Dutch towns near the Reich's frontier.

While Supreme Headquarters did not say where the thousands of American, British and Polish sky troopers landed, the Germans declared they hit Dutch soil in force at Nijmegen, 12 miles west and slightly north of where the already breached Siegfried Line ends at Kieve.

Simultaneously, the British Second Army broke across the Dutch frontier south of the landings in a great offensive timed perfectly with this first entirely airborne operation in military history.

The Germans said part of Lt. Gen. Lewis H. Brereton's airborne army came down at Tilburg and Eindhoven, eight to ten miles inside Holland and close to where the British Second Army is fighting up from the south. A field dispatch said the British were two miles inside Holland and driving toward these cities.

Troops Land on Rhine

But the most important stroke appeared to have fallen at Nijmegen, which is on the Rhine and only six miles from the German frontier. Here Berlin is 315 miles to the east. . . .

While it was believed only a matter of time until the airborne divisions and Lt. Gen. Miles C. Dempsey's Second British Army will wheel on or around the Siegfried Line, the U.S. First Army

Brig. Gen. Anthony C. McAuliffe, artillery commander of the 101st Airborne Division, gives his glider pilots last-minute instructions in England on Sept. 18, 1944, before their takeoff during Operation Market Garden, the Allied air assault on the German-occupied Netherlands and the largest airborne operation of the war.

Parachutes open overhead as waves of paratroops land in the Netherlands during operations by the First Allied Airborne Army, Sept. 17, 1944.

Salt Lake Tribune, Salt Lake City, Sunday, September 17, 1944

GERMANY FEELS FIRST HOME INVASION SINCE NAPOLEON

By ROBERT N. COOL
Associated Press Writer

The shortest road to Berlin from the west is an end run through the Lowlands, flanking the Siegfried Line. That is one route the Allies are embarked on, while all along the German border other armies probe and smash at narrower gates to the Reich. This is in the historic pattern of war between Germany and France. Yet not since Napoleonic times have Germans been on the receiving end of the operation.

Now the Lowlands approach spells disaster in a special sense for the Nazi war machine. It is a shortcut to the Ruhr, that all-important region of coal and iron where great steel mills are clustered. When the Allies sweep from Belgium and Holland into the Ruhr, the Wehrmacht will stutter like an engine running out of gasoline.

This region, less than 50 miles square, is the solar plexus of German war-making power. Nature placed it only 25 miles from the Netherlands border. Hitler's West Wall, affording only partial protection, ends amid the coalpits and smokestacks just above Essen, Dusseldorf and Aachen.

It is not likely that the German high command ever really intended to defend this important area at such close quarters. The battle for the Ruhr was clearly meant to be fought in France, or along the Atlantic wall. But the Allies were too strong and too fast.

In 1940, it is now asserted, the French high command had failed to extend the Maginot Line to the channel because they could not afford to fight in a rich industrial area needed for production. Their strategy was based on defending France in Belgium.

Hitler Lacks Resources

They failed, and Hitler's legions conquered the country on the Flanders plain.

In both World War I and World War II the tide for France was turned by inexhaustible new resources from overseas. But Hitler has no such resources. That is why the British Second Army and the U.S. First Army are driving hard through Belgium toward the Ruhr, while farther south the U.S. Third and Seventh hammer at the frontal approaches to the Siegfried Line, which alone guards Germany from invasion.

was hammering away through a hole in the fortifications 25 miles from the Rhineland city of Cologne.

German commanders fell back on old World War I tactics and sent wave after wave of infantry against Americans fighting on the German side of the Siegfried Line east of Aachen, and these were cut down in a storm of fire. . . .

The bold aerial D-Day by daylight was preceded by a shattering barrage from 1,000 Flying Fortresses, which dropped tons of bombs on German defenses in a virtually unopposed operation that cost two bombers. Not a fighter place was lost.

They were paced by squadrons of fighters and fighter-bombers that challenged the few German fighters venturing out of the clouds, or flew low and blasted anti-aircraft positions.

The widespread operation was accompanied by a call from Eisenhower to Dutch patriots to rise and fight, and a summons by the Dutch government in London for a general strike of Netherlands railroad workers to paralyze enemy troop movements. . . .

Supreme Headquarters gave few details of the assault by Gen. Brereton's "secret weapon" airborne army, formed of American and British troops and fliers, weapons and planes in size approximating a full ground army. Its existence was disclosed only August 10.

It was in Holland that the Germans in May 1940 made the first large-scale use of parachute troops, and Holland witnessed the first employment of Brereton's mighty sky army.

★ ★ ★

BELOW: A panoramic view of the city of Nijmegen, the Netherlands, and the Nijmegen Bridge over the Waal River (a tributary of the Rhine) in the background, Sept, 28, 1944. The Allies secured the hard-fought bridge during Market Garden but the city, while liberated, was largely destroyed by German and Allied bombardment and shelling.

The Delta Democrat-Times

48th Year　(NEA)　GREENVILLE, MISSISSIPPI, Tuesday, September 26, 1944　Associated Press (AP)　No. 331

Allies Cloak Big Arnhem Battle In Secrecy; Nazis Say British Airborne Troops Wiped Out

1700 Allied Planes Attack German Cities

LONDON (AP)—Armadas of 1,700 American British heavy bombers, operating in support of land troops, attacked Osnabruck, Hamm and the besieged port of Calais today.

Forces of 1,100 Fortresses and Liberators bombed the German cities. The RAF sent 500 Lancasters and Halifaxes against the French channel port which Canadians are attacking.

Osnabruck lies 83 miles northeast of the Dutch battleground at Arnhem, Bremen, a leading German port on the Weser river, is 150 miles northeast of Arnhem. Hamm, one of the chief rail junctions of northwest Germany, is 82 miles southeast of the Dutch city.

Allied planes again supported hard-pressed airborne troops in the Arnhem area of Holland today with rocket and machinegun attacks on German troop concentrations, gun emplacements and other targets along the Eindhoven-Nijmegen corridor.

British Mosquitos before dawn bombed Mannheim on the Rhine opposite Ludwigshafen, which American planes worked over yesterday.

Unescorted Liberators from Italian fields attacked Greek har-

RIGHT ATTACK INTO BELGIUM: Here's that picture again—of a Yank who didn't miss the bus when his outfit rolled into a city. He erected from the Germans. This one's from Liege, and shows a century blonde Belgian lass giving a pleasant welcome to Pvt. Kabe Quinn, of Louisville, Miss.

Nazi Casualties In Home Defense Near One Million

SUPREME HEADQUARTERS ALLIED EXPEDITIONARY FORCE (AP)—German casualties on the western front — in killed, wounded and captured or troops hopelessly cut off — were estimated tonight at close to 1,000,000 since D-Day.

The casualties included at least 100,000 Allied, well over 200,000 badly wounded, more than 800,000 captured and the rest sealed off in the Channel islands, the last holdout ports of France and in various pockets along the coast and the Bay of Biscay.

The million casualties are well over twice the German force now believed to be lined up along the west wall for the homeland stand.

The Germans announced or estimated capture by the Allies in France and the low countries since June 6 total 520,789, of which 385,739 surrendered to American armies.

The U. S. First Army captured 183,827; the U. S. Third Army 92,600; the U. S. Seventh Army more than 90,000; and the U. S. Ninth Army 19,312 through last announced figures two days ago.

The British Second Army was credited with 75,000 captives and the Canadian First Army 60,000 at the time.

North Bank Stand Of Famed "Red Devils" In Ninth Day

LONDON (AP)—Silence cloaked the ninth day of one of the most dramatic battles of the invasion—the north bank stand of isolated British "Red Devils" who fought to keep a foothold across the Dutch Rhine.

General Eisenhower's headquarters, imposing a security dimout of news from middle Holland, called the situation fluid. The British press declared it critical. And the German International Information bureau, a propaganda agency, said the British paratroops had been wiped out.

Nothing was disclosed at supreme headquarters to indicate whether this was true or false.

Allied air commanders, in an attempt to stop the flow of enemy troops and material to the Moselle and Dutch fronts, flung 1,100 Fortresses and Liberators against two vital German freight yards. With almost 3,500 tons of bombs these heavy bombers blasted the yards at Osnabruck, through which the enemy has been funneling supplies to his forces in Holland, the very large yards at Hamm and unspecified targets at Bremen.

The latest information at supreme headquarters on the Arnhem troops was more than 24 hours old. This was that the British were holding on, desperately thinly supplied by night across the quarter-mile-wide Rhine.

There was no attempt to minimize the hazard of their position nor any indica-

Neutral Havens For War Criminals Blasted By British

LONDON (AP)—Prime Minister Churchill reiterated today that the British government insists German war criminals find no haven in neutral territories.

Some neutrals already have made satisfactory statements on the matter, Churchill told Commons, but he has not "noticed any particular pronouncement" from Spain in this connection. His statement about Spain was in reply to a direct question.

Cheered from all quarters of Commons as he resumed his seat following the Quebec conference, Churchill planned a full-dress statement Thursday. A two-day debate starting then may disclose Britain's attitude on what to do with Germany after the war—a question which already has through divided opinion in President Roosevelt's

★ ★ ★ BATTLE OF LEYTE AND LEYTE GULF, OCTOBER 17–26, 1944 ★ ★ ★

Harrisburg Telegraph, Harrisburg, PA, Friday, October 20, 1944

U.S. TROOPS SEIZE 3 BEACHHEADS, PRESS INLAND UPON LEYTE ISLAND; FDR REPORTS CASUALTIES "LIGHT"

By The Associated Press

"I have returned," General Douglas MacArthur told the Filipino people in a broadcast today calling upon them to "rise and strike" the Japanese. Here is the text of his broadcast over the "Voice of Freedom" radio, as reported by the Office of War Information:

"This is the Voice of Freedom, General MacArthur speaking:

"People of the Philippines: I have returned. By the grace of Almighty God our forces stand again on Philippine soil—soil consecrated in the blood of our two peoples. We have come, dedicated and committed, to the task of destroying every vestige of enemy control over your daily lives, and of restoring, upon a foundation of indestructible strength, the liberties of your people.

"At my side is your president, Sergio Osmeña, worthy successor of that great patriot, Manuel Quezon, with members of his cabinet. The seat of your government is now therefore firmly re-established on Philippine soil. The hour of your redemption is here. Your patriots have demonstrated an unswerving and resolute devotion to the principles of freedom that challenges the best that is written on the pages of human history. I now call upon your supreme effort that the enemy may know from the temper of an aroused and outraged people within that he has a force there to contend with no less violent than is the force committed from without.

"Rally to me. Let the indomitable spirit of Bataan and Corregidor lead on. As the lines of battle roll forward to bring you within the zone of operations, rise and strike! Strike at every favorable opportunity. For your homes, and hearths, strike! For future generations of your sons and daughters, strike! In the name of your sacred dead, strike! Let no heart be faint. Let every arm be steeled. The guidance of Divine God points the way. Follow in his name to the Holy Grail of righteous victory!"

MacArthur's call for guerrilla warfare was a summons to thousands of Filipinos who have been operating in roving bands throughout the islands, sometimes under American leadership, since the fall of Bataan. And it was a plea for others to join their numbers.

The extent of guerrilla activities was recognized by the puppet government a year ago when it voted to grant amnesty to any guerrilla who would swear "to become a good citizen." Guerrilla activity could be of immeasurable value to MacArthur's men in the scattered islands, garrisoned by hated enemy troops.

★ ★ ★

In this iconic image taken on Oct. 20, 1944, Gen. Douglas MacArthur wades ashore at Leyte Island, on his way to announce to the people of the Philippines: "I have returned." At far left in the pith helmet is Philippine president Sergio Osmeña, returning to his country from exile.

ABOVE: Gen. MacArthur speaks during a ceremony restoring constitutional government to the Philippines, on the steps of the capitol building in Tacloban, Leyte, Oct. 23, 1944. President Osmeña is to the right of MacArthur on the step behind, in a pith helmet.

RIGHT: Crewmen on USS *Birmingham* train fire hoses on the burning USS *Princeton* as their ship comes alongside to assist in damage-control measures during the Battle of Leyte Gulf, the largest naval battle in history, Oct. 24, 1944. Despite heroic efforts, the firefighting crews were unable to bring the flames under control and a massive explosion blew 130 feet of the *Princeton*'s stern off above the waterline. Shrapnel and massive chunks of debris from the explosion rained down on the deck of the *Birmingham* killing 233 of her officers and crew and wounding more than 400.

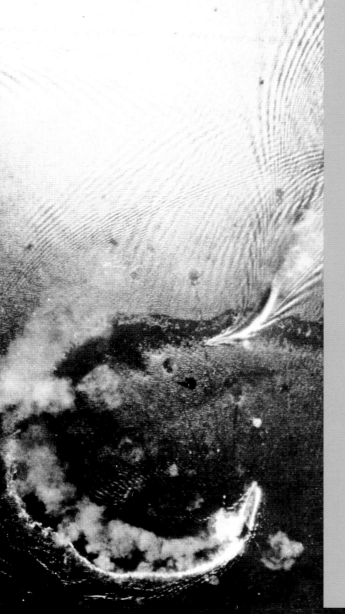

The Japanese battleship *Yamato* (lower center) and other ships maneuver while under attack by U.S. Navy carrier-based aircraft in the Sibuyan Sea, Oct. 24, 1944, during the Battle of Leyte Gulf. The shadow of one plane is visible on a cloud in the lower right center.

Port Huron Times Herald, Port Huron, MI, Wednesday, October 25, 1944

GREAT SEA BATTLE RAGES

Each Navy Loses Carrier; Jap Battleships Damaged; Tokyo Claims Eleven U.S. Warships Sunk in Fight

By CHARLES H. McMURTRY
Associated Press Staff Writer

U.S. PACIFIC FLEET HEADQUARTERS, PEARL HARBOR, Oct. 25— Carrier planes of the U.S. Third Fleet have sunk a large Japanese carrier and have damaged two other large carriers, five or six battleships, one cruiser and several other unidentified warships in a great naval battle which is still continuing near the Philippines.

The USS *Princeton*, a light carrier in Adm. William F. Halsey's force, was lost when, already badly crippled, its magazines exploded and it had to be sunk by American ships.

No mention was made in the 1:30 a.m. communiqué issued by Adm. Chester W. Nimitz of any great sea battle between American fleets and the Japanese fleet, as claimed by the Japanese radio since late Tuesday. The Tokyo radio has admitted the loss of two cruisers and a destroyer in the action, while claiming to have sunk 11 ships and damaged five others.

The *Princeton*'s captain and 1,360 of its officers and men were rescued.

In addition to the fleet units sunk or damaged, the Japanese lost 150 planes.

The action began Monday afternoon (U.S. time), extended through Tuesday and general "action is continuing," Nimitz said. Nimitz said a strong force of land-based Japanese planes attacked one U.S. task group Monday and succeeded in seriously damaging the *Princeton*, which is the first American carrier lost since the *Liscome Bay* went down in flames off the Marshall Islands in [November] 1943. Approximately 150 of these enemy planes were shot down during the attack, Nimitz said.

Abilene Reporter-News, Abilene, TX, Sunday, December 17, 1944

GERMANS LOOSE BARRAGE OF SHELL AND FIRE ALONG 200-MILE WESTERN FRONT

SUPREME HEADQUARTERS ALLIED EXPEDITIONARY FORCE, PARIS, Dec. 16 (AP)—German counterattacks were opened today at a dozen points on the 70-mile first U.S. Army front between Düren and Trier, the heaviest fighting occurring in the Ardennes forest. The counterthrusts were an apparent effort to draw off pressure against the Düren sector.

The thunder of explosions set off by the Germans destroying the last bridges across the Roer River indicated that they had given up hope of holding back the First Army on the west bank of that stream.

The Germans counterattacked for the first time in two weeks against the U.S. Ninth Army north of Lindern, but were thrown back.

The U.S. Third Army bored 300 yards deeper into the Siegfried Line in the Western Saarland, and infantry crossed the southern border of the basin at a new point nine miles east of Sarreguemines.

(U.S. Seventh Army doughboys are driving deeper into Germany and have seized Scheibenhard, a German border town near the Rhine, and a number of Reich villages, a dispatch from Thoburn Wiant and Robert C. Wilson, Associated Press correspondents, reported. They also said that Wissembourg and Lauterbourg, Alsatian border cities, had been seized by the Seventh.)

There were four crossings on a 17-mile front into the old Bavarian palatinate—a region of war industry and agriculture, and already the Seventh was drawing off German strength and relieving pressure father north on the western front. The German high command was aware that to leave the Siegfried Line lightly defended here was to invite a breakthrough that not only would menace such arsenal cities as Ludwigshafen and Mannheim, 35 miles farther down the Rhine, but might outflank the entire Saar basin, a coal and steel region of the first importance. . . .

The 45th Division was believed to be about two miles inside the palatinate west of Wissembourg, the 103rd Division invaded in the same general area and the 79th forged two bridgeheads across the borderline river near Lauterbourg, near the Rhine. The heaviest fighting appeared to be on the 79th sector where the Germans had the advantage of the bunker-studded forest of Bienwald. Twenty-three miles west of Wissembourg around Bitche the Germans were fighting fiercely from the Maginot Line, swinging the fortifications' guns around and blazing away at the Americans attacking from the south.

Other diversionary attacks were aimed by the Germans far to the south in Alsace around Colmar, but there the French First Army and elements of the U.S. Seventh held foothill positions and, fighting from behind flooded streams, could not be dislodged easily.

★ ★ ★

German soldiers, wearing heavy winter gear, walk past a burning American half-track in the western front during the Battle of the Bulge, December 1944. This photo is from a batch of film captured from the Germans by American forces.

LEFT: A soldier runs past a burning German half-track in the recaptured town of La Glieze, Belgium, during the Battle of the Bulge, early January 1945. American forces recaptured the town on Christmas Eve 1944, when, surrounded by American forces, 800 survivors of the 1st Panzer SS lead by the notorious Lt. Col. Joachim Peiper—who would later be convicted of war crimes for the Malmedy massacre—fled, leaving behind 135 armored vehicles. During the Malmedy massacre, a German Waffen-SS unit shot and killed 84 American POWs on Dec. 17, 1944; 73 members of the Waffen-SS involved were tried for war crimes in 1946 for this and other massacres.

BELOW: Refugees evacuate Bastogne as U.S. troops hold the town against the power thrusts of the enemy, December 1944.

San Bernardino County Sun, San Bernardino, CA, December 18, 1944

GERMANS REINVADE BELGIUM AND LUXEMBOURG IN GREAT OFFENSIVE

U.S. First Army Line Dented on 60-Mile Front

By EDWARD KENNEDY

PARIS, Dec. 18 (Monday) (AP)—The German army reinvaded Belgium and Luxembourg in an all-out offensive yesterday, denting U.S. First Army lines with thousands of troops and scores of tanks attacking on a 60-mile front.

This first major counteroffensive since Normandy was gaining in intensity. At some points along a front between Monschau, 16 miles southeast of Aachen, on southward to the German fortress of Trier, the enemy had advanced some miles while other thrusts were being held by the Americans.

(The depths of the German penetrations were not given. Kennedy reported that some of his dispatches were altered by censorship.)

Seizing the initiative for the first time since D-Day, the Germans swept back along the paths of their 1940 conquest, spurred by an order from Field Marshal von Rundstedt that "your hour has struck."

10 Miles from Malmedy

What appeared to be the main blow carried to within 10 miles of the Belgian city of Malmedy, 23 miles south of Aachen. Malmedy is 14 miles west of the German border and, assuming American lines were at the frontier, that would mean a penetration of four miles. However, Allied lines on that long-quiet sector near the Ardennes Forest are ill-defined.

An inferno of artillery fire plunged into the American lines. Parachute troops in considerable numbers dropped behind the American positions in two corps areas on the First Army front and also behind the U.S. Ninth Army. Dropping in groups of four to eight, many were captured.

Nazis Lose 143 Planes

The long-hidden German Air Force roared out at least 450 strong and by nightfall had lost 143 planes in terrific air battles that cost the Americans 33 fighters. It was the enemy's greatest show of air power since the Allies stormed the French coast. The battle flared along a 60-mile front from Roetgen, 10 miles southeast of Aachen, on south into Luxembourg, where at least two small penetrations were made before the Americans held.

Associated Press correspondent William F. Boni said the land assault was concentrated some 23 miles south of Aachen, where German infantry and from 30 to 50 tanks overran advance American positions in the area of Honsfeld on the route to the Ardennes Forest. From Honsfeld, two miles inside Belgium, the Germans pressed on west to within 10 miles of Malmedy before the attack eased late in the afternoon. The doughboys appeared to have the situation fairly well under control. . . .

Supreme Headquarters said that while the German drive represented a major effort which is not underestimated, there was no reason for alarm or anxiety. . . . A dispatch from the First Army front said the German intent appeared to be to ease pressure on the Düren front east of Aachen and on the Saar and Palatinate fronts. One from the Ninth Army front said it was doubtful if the German high command hoped to capture and hold any large amount of territory.

The German army does not appear to have resources for such adventures, and it seemed likely the main objective was to disrupt Gen. Eisenhower's winter offensive.

Nebraska State Journal, Lincoln, NE, Sunday, December 24, 1944

MAJ. GLENN MILLER REPORTED MISSING

DUARTE, CALIF. (AP)—Maj. Glenn Miller, peacetime dance bandleader, is reported missing in action in France, his wife's parents announced here Saturday night.

Mr. and Mrs. Fred W. Burger said the word came by telephone from their daughter. Mrs. Miller called from Tenafly, N.J., where she had gone to accompany a girl, recently adopted by the Millers, to California.

Mrs. Miller said that the bandleader had been in England for some time, directing musicians' groups in an armed forces entertainment program, and that he went to France about two weeks ago.

A .50-caliber machine-gun crew from the 120th Regiment, 30th Division, is set to repel advancing Germans near Malmedy, Belgium, Dec. 22, 1944. The red censor marks on the photograph would have printed black in the newspaper; as noted in the *Code of Wartime Practices for the American Press* (June 1942): "Care should be exercised in publishing photos of service men to prevent disclosure of military or naval units outside the country through insignia."

Decatur Daily Review, Decatur, IL, Wednesday, December 27, 1944

NAZIS GET FIRST SERIOUS SETBACK; NEWS BAN HIDES DETAILS OF DRIVE

Push Halted, Early Tuesday Report States

By JAMES M. LONG
Of The Associated Press

PARIS, Dec. 27—American troops have thrown back German armored columns that thrust within four miles of the Meuse River, and a front dispatch today declared doughboys were slowly regaining the initiative on flanks of the German drive into Belgium.

The German offensive—believed to be powered with some 250,000 troops—had sent light armored combat teams to Celles and Ciney in a bid to reach the Meuse. But doughboys in a Christmas Day battle rolled them back one to two miles, Supreme Headquarters disclosed.

A dispatch from the field today declared U.S. armor and infantry "slowly regaining the initiative, have locked in a series of sharp battles with probing Germans on both flanks of the 20-mile gap between the Hotton and Bastogne areas." Fighting still is extremely fluid in this sector, it added.

Trying to Relieve Bastogne

Supreme Headquarters said Field Marshal Karl von Rundstedt had been held virtually without gains in the 24 hours up to Tuesday morning.

But the German southern flank at that same time stiffened against the American push to relieve the encircled garrison at Bastogne. The Yanks at last official reports still were 4½ miles south of the city. Hundreds of tons of supplies were parachuted today to the Bastogne garrison.

Another front dispatch today said the front was comparatively, and almost ominously, quiet today with each side thrusting tentatively and ineffectually at opposing defenses. . . .

Bastogne Garrison Holds On

The surrounded Bastogne garrison of several thousand doughboys still held out in an epic stand. . . .

Field Marshal Karl von Rundstedt was pushing hard to the northwest—toward the Antwerp supply route—from his reinforced

Standing on a snow-covered battlefield, these American infantrymen of the 4th Armored Division fire at German troops in an advance to relieve pressure on surrounded U.S. airborne units near Bastogne, Belgium, Dec. 27, 1944.

line along the Hotton-Marche road, but "our positions have been maintained," said the Allied communiqué covering actions two days old.

It still was a grinding battle of huge cost in which von Rundstedt's next moves yet were to shape up. The terrific American defense had slowed but not yet stopped the German armor.

Along the northern rim of their bulge, Germans captured Manhay, 10 miles southwest of Stavelot.

Von Rundstedt kept bloody Bastogne near the middle of the bulge under incessant day and night attack, hurling in tanks which the defenders methodically knocked out as fast as they came up.

There was no indication how much longer the Bastogne force, originally numbering several thousand men, could hold out, but neither was there any suggestion they were anywhere near the end of their power or determination to resist.

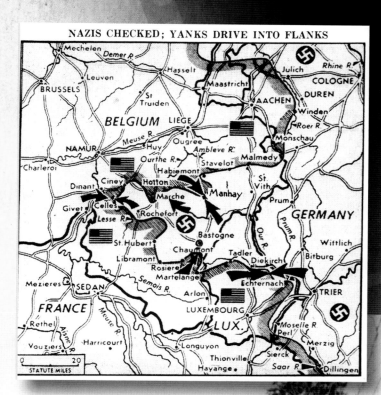

NAZIS CHECKED; YANKS DRIVE INTO FLANKS

RIGHT: Germans driving into Belgium squeezed out a bulge into American territory west of St. Vith. Arrows indicate action on both sides. A German armored thrust to Celles, near the Meuse River, was checked on Dec. 25, 1944.

BELOW: Members of the 101st Airborne Division move out of Bastogne to drive the Germans who had besieged them for 10 days out of a neighboring town, Dec. 29, 1944.

Plain Speaker, Hazleton, PA, Friday, December 29, 1944

GEN. MCAULIFFE REPLIED "NUTS"

BASTOGNE, Dec. 29. (AP)—Fresh details of the Bastogne siege released today disclosed that Brig. Gen. A. C. McAuliffe, acting commander of the trapped 101st Airborne Division, gave the "nuts" reply to a German demand Dec. 22 for surrender.

McAuliffe took charge of all troops in the Bastogne pocket until the arrival of the 101st commanding officer, Maj. Gen. Maxwell D. Taylor, who left Washington Christmas Eve when he heard of his outfit's predicament and flew the Atlantic.

Taylor arrived in Belgium Dec. 26, made his way through enemy lines and reached Bastogne early Dec. 27. Armored elements and stragglers from various infantry units were hemmed in the town along with the 101st.

The relief corridor from the south was opened by Lt. Gen. George S. Patton, Jr., waging a kind of war that is to his liking. Patton used the veteran 4th Armored Division and units of the 80th and 26th Infantry Divisions to smash the encirclement of Bastogne.

Other Third Army units which were trapped with the 101st Airborne Division in Bastogne were from the 9th and 10th Armored Divisions.

Brig. Gen. Anthony McAuliffe, fourth from the left, and his staff gather inside the basement of Bastogne's Heintz Barracks for Christmas dinner, Dec. 25, 1944. This military barracks served as the 101st Airborne Division's main command post during the siege of Bastogne. The facility is now a museum known as "Nuts Cave."

Two other Third Army divisions, the 4th and 5th Infantry Divisions, were disclosed to be fighting the Germans in the area northeast of the city of Luxembourg. Troops of the 101st "Screaming Eagle" Division had been rushed into Bastogne by trucks just before the German encirclement was completed. The hard-fighting youths, who participated in airborne operations in Normandy and Holland, were spoiling for action and they found it here.

"In Normandy and Holland I jumped out of a C-47; here I jumped out of the rear of a truck," said a dismounted parachute trooper who started fighting less than an hour after arriving in Bastogne and kept on until he was carried off wounded.

Maj. Charles Fife of Los Angeles, member of an armored force headquarters staff, said "these parachute troopers were the best morale bucker-uppers we had.

"Those boys fought hard from the word go," he said. "They know their stuff and they proceeded to show it." . . .

McAuliffe, who was in command of the besieged forces, is 46 years old and one of the youngest generals in the army. He is a native of Washington, D.C. His wife and two children, Patricia and John, live in Washington.

ABOVE: Snowsuited U.S. troops of the 48th Armored Infantry Battalion march through snowdrifts while on patrol in St. Vith, Belgium, during the Battle of the Bulge, January 1945.

RIGHT: Surveying the damage in Bastogne during a tour of the front, from left to right: Lt. Gen. Omar Bradley, commander, U.S. Twelfth Army Group; Supreme Allied Commander Dwight D. Eisenhower; and Gen. George S. Patton, commander, U.S. Third Army, Feb. 5, 1945.

CHAPTER SEVEN

1945

The shock of the Battle of the Bulge darkened Christmas in many anxious American homes at the close of 1944, but 1945 opened with news, on Jan. 3, that the Allies had pushed a massive counteroffensive east of the Bulge. The German armies were spent. Nevertheless, the Bulge proved the costliest U.S. battle in Europe, with more than 80,000 American casualties.

In the Pacific, the Japanese had been defeated in every meaningful strategic sense, yet the toll on American lives only continued to increase. The great Battle of Leyte Gulf had ended in late October 1944, but on the twenty-fifth of that month, Japanese naval aviators launched the first kamikaze attack of the war. On Jan. 2, 1945, a U.S. convoy was hit by a much larger kamikaze attack. For the next eight months, Japan would use this suicide tactic to awful effect. By the end of the war, some 2,800 suicide attacks had sunk 34 U.S. warships, damaged 368 more, killed 4,900 sailors, and wounded almost as many.

At the height of his wartime success, Adolf Hitler held territory from the Caucasus in the east, to the northern tip of Norway in the north, to the Greek island of Gavdos in the south, to the French channel island of Ushant in the west. On Jan. 15, Hitler and his mistress, Eva Braun, confined themselves to the subterranean Führerbunker beneath the garden of the Reich Chancellery. Here they would live until their double suicide on April 30.

On Jan. 17, the Red Army liberated Warsaw, and the next month, on Feb. 4, Stalin, Churchill, and Roosevelt convened at the Black Sea town of Yalta to discuss how their nations would preside over the entire postwar world.

In four raids from Feb. 13 through Feb. 15, some 1,290 U.S. and British bombers dropped high-explosive and incendiary bombs on Dresden, Germany, creating at one point a firestorm that peaked at 1,800 degrees Fahrenheit. As many as 35,000 civilians perished, and much of the medieval city was destroyed.

Most historians have condemned the Dresden raid as a war crime without strategic purpose, but few Americans felt sympathy for the people of Dresden—or for the Japanese, on whom U.S. forces were inexorably closing. On Feb. 23, Associated Press photographer Joe Rosenthal took the most celebrated photograph of World War II, documenting marines raising the Stars and Stripes atop Mount Suribachi on Iwo Jima, a fortified Pacific island some 750 miles southeast of Tokyo. The photograph became an icon of the American will to victory, generating many millions of dollars in desperately needed war bond sales.

The Battle of Iwo Jima would grind on for more than a bloody month after the flag-raising. In the meantime, at the Battle of Remagen, in Germany, the U.S. First Army captured Cologne on the west bank of the Rhine on March 6. On the seventh, it took the Ludendorff Bridge and began marching across the Rhine on March 7.

With the Allies now penetrating the very heart of Germany, Hitler issued from his bunker the "Nero Decree" of March 19, ordering the destruction of "anything . . . of value within Reich territory, which could . . . be used by the enemy." His minister of armaments and war production, Albert Speer, charged with executing the destruction, quietly ignored the order.

On April 1, 1,500 U.S. ships landed 50,000 men on Okinawa, gateway to Japan itself. It was the greatest invasion since D-Day. By the time the operation ended on June 22, 110,000 Japanese troops and some 100,000 Okinawan civilians (an estimated 25 percent of the population) lay dead. Twelve thousand Americans lay with them, making it the costliest Allied victory in this theater.

Triumphs came at great cost, but some were nothing short of deliverance. On April 11, lead elements of the U.S. 9th Armored Infantry Battalion of the 6th Armored Division liberated Buchenwald concentration camp outside of Weimar, Germany. The time was 3:15 p.m.—today preserved on the stopped clock at the entrance gate. (Eisenhower would bring groups of legislators and journalists to tour Buchenwald later in April, telling them "You saw only one camp. There are many others. . . . The barbarous treatment these people received in the [camps] is almost unbelievable. I want you to see for yourselves.")

The liberation of Buchenwald was followed on the next day, April 12, by devastating news from FDR's "Little White House" at Warm Springs, Georgia. The president—war leader of the Free World—had suffered a fatal cerebral hemorrhage. Vice President Harry S. Truman took the oath of office. "I felt like the moon, the stars, and all the planets had fallen on me," he candidly told reporters the next day.

Roosevelt did not live to see Zhukov's Red Army begin the Battle of Berlin on April 16. He also missed the linkup of U.S. and Soviet forces at Torgau, on the Elbe River, on the twenty-fifth. He died little more than two weeks before Hitler and his bride killed themselves on April 30.

On May 2, a Red Army soldier was photographed by Yevgeny Khaldei raising the Soviet Hammer and Sickle flag over the ruins of the Reichstag. Surrender negotiations began at Reims, France, on the fifth and were signed on the morning of the seventh, at 2:41. V-E (Victory in Europe) Day was proclaimed on May 8, Hitler's "Thousand-Year Reich" having lasted for less than a dozen.

Even as the war against Japan continued, a charter creating the United Nations was signed in San Francisco on June 26, and Gen. Douglas MacArthur, having waded ashore at Leyte on Oct. 20, 1944 ("People of the Philippines, I have returned!"), announced the liberation of those islands on July 5. From July 17 through Aug. 2, the "Big Three"—now Churchill, Stalin, and Truman—met in the Berlin suburb of Potsdam both to decide the fate of postwar Europe and to affirm their demand for Japan's unconditional surrender.

It came only after the United States dropped two atomic bombs on Japan—the first, on Hiroshima, Aug. 6, and the second, on Nagasaki, Aug. 9. Together, they instantly killed 130,000 to 240,000 Japanese people, mostly civilians. Thousands more died later as the result of radiation sickness and cancer.

In Tokyo, Emperor Hirohito recorded a surrender announcement that was broadcast on Aug. 15 to Japan and to the world. The formal surrender took place on what Truman proclaimed as V-J (Victory Japan) Day, Sept. 2, in a ceremony on the deck of the U.S. Navy battleship *Missouri* riding at anchor in Tokyo Bay, presided over by General of the Army Douglas MacArthur.

Lt. Gen. Kataoka Tadasu of the Japanese 35th Army (center) hands over his sword to Maj. Gen. William H. Arnold, commander of the Americal Division, after surrendering his army of 10,000 troops in Cebu, the Philippines, Aug. 28, 1945.

★ ★ ★ BOMBING OF DRESDEN, FEBRUARY 13–15, 1945 ★ ★ ★

Atchison Daily Globe, Atchison, KS, Wednesday, February 14, 1945

BOMBERS HIT DRESDEN IN STRONG FORCE

LONDON, Feb. 14 (AP)—More than 2,250 U.S. bombers and fighters struck Germany in widespread attacks today, delivering a main blow at Dresden which was already burning from a night assault by 800 heavy RAF bombers.

Dresden is only 68 miles or less from advancing Russian troops, and is a nerve center of Nazi defenses in central Germany. The day and night air blows were in direct and coordinated support of Marshal Ivan Konev's First Ukrainian army.

The RAF bombed Dresden twice in attacks three hours apart.

Part of the American force, consisting of more than 1,350 Flying Fortresses and Liberators and 900 fighters, also bombed transportation and industrial targets at Chemnitz, 35 miles southwest of Dresden, and at Magdeburg, 70 miles west of Berlin.

A fourth formation was assigned to knock out an important Rhine bridge at Wesel 19 miles ahead of the Canadian First Army on the western front.

Rail Center

Announcing the night operations, the British air ministry declared: "As the center of a railway network and a great industrial town it (Dresden) has become of the greatest value for conducting any defense the Germans may organize against Marshal Konev's armies."

Altogether the RAF dispatched 1,400 aircraft to Germany during the night. Other targets were a synthetic oil plant at Böhlen south of Leipzig, objectives at Magdeburg 75 miles southwest of Berlin and the railroad towns of Nuremberg, Bonn and Dortmund. All the night operations were at a cost of 16 bombers missing.

Soon after breakfast this morning the German radio began interrupting its programs every few minutes to warn listeners to take cover from approaching planes. At noon the U.S. Army Air Forces announced officially its bombers were over Germany.

Ineffective Defense

The British blow against Dresden, Germany's seventh largest city, was the first major attack ever made there. A striking feature was the lack of anti-aircraft fire.

When the first wave hit about 10 p.m. clouds obscured the target. When the second arrived three hours later the sky was clear. The crews said fires could be seen for 200 miles.

Dresden is 93 miles south of Berlin and is overflowing with refugees fleeing ahead of the Russians. Some German government offices also are said to have been shifted there.

The demolished city of Dresden after the fatal Allied forces' firebombing raids of Feb. 13–15, 1945. An estimated 3,000 tons of bombs were dropped on the city just that month alone, creating a giant firestorm that obliterated an area of 1,600 acres and killed an estimated 25,000 people.

Together, American and British tactical forces on the continent yesterday flew more than 2,100 sorties against battle area targets and Nazi supply lines. The pilots reported meeting the stiffest anti-aircraft opposition to these battle line attacks since the German Ardennes offensive was checked.

Their combined claims for the day included 103 locomotives, 307 railcars and 278 motor vehicles wrecked and 48 rail cuts.

The U.S. Ninth Air Force, which lost 11 aircraft, claimed two Nazis shot down and three more damaged.

★ ★ ★

View from the destroyed Dresden Cathedral overlooking the ruins of Dresden Castle and the
Sophienkirche (Saint Sophia's Church) to the left, c. 1946.

Richmond Times-Dispatch, Richmond, VA, Friday, February 16, 1945

BERLIN'S OUTER RING OUTFLANKED

Dresden Called "Burning Inferno"

LONDON, Feb. 16 (AP)—The Red Army, paced by attacking American heavy bombers, outflanked Berlin's eastern defenses yesterday in a powerful 30-mile breakthrough which toppled the Brandenburg Province stronghold of Sommerfeld, 67 miles from the imperiled Reich capital. . . .

Marshal Ivan S. Konev's First Ukraine Army cut in behind a 75-mile stretch of the Oder held by the enemy between Fürstenberg and Neusalz, thus destroying the effectiveness of that defense line guarding the capital on the southeast. . . .

Front dispatches said that Konev's lower wing also had driven to within 45 miles of Dresden, capital of Saxony, after reaching the Neisse River in the area of Görlitz, 74 miles northeast of Prague, Czechoslovak capital.

An eye-level view of the devastation in Dresden after the Allied firebombing of the city, c. 1946.

A Stockholm dispatch said that Dresden was a "burning inferno" because of heavy United States bomber attacks paving the way for the Soviet ground drive, and that "tens of thousands" of persons had been killed there. . . .

Dresden also was attacked for the fourth time since the great Allied air assault began Tuesday night. Two hundred American heavyweights brought to 4,000 tons the weight of explosives dropped on that Saxon citadel. . . .

CITY "HEAP OF RUBBLE"

LONDON, Feb. 15 (AP)—The German radio tonight described Dresden, Germany's famed art center now lying in the path of the Red Army, as "smoking heaps of rubble" left by the massive Allied air attacks.

Attacked four times since the great aerial offensive was launched Tuesday night, the historic capital of Saxony became a prime target because it is a strategic communications center for Nazi troops on the eastern front.

But the German radio confined its propaganda score sheet on the damage to celebrated art treasures.

Pomona Progress Bulletin, Pomona, CA, Friday, February 23, 1945

MARINES TAKE IWO VOLCANO FORTRESS AS JAPS LEAP TO DEATH FROM CLIFFS

U.S. Casualties Rise in Counterattacks

By LEONARD MILLIMAN
Associated Press War Editor

The most famous image from World War II, taken by Associated Press photographer Joe Rosenthal on Feb. 23, 1945, depicts U.S. Marines of the 28th Regiment, 5th Division, raising the American flag atop Mt. Suribachi, Iwo Jima, the site of one of the bloodiest battles of World War II against Japan. Rosenthal received the Pulitzer Prize in 1945 for his photo.

American marines scaled the summit of Suribachi volcano fortress on the southern tip of Iwo Jima today in the most dramatic feat of that costly campaign, while forces in the center of the island renewed their northward drive after beating off two heavy nighttime counterattacks. Japanese leaped to their death from the rim of the volcanic crater as marines climbed up its sheer height and began mopping up by-passed pockets with flamethrowers. Suribachi's capture eliminated enemy artillery and mortar positions firing on the rear of other marines slowly battling toward the center fighter strip.

In a futile gesture of defiance, Adm. Chester W. Nimitz reported, Japanese swimmers landed on the southwest coast of Iwo in an attempt to attack the American rear.

The Japanese counteroffensives on Iwo were launched yesterday afternoon, nearly 24 hours after marine casualties had risen to 5,372. That figure, covering only the first 58 hours of the invasion of the airbase island 750 miles south of Tokyo, is by far the heaviest for a comparable period of the Pacific War.

Marines start the drive to the interior of Iwo Jima, March 3, 1945. Running at a crouch, they dart across the plateau-like tableland in the shadow of Mt. Suribachi, taking advantage of the scant protection offered by the small rises in the volcanic sand.

Marine casualties included 644 killed, 560 missing, 4,168 wounded. The 72-hour Tarawa battle claimed a little over 3,000 marine casualties. More than 15,000 Americans were killed or wounded in nearly a month of fighting for Saipan. Americans are still killing Japanese on Saipan and other Marianas Islands where B-29s are based. The 24th (Negro) Regiment recently fought a pitched battle with 350 Japanese on Saipan. Last Saturday was the first day in seventh months that no enemy soldiers were killed on Guam.

The Japanese cabinet met today to hear an obviously unfavorable war report. In preparation for this session the war ministry has twice shaken up its ranking generals in the last three days.

Tokyo broadcast unconfirmed claims that a total of 28 American warships have been sunk or heavily damaged off Iwo Jima. Admittedly some U.S. warcraft were damaged in the first of four Japanese air attacks. Nimitz said the other three attacks were beaten off. These ships, with their carrier planes, have poured more than 20,000 tons of explosives on Iwo. That is more than a ton for each Japanese on the island.

"Our fanatical enemy will fight to the bitter end," said Marine Lt. Gen. Holland Smith. "They have caused us some difficulties."

And Vice Adm. John H. Hoover, who has been in on most of the Pacific amphibious operations, said Japanese firepower on Iwo was "far stronger than any other place we've attacked." For a time on D-Day, he said, it didn't look as if the marines would be able to stick on the beaches.

The Yanks are still puzzled by the absence of Japanese tanks on the island, where the enemy is believed to have a heavy armored force.

Thirteen Japanese planes have been shot down off Iwo. Gen. Douglas MacArthur reported destruction of 18 more in Philippines-based air sweeps from the Ryukyu Islands to Indo-China. Ten small Japanese ships were sunk or damaged in these strikes. MacArthur also announced the seizure of great quantities of materiel and capture of Muntinlupa 12 miles south of Manila.

This outtake by Joe Rosenthal shows the 28th Regiment marines cheering after the flag-raising atop Mt. Suribachi.

★ ★ ★ BATTLE OF OKINAWA, APRIL 1–JUNE 22, 1945 ★ ★ ★

Santa Cruz Sentinel, Santa Cruz, CA, Sunday, April 1, 1945

YANKS ON RYUKYUS

SAN FRANCISCO, Sunday, April 1 (AP)—American troops swept ashore on Okinawa Island in the strategic center of the Ryukyu chain Sunday morning (Japanese time) after having landed on two small nearby islands Saturday, an imperial headquarters communiqué recorded by the federal communications commission reported today.

The newest landings were made in southern Okinawa, the enemy communiqué said. Okinawa is only 325 miles from Kyushu, southernmost of the Japanese home islands.

Saturday's landings were made on Kamiyama and Mae Islands, 15 miles north of Okinawa's northern extremity, the broadcast said. That would indicate a feint to stick Japanese defenders to the northern end of Okinawa, which is 65 miles long.

The communiqué was issued at 3 p.m. Sunday (Tokyo time; 2 a.m. Sunday Eastern War Time).

Storming ashore from amtracs, U.S. marines hurry along the beach of Okinawa, Japan, as they invade the island, April 1, 1945. The assault brought American forces to within some 300 miles of the Japanese mainland.

Claim U.S. Ships Sunk

In usual Japanese braggadocio fashion in the face of defeat or amphibious invasions of its territory, the communiqué reported—wholly without American confirmation—that Nipponese air and surface units sank or damaged 16 American ships. These were reported as including one aircraft carrier, two battleships or cruisers, two cruisers and three destroyers. The imperial communiqué, broadcast domestically by Tokyo, said the principal landings were on southern Okinawa beaches.

A few minutes earlier, Tokyo had reported landings of 1,500 American troops—unidentified as to soldiers, marines or both—reinforced by 100 tanks, on an unidentified island near strategic Okinawa.

On Good Beaches

Tokyo said landings were made on southern Okinawa. That portion of the island is fairly flat, with low, rolling hills a few miles back from the shore, affording rather good beaches.

Blue Network reported this text of the Tokyo broadcast:

"Enemy invading forces around the waters of the southwestern islands at 8 o'clock on Saturday morning began landing on Hidashi Kimana and Nishi Kamimama Islands in the Keisi group lying 10 kilometers west of Naha on Okinawa Gunto. The enemy landed by the same evening about 1,500 men, equipped with 100 amphibian tanks and 10 artillery pieces."

★ ★ ★

LEFT: The polka-dot pattern of rain-filled shell holes and the splintered stumps of leafless trees on an Okinawa battlefield attest to the deluge of Tenth Army artillery poured on strong Japanese positions around Shuri Castle in 1945. The demolished Japanese radio tower in the left foreground was one of 11 such installations around this nerve center of the defensive system manned by Japanese troops.

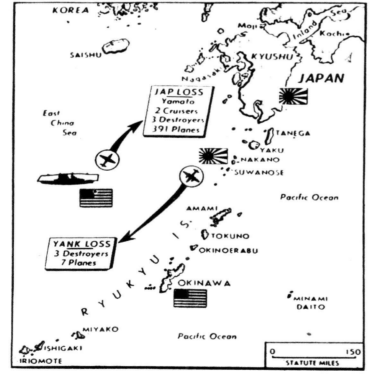

This AP map printed in the *Atlanta Constitution* on April 8, 1945, shows the action in the Ryukyu Islands during a two-day sea battle that saw the world's largest and most powerful battleship—the 72,800-ton *Yamato*—sunk, along with 2,500 of her crew. Japanese and American losses are denoted in the boxed notes. By the end of the battle, more than 3,600 Japanese sailors had died, and the Imperial Japanese Navy was destroyed.

Army tanks of the Tenth Army hit the beach at Okinawa, June 6, 1945. Enemy opposition was light, beachheads were secured quickly, and the landing of supplies followed within a few hours of the initial landings.

San Pedro News-Pilot, San Pedro, CA, Monday, April 16, 1945

KAMIKAZE CORPS MEN DO DAMAGE BUT OFTEN SACRIFICE LIVES IN VAIN

By MURLIN SPENCER

GUAM (AP)—A single plane diving through a tropical sky spattered with flak and crashing in a great sheet of flame on a destroyer's stern was my introduction to the Kamikaze (suicide) corps of Japan.

It was the first but not the last time I watched battles with Japan's fanatic group of suicide pilots who die without rhyme or reason, a Japanese flag wrapped around their heads and their bodies clothed in bright ceremonial colors. Their minds, too, are reportedly warped by pre-death ceremonial honors such as few Japanese warriors ever before them were accorded.

ABOVE: 20mm anti-aircraft gunners, center foreground, pour a deadly stream of fire into the already burning Japanese kamikaze plane plummeting toward the flight deck of the USS *Sangamon*, a navy escort carrier, during action in the Ryukyu Islands, May 4, 1945. The suicide plane landed in the sea close to the carrier. Another Japanese aircraft later succeeded in hitting the ship deck, inflicting heavy damage.

LEFT: Scene on the flight deck of the USS *Bunker Hill* aircraft carrier, looking aft, while her crew was fighting fires caused by kamikaze hits off Okinawa, May 11, 1945.

The plane which bashed onto the destroyer came in afire, a P-38 on its tail pumping machine gun slugs into the cockpit.

"He's too close—too close, they can't stop him now," murmured a seaman at my side. Almost in a trance, we watched the Japanese pilot plunge straight into the destroyer. He had not fired a shot, or dropped a bomb. Death was his mission, his own and for a considerable number of Americans aboard the destroyer. He didn't sink the destroyer but he made a trade.

"Divine Tempest"

This is not an attempt to minimize or exaggerate the work of Japanese suicide pilots whose title, Kamikaze, means in effect, "Divine Tempest." Like the Japanese army and navy, there are times when there is no logical explanation for the Kamikaze corps' actions. They go after battleships, aircraft carriers, cruisers, destroyers, transports, PT-boats and even barges. Three suicide planes went after one PT-boat, missed, and crashed into the water. It was a costly price in pilots and planes to pay in an attempt to destroy such a small craft. . . . After a Kamikaze commits himself to a dive it is too late to change a decision or come back for another run.

Their attacks are fascinating to watch. Three times I watched them and there appeared to be no set pattern of attack. . . . The gunners know it isn't enough to set him afire. A pilot must be killed or the plane destroyed in the air to keep him from completing his mission. . . . It isn't until the last minute that a ship in a convoy can tell if it is a Kamikaze's target. There isn't much time to be afraid. The Japanese either hits or misses, and he never lives long enough to make a second try.

ABOVE: A Corsair fighter looses its load of rocket projectiles on a run against a Japanese stronghold on Okinawa. In the lower background is the smoke of battle as marine units move in to follow up, June 1945.

BELOW: Men of the 1st Marine Division keep close to the ground on May 19, 1945, while under heavy Japanese mortar and machine-gun fire on the crest of the newly won hill bounding the "Awacha Pocket." The marines sealed off the pocket, south of the town of Awacha on Okinawa, after three days of bitter fighting.

Cincinnati Enquirer, Cincinnati, OH, Tuesday, April 17, 1945

21,000 FREED!

Americans Release Victims Jammed Back to Back into Buchenwald Holes

By ALVIN J. STEINKOPF

WEIMAR, GERMANY, April 16 (AP)—Young Americans of the 80th Division broke into the notorious Buchenwald concentration camp, a few miles outside of Weimar and brought fresh air, hope and liberty to 21,000 miserable, sick, and ragged men.

Tens of thousands of other prisoners had died before the Americans got there, and many of the liberated were too far gone to be saved. In the first 24 hours of American administration a few more than 150 succumbed of malnutrition and disease. In the next six hours, 39 more died. . . .

There once were more than 50,000 prisoners at Buchenwald, but shortly before the Americans came the Nazis marched 20,000 to 30,000 eastward. I saw several inmates die in Barracks 61. Bodies were hauled to a six-burner crematorium.

Barracks 61 of the hospital section, which inmates said was the worst in the compound, looks like a conventional one-story wooden army barracks. Inside it is divided into two rows of four-tier shelves divided at five and one-half foot intervals by upright partitions.

In each hole, approximately 18 inches high, as many as six men were quartered. Three in a cubby hole could lie comfortably on their backs. With six, the men had to lie on their sides. There were no mattresses on the boards and few had blankets. The patients had pneumonia, dysentery, typhus and almost every type of disease.

★ ★ ★

An American soldier of the 80th Infantry Division took this photograph of Buchenwald inmates inside their barracks on April 16, 1945, several days after U.S. Third Army troops liberated the concentration camp near Weimar. The young man in the second row from the bottom, seventh from the left, is sixteen-year-old Elie Wiesel, who would later become an acclaimed author, activist, and Nobel Peace Prize laureate.

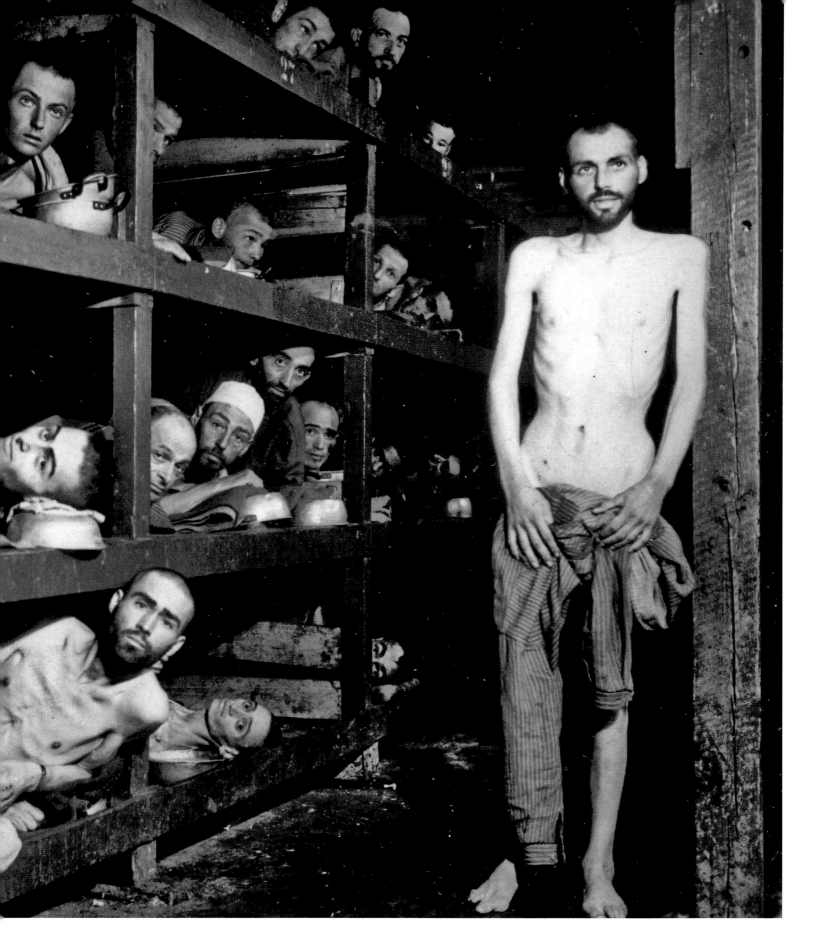

Ottawa Journal, Ottawa, Ont., Canada, April 23, 1945

"BARBARISM AT ITS WORST" SAY SHOCKED U.S. CONGRESSMEN

By DON WHITEHEAD

BUCHENWALD PRISON, GERMANY, April 22 (AP)—Eight American congressmen walked among the horrors of Buchenwald prison today and got shocked eyewitness proof of a Nazi world in which human life was not worth that of an animal.

They came at the personal invitation of Gen. Eisenhower, who wanted them to see for themselves this village where decency was torn aside and men died like beasts in one of Germany's worst butcher shops. "This is barbarism at its worst," said Rep. Gordon Canfield (R–N.J.), one of the group.

Each of his companions said he was shocked almost beyond belief at what he saw and was told by the prisoners. That is the reaction of everyone who goes through this camp of horrors—a camp where emaciated bodies are still stacked like cordwood, where bodies were shoved into furnaces and burned, where men were hung on spikes like sides of beef until they died, and where thin, emaciated children look at you from great lifeless eyes because they remember nothing but prison life.

The Americans liberated 21,000 prisoners in Buchenwald 11 days ago and conditions have improved considerably since then, but there is no way to erase this tragedy as long as the shambles of humanity who were the prisoners wander about the place waiting until somebody takes them home.

Hundreds of Americans, British—and German civilians from the nearby town of Weimar—visit the camp daily to see the living dead and be convinced that the report of Nazi atrocities is not just propaganda.

Behind one building was the most gruesome sight I have ever seen—bodies piled up on each other like logs ready for mass burial. They were pitifully thin and wasted, with the skin tight over bones and purple faces contorted into expressions of suffering. They simply starved to death.

Beside this stack of 40 bodies was a truck with some 60 naked dead. Their bodies with names and prison numbers tattooed on the arms were like something out of a nightmare.

In the courtyard nearby was a pile of ashes and bits of bones—the remains of the dead burned in the 12-furnace crematory. In the furnace grates lay blackened portions of skulls, and in one was a body which the fire had not entirely consumed.

Below the furnaces was a room from which the prisoners said none of their number emerged alive. Along the walls were hooks like those in a butcher shop. Bodies—and the prisoners said some that still had life—were hung there until the furnaces were ready.

Yet somehow the dead were not as pitiful as those hulks of men and boys walking about the place. There was death in their eyes, but they still moved and talked—zombies created by the Nazis.

BELOW: Pfc. Albert of Brooklyn, New York, views the charred remains of a cremated victim at Buchenwald, April 19, 1945. The SS imprisoned approximately 250,000 people in Buchenwald from July 1937 until the camp was liberated in April 1945. It is estimated that at least 56,000 prisoners were murdered in the Nazi camp, some 11,000 of them Jews.

LEFT: American soldiers stand guard while German civilians gaze at a pile of bones that are the remains of about 400 prisoners killed at Buchenwald, April 1945. Gen. Patton requested that over 1,000 German citizens from Weimar tour the camp and be forced to view the atrocities committed there.

BELOW: American soldiers and liberated prisoners on the grounds of Buchenwald, April 27, 1945.

★ ★ ★ U.S. MOURNS ROOSEVELT; TRUMAN SWORN IN, APRIL 12–15, 1945 ★ ★ ★

Brownsville Herald, Brownsville, TX, Friday, April 13, 1945

TRUMAN ASSUMES PRESIDENCY; ROOSEVELT FUNERAL SATURDAY

Stunned Nation Is Assured War Will Be Pressed

WARM SPRINGS, Ga. (AP)—A special train bearing President Roosevelt's body to Washington left here at 10:15 a.m., C.W.T.

By JACK BELL
Associated Press Political News Editor

WASHINGTON—A dazed and questioning world today watched Harry S. Truman pick up the banners of war and peace that slipped yesterday from the lifeless fingers of Franklin Delano Roosevelt.

Stunned by the shock of its leader's passing, a mourning nation gave solid backing to the gray-haired man in the gray business suit who became President of the United States at 7:09 p.m. last night.

Truman to "Carry On"

The new president himself announced simply that he would try to carry on as he believes President Roosevelt would have done. Then, swiftly, he asked the Roosevelt cabinet to stay on. He gave assurance that the United Nations conference would open in San Francisco April 25, on schedule. He issued a statement that the war would be prosecuted to the utmost on all fronts.

Today as international friends and enemies looked on, as men high and low maneuvered to find their place in a new U.S. orbit, these prospects loomed:

1. A speedy summoning of Gen. George C. Marshall and Adm. Ernest J. King for the most important fill-in on the military situation any world leader ever needed at such a critical hour.

2. A conference with Secretary of State Stettinius on pressing and complicated international situations.

3. The sorrowful duty of helping arrange for a White House funeral at 4 p.m. Saturday (E.W.T.), for his predecessor, the nation's first fourth-term president.

These transcended such important questions as the likelihood that the new chief executive will want to meet as soon as possible with Prime Minister Churchill, whom he knows slightly, and Premier Stalin, whom he knows not at all. Domestic problems could be pushed aside temporarily too, left to a cabinet that stays on now, but may see some changes later.

To the 60-year-old, ruddy-complexioned new president fell the immediate and sorrowful task of burying a chief executive for whom he had boundless admiration and unfaltering loyalty.

Mr. Roosevelt was struck down by a cerebral hemorrhage as he posed for a sketching artist in his cottage at the Warm Springs Infantile Paralysis Foundation where he had gone last month for a rest. Carried into the bedroom of the little white cottage on Pine Mountain that was his vacation home, he died without regaining consciousness.

It was as simple as that; the blow that struck the nation to its heart as it read of climactic military successes in Germany and of a quickening of the war in the Pacific, and speculated on the success or failure of the forthcoming conference to form an organization Mr. Roosevelt hoped would prevent future wars.

Mrs. Roosevelt Informed

Mrs. Roosevelt, at a charity benefit, received the news by telephone. Without a word, she went to the White House. The call went out for Mr. Truman. He rushed there with a hastily assembled Secret Service escort. His first words to Mrs. Roosevelt were of her and the four Roosevelt sons. Mrs. Roosevelt had sent them a message that their father had slipped away. He did his job to the end as he would have them do, she said. "What can I do?" asked the new president. "Tell us what we can do," Mrs. Roosevelt replied bravely, "Is there any way we can help you?"

Outside on the street, a quiet, unbelieving crowd gathered quickly. Confused and dazed, hundreds stood in Lafayette Park, across from the White House square, far into the night.

Long since, Mr. Truman had been sworn in by Chief Justice Stone in the cabinet room. Placing his hand on a red-edged Bible, the new president repeated the oath, reading from a small slip of paper. He, his wife and their daughter, Margaret, left from a rear entrance for their apartment home where they spent the night, guarded closely by the secret service and police. . . .

There came pledges of support for the new chief executive, mixed with grief at the death of the old. Prime Minister Churchill arranged to address the House of Commons today on the world's loss.

From Premier Stalin came a personal message to Mrs. Roosevelt characterizing the president as "a great organizer of the struggles of freedom-loving nations against the common enemy."

Gen. Charles de Gaulle, president of the Provisional Government of France who recently declined to meet Mr. Roosevelt in Algiers, told of the sympathy of the French people in a telegram to Mr. Truman.

The German radio said Mr. Roosevelt would go down in history as the man on whose instigation the present war turned into a second world war. The Japanese radio told only of his death.

Expressions of sympathy and grief came from far and wide in this country. . .

There came, too, pledges of support for Mr. Truman's regime. . . . Sen. Wheeler (D-Mont.), who criticized Mr. Roosevelt's foreign policies, said "I think Mr. Truman will make a good president." The *Chicago Tribune*, also critical of Mr. Roosevelt's dealings with other nations, said editorially of Mr. Truman: "He will receive the support of us all."

Thus the former Kansas City haberdashery clerk who became a county judge and then climbed to the Senate . . . goes into the White House with the nation's best wishes.

★ ★ ★

Harry S. Truman takes the oath of office as president of the United States at 7:00 p.m., April 12, 1945, in the Cabinet Room of the White House, shortly after President Franklin Delano Roosevelt's death. Chief Justice Harlan F. Stone administered the oath of office.

RIGHT: Stunned citizens in Washington, D.C., gather on the North Lawn outside the White House after learning of the death of President Roosevelt, the morning of April 13, 1945.

BELOW: The flag-draped coffin of President Roosevelt is borne on a caisson drawn by white horses, at center, along Constitution Avenue in Washington, D.C., April 14, 1945, as crowds line the route from Union Station to the White House.

The funeral for Franklin D. Roosevelt held in Hyde Park, New York, April 15, 1945.

NEW LEADER ACTS TO SPEED UP WAR

By The Associated Press

WASHINGTON—President Truman called the nation's top military chiefs into conference on the war situation today as he took up the reins of government.

The White House announced a presidential conference this morning with Fleet Adm. William D. Leahy, the late President Roosevelt's military adviser; Fleet Adm. Ernest J. King, chief of the navy; Gen. of the Army George C. Marshall, army chief of staff; Secretary of War Stimson; and Secretary of the Navy Forrestal.

The new president thus put into immediate effect the statement he made shortly after he was sworn in last night that one of his prime tasks would be to prosecute the war vigorously on all fronts. . . .

As one of his first official acts, President Truman was putting the finishing touches to a proclamation calling for a national day of mourning tomorrow in tribute to the memory of his predecessor, Franklin Delano Roosevelt, who died at Warm Springs, Ga., yesterday.

Funeral services for the late president will be held in the State House East Room tomorrow with burial in the family plot at Hyde Park, N.Y., Sunday morning.

Fighting men of the 165th Regiment, 2nd Battalion of the 27th Division, from New York, kneel during memorial services for President Roosevelt on Okinawa, April 21, 1945. Chaplain C. J. Wartman (background) stands before a tomb as he conducts the service.

Salt Lake Telegram, Salt Lake City, UT, Friday, April 27, 1945

YANK, RED ARMIES JOIN

Yanks, Russ Mark Link with Wild Celebration

By DON WHITEHEAD

WITH KONEV'S FIRST UKRAINIAN ARMY EAST OF THE ELBE, April 26 (Delayed) (AP)—There was singing and dancing and music on the banks of the Elbe today as doughboys of Gen. Hodges' First Army and jubilant troops of Marshal Ivan Konev's First Ukrainian Army celebrate the historic junction symbolizing the defeat of Nazi Germany.

Americans and Russians slapped each other on the back, gave each other bear hugs, and sat in the warm sunshine drinking Champagne from beer mugs and toasting the great occasion of the meeting of the two armies Thursday.

Not in all this long war have there been scenes such as those enacted in the town of Torgau, on the west bank of the Elbe, and across the river in the Red Army encampment where Russian and American troops saw each other for the first time, and began to get acquainted despite the handicaps of language. It was enough that they were Allies and had whipped the enemy to open the way for this joining of armies in weird Torgau. Parts of the city are deserted and ghostly. In other sections Russian and American troops whooped, sang and formed fast friendships within a few minutes of meeting. . . .

This April 25, 1945, map from the *Salt Lake Telegram* shows the reduced remaining German-held territory (shaded) and the area where two Red Army divisions joined southeast of Berlin, fought in the city and nearly cut off the capital in the west. In the south, the Russians fought along the Elbe, where they would link with U.S. troops at Torgau.

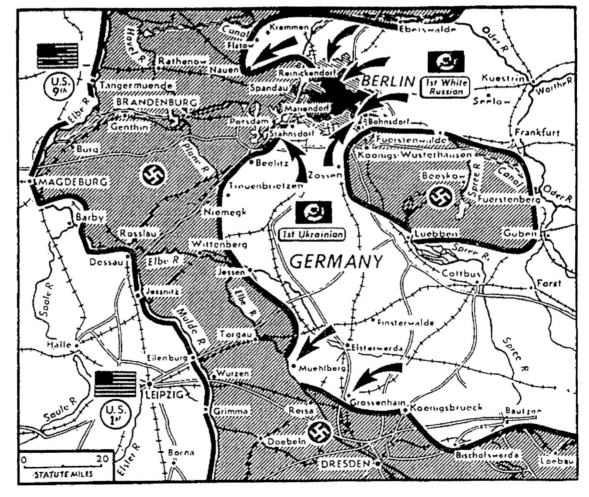

Fantastic Day

The whole day was almost too fantastic to believe, from the time a column set out in the morning to meet the Russians until dusk settled over the Elbe and there was nothing more to be wrung from hours crammed with emotional outbursts.

This is the story of the memorable day which began when a U.S. column set out for Torgau, where the 69th Infantry Division made the first contact with Soviet troops Thursday.

The road from the Mulde River to the Elbe was a vivid picture of defeated Germany etched in the pain, misery and fear of people fleeing along the roads by thousands before the Russians, and hoping vainly to find safety within American lines. Never before have American troops looked on scenes which showed so clearly Germany's defeat. . . .

Voluntary Captives

One of the strangest sights consisted of columns of German soldiers marching along the road to the west without anyone to guard them. Some of them still were carrying arms, but nobody had taken the trouble to disarm them and they made no pretense of resistance. They voluntarily were marching into captivity. . . . These scenes were comical at times. It was not unusual to see liberated British prisoners of war walking in long columns alongside of German soldiers and Hitler youth whose Nazi indoctrination melted in their fear of the Russians.

Firm contact was established between ground forces of the First American Army and those of the Russian Army in Germany on April 25, 1945. The historic meeting took place in the town of Torgau on the Elbe River, 75 miles south of Berlin, when First Army troops met forward elements of the Russian Guards Division. Here, U.S. and Russian troops meet on the wrecked bridge over the Elbe. The Americans, left, and Russian soldiers, right, reach out to grasp each other's hands.

MUSSOLINI EXECUTED; HIS BODY EXHIBITED FOR CROWDS TO REVILE

ROME, April 29 (AP)—Benito Mussolini was executed Saturday in Northern Italy and his body, with that of 17 other executed fascist leaders, was on exhibition Sunday night before a huge crowd in Milan square, Allied headquarters announced, quoting two British correspondents who saw the bodies. . . .

The Milan radio said Mussolini, his young sweetheart Claretta Petacci, and 16 other fascists were executed. American columns pushing into Milan Sunday came to a "gruesome, horrible sight," the eyewitness said. "Suspended with heads downward were seven bodies. In the center was the body of Mussolini, disfigured by blows from the crowd which has passed through the square since early morning." . . .

The Rome newspaper *Il Momento* . . . said the bodies of Mussolini, Miss Petacci and several others were strung up on a large sign before a department store and that a woman had fired revolver shots at Mussolini's body, shouting "Those are for my five sons you killed!" . . .

On Friday the Swiss radio reported that Mussolini had been denied permission to cross the Swiss frontier and the same day the Milan station said the former dictator, "yellow with fury and fear," had been captured. . . . At the last, when Mussolini fled for his life before an uprising of patriots against his new government, he was reported to have lamented that "even Hitler" had bereft him and that he had no friends.

Wisconsin Rapids Daily Tribune, Wisconsin Rapids, WI, May 1, 1945

HITLER IS DEAD!

KILLED AT HIS COMMAND POST THIS AFTERNOON

BULLETIN
By The Associated Press

LONDON—The German radio has announced the death of Adolf Hitler—11 days after the German führer reached his 56th birthday, and 48 hours after Benito Mussolini was shot to death in north Italy.

The death of Hitler was announced by the Hamburg radio—the only station remaining in Nazi hands. The German broadcaster, Lord Haw-Haw, went on the air and told the German people to stand by for a grave and important announcement. A short time later, the Hamburg station announced that Adolf Hitler was killed this afternoon.

The German broadcast said Hitler was killed in his command post at the Reich's chancellery in Berlin. The Hamburg broadcast said Hitler has been succeeded by Adm. Karl Doenitz, commander of the German fleet. The announcement went on to say that Hitler fought up to his last breath against Bolshevism. Whether all of these German-announced facts on the details of Hitler's death are true, cannot be determined now. But, it is recalled that in his order to German armies to invade Poland in September of 1939, Hitler said he would stay in uniform until death or victory.

The Hamburg broadcast on the death of Hitler said: "At the Führer's headquarters, it is reported that our Führer Adolf Hitler has fallen in his command post at the Reich Chancellery, fighting up to his last breath against Bolshevism."

The new Nazi leader, Adm. Doenitz, appealed to the German people. He said—quote—"Give me your confidence. Keep calm and be disciplined. . . . Only in that way will we be able to stave off defeat." . . . .

The death of Hitler ends an infamous career which began its real ascendency on January 30, 1933 when Hitler became chancellor of Germany. The German announcement of Hitler's death made no mention of Gestapo chief Heinrich Himmler, who had been reported dickering for surrender of Germany to the Allies. Adolf Hitler, who died in Berlin today, was born on April 20, 1889, at Braunau, Austria.

Leader-Telegram, Eau Claire, WI, Thursday, May 3, 1945

AGREE HITLER IS DEAD BUT NOT HOW HE DIED

By The Associated Press

The Germans and the Allies appeared agreed today that Adolf Hitler was dead, but they disagreed on how he met his end. There were at least these three versions:

Russian—He committed suicide. (Soviet communiqué)

German—He met a hero's death in the battle of Berlin. (Hamburg Radio)

American—He died or was dying of a cerebral hemorrhage. (Supreme Headquarter's statement attributing the report to Heinrich Himmler)

In Washington, President Truman said he had it on best authority that Hitler was dead, but didn't know how the death occurred.

U.S. soldiers on leave in Paris read the news of Hitler's death in the May 2, 1945, edition of the *Stars and Stripes*.

Owensboro Messenger, Owensboro, KY, Tuesday, May 1, 1945

GERMANS ADMIT FALL OF BERLIN NEAR

RUSSIANS CAPTURE REICHSTAG IN HEART OF BLAZING CAPITAL

Seize 200 City Blocks in Center of Berlin's Business District

By ROMNEY WHEELER

LONDON (AP)—Red Army troops captured the gutted shell of the German Reichstag in the blazing heart of Berlin Monday night, hoisting the Russian "flag of victory" over the Nazi shrine as the Germans admitted that the 10-day battle for Berlin was lost.

The fall of Berlin was imminent, perhaps to be announced in a May Day proclamation in Moscow later today.

Moscow's nightly war bulletin announced the capture of the famous building, which was wrecked by fire in February 1933, and was used by the Nazis as an excuse to seize dictatorial powers and persecute the Communists. . . .

Along with the Reichstag building, Soviet troops captured Heinrich Himmler's ministry of the interior and 200 city blocks in the heart of Berlin. The central post office building also was seized. The fall of these buildings placed Red Army storm troops at both ends of Unter den Linden and at Berlin's triumphal arch, the Brandenburg gate.

As German troops continued to surrender by the thousands in the capital, giving up the suicidal struggle, the Russians laid siege to Hitler's underground fortress headquarters in the Tiergarten. North of the dying capital, Red Army troops rolled forward another twenty miles along the Baltic coast and seized the great German port of Greifswald.

While peace rumors engaged Allied and neutral capitals, in tottering Berlin the Red Army's grim, unshaven Tommygunners, sappers, rocket-gun crews and tankmen smashed inexorably down Unter den Linden and were reducing the last barricades. . . .

Nazis Admit End Near

The Russian stepped up their overwhelming struggle for the Nazi capital to unprecedented proportions in an apparent all-out bid to capture the city by today, when Moscow will hold its annual May Day celebrations.

ABOVE: Victorious Red Army soldiers listen to their favorite song, Tchaikovsky's "Moscow," on a Victrola they set up on a Berlin street, May 1, 1945.

OPPOSITE PAGE: This famous image of a Red Army soldier raising the Soviet flag over the ruins of the Reichstag in Berlin on May 2, 1945, by Soviet naval officer and photographer Yevgeny Khaldei, symbolized Russian victory in what Stalin called the "Great Patriotic War."

As the battle neared its end, the German radio admitted only a few strongholds still held out in the heart of the desolate capital. Nazi lamentations indicated the Germans had given up all hope of holding out much longer. "The hard battle for Berlin reached its climax Monday," the Hamburg radio said. "A heroic, gruesome fate has befallen Berlin. This vast European town has ceased to exist. These are the hours of her last heave."

In the dwindling heart of Berlin, the combined First White Russian and First Ukrainian Armies hurled back the Nazi defenders into an area little more than ten square miles in area, and the German-controlled Oslo radio said fresh Russian tank forces had been thrown into the gigantic struggle for the city's central core.

Oakland Tribune, Oakland, CA, Monday, May 7, 1945

GERMANY UNCONDITIONALLY SURRENDERS TO ALLIES

Mighty Struggle Comes to End at Gen. Eisenhower's H.Q.

By The Associated Press

LONDON, May 7—The war against Germany, the greatest in history, ended today with the unconditional surrender of the once mighty Wehrmacht.

The surrender to the Western Allies and Russia was made at Gen. Eisenhower's headquarters at Reims, France, by the German high command.

The British government announced that tomorrow will be celebrated as V-E Day. Prime Minister Churchill will broadcast at 6 a.m., P.W.T., and King George VI at 12 p.m., P.W.T.

In Washington, microphones were made ready for a broadcast by President Truman. Prime Minister Churchill, after a busy day at 10 Downing St., went to see King George VI.

News of the surrender came in an Associated Press dispatch from Reims, at 6:35 a.m. (P.W.T.) and immediately set the church bells tolling in Rome and elsewhere.

In the hour before the news from Reims, German broadcasts told the German people that Grand Adm. Karl Doenitz had ordered capitulation of all fighting forces, and called off U-boat warfare.

The surrender was signed for Germany by Col. Gen. Gustav Jodl, chief of staff of the German army. It was signed for the Supreme Allied Command by Lieut. Gen. Walter Bedell Smith, chief of staff for Gen. Eisenhower. It was also signed by Gen. Ivan Susloparov for Russia and by Gen. François Sevez for France. The Germans were asked sternly if they understood the surrender terms imposed upon Germany and if they would be carried out by Germany. They answered yes.

Germany, which began the war with a ruthless attack upon Poland, followed by successive aggression and brutality in internment camps, surrendered with an appeal to the victor for mercy toward the German people and armed forces.

After signing the full surrender, Jodl said he wanted to speak and was given leave to do so. "With this signature," he said in soft-spoken German, "the German people and armed forces are for better or worse delivered into the victors' hands. In this war, which has lasted more than five years, both have achieved and suffered more than perhaps any other people in the world." Joy at the news was tempered only by the realization that the war against Japan remains to be resolved, with many casualties still ahead.

The end of the European warfare, greatest, bloodiest and costliest war in human history—it has claimed at least 40,000,000 casualties on both sides in killed, wounded and captured—came after five years, eight months and six days of strife that overspread the globe. . . .

London went wild at the news. Crowds jammed Piccadilly Circus. Smiling throngs poured out of subways and lined the streets. (Cheers went up in New York, too, and papers showered down from skyscrapers). . . . The BBC said telephone conversations were going on between London, Washington and Moscow in order to fix the exact hour of the V-E Day announcement by President Truman, Prime Minister Churchill and Premier Stalin.

An announcement on the wavelength of the Flensburg radio, which has been carrying German communiqués and orders for several days, said: "German men and women! The High Command of the armed forces has today, at the order of Grand Admiral Doenitz, declared the unconditional surrender of all fighting German troops." The announcement was attributed to the new German foreign minister, Count Schwerin von Krosigk. . . . "After a heroic fight of almost six years of incomparable hardness Germany has succumbed to the overwhelming power of her enemies. To continue the war would only mean senseless bloodshed and a futile disintegration. A government which has a feeling of responsibility for the future of its nation was compelled to act on the collapse of all physical and material forces and to demand of the enemy the cessation of hostilities.

"It was the noblest task of the admiral of the fleet and of the government supporting him—after the terrible sacrifices which the war demanded—to save in the last phase of the war the lives of a maximum number of fellow countrymen. . . .

"We end this gravest hour of the German nation and its Reich."

★ ★ ★

LEFT TOP: President Harry S. Truman, back center, gestures as he tells reporters and staff details about the surrender of Germany during a press conference at the White House, May 8, 1945.

LEFT BOTTOM: Prime Minister Winston Churchill, center, joins the royal family, from left, Princess Elizabeth, Queen Elizabeth, King George VI, and Princess Margaret, on the balcony of Buckingham Palace, London, England, on V-E Day, May 8, 1945.

Baltimore Evening Sun, Baltimore, MD, Sunday, May 7, 1945

NAZIS KILLED FOUR MILLION IN POLISH CAMP, REDS SAY

MOSCOW, May 7 (AP)—More than 4,000,000 persons were put to death by the Nazis in the "most horrible crime against the peoples of Europe" at the Oswiecim concentration camp in Poland, an official report of the Extraordinary State Commission declared today.

(This was the first official Soviet report on the number of persons killed at Oswiecim. On April 11, Dr. Bela Fabian, president of the dissolved Hungarian Independent Democratic party, in an interview near Erfurt, Germany, accused the Germans of killing 5,000,000 Jews at Oswiecim, from which he himself narrowly escaped. He said the executions had been carried out over a ten-month period.)

BELOW: The main guardhouse and rail entrance to the Auschwitz II-Birkenau extermination camp, the largest of the camps and subcamps in the Auschwitz complex in Oswiecim (Auschwitz, in German), Poland. An estimated 1.3 million people from throughout Europe were deported to the complex between 1940 and 1945. The AP article here reported at the time that it was believed that more than 4,000,000 had been put to death at Auschwitz; the actual number of victims was 1.1 million men, women, and children, including nearly 1 million Jews. This photograph was taken in late January 1945 after the camp was abandoned by the Germans fleeing the approaching Red Army (60,000 of the camp's prisoners were forced by SS units on a death march to other camps in the region). The Soviets entered Auschwitz on Jan. 27, 1945, liberating more than 6,000 dying and ill prisoners. More than 6 million Jews were murdered by the Nazi state and its collaborators during the Holocaust.

Male survivors of Auschwitz stand behind a barbed wire fence in the camp, late January–early February 1945. This photograph is a still from a Soviet film produced on the liberation of Auschwitz, created by the film unit of the First Ukrainian Front.

Oswiecim Surpasses All Others

The committee report said the dead included citizens of Russia, Poland, France, Belgium, Holland, Czechoslovakia, Romania, Hungary, Yugoslavia and "other countries," and that they had been killed by various means, including torture, poison, gas and cremation. The committee stated that Oswiecim surpassed anything heretofore disclosed as perpetrated by the Nazis against the people of Europe.

Medical experts and scientists from France, Poland, and Czechoslovakia participated with the Russians in the inquiry, conducted during February and March. The report was made on the basis of the questioning of persons who escaped from the horror camp and from captured German documents. Other evidence included crematory stoves and gas chambers.

As part of the camp's routine, German doctors had carried out systematic experiments on living men, women and children, which included sterilization and castration. Children were infected with typhus, cancer and malaria, the report added, and the reaction of young children to certain poisons was "observed" by the Nazi medical men.

Himmler Blamed

The report said investigators found the most extensively and elaborately equipped Nazi death laboratories yet. Gas chambers where thousands lost their lives had signs above the doors reading "Special Baths," "Disinfection Point" or simply "Entrance to Baths."

The investigating committee placed the full blame on Heinrich Himmler, declaring him the organizer of the camp in 1939 for the special purpose of wiping out citizens of occupied Europe.

Bakersfield Californian, Bakersfield, CA, Wednesday, May 9, 1945

GÖRING, KESSELRING NABBED

By A. I. GOLDBERG

SIXTH ARMY GROUP HEADQUARTERS, May 9 (AP)—Hermann Göring, once the second-ranking Nazi, was captured last night by the American Seventh Army and declared today that he had been arrested by the Germans on orders of Hitler because he wanted to conclude a surrender.

The fat Reichsmarschall said he was seized by the Germans on April 21, held at Berchtesgaden and ordered executed. He last saw Hitler on April 22 in Berlin, he asserted. He said he believed Hitler died on April 27 or 28. Field Marshal Albert Kesselring, German commander on the western front until March, also was captured. . . .

Göring said he was in Berchtesgaden on April 24 and talked to Hitler by telephone, recalling Hitler's previous assertions that Göring was to be his successor. The marshal said he suggested to Hitler that perhaps that time had arrived as "it looks like the end." Göring said Hitler was enraged and accused him of losing faith. Göring added that Hitler told him he had signed his death warrant, "but if you renounce all of your titles and high honors, you will be forgiven."

The marshal said he complied, but that Hitler let the order stand and ordered SS troops to place him under arrest. His air force followers shot their way through the SS men and took him to a mountain hideaway, Göring said. The marshal indicated he did not know what was in store for him. His spirit seemed high and he told his captors to "guard me well."

LEFT: Reichsmarschall Hermann Göring is shown during an interview with reporters in Augsburg, Germany, May 11, 1945. He surrendered to the U.S. Army in Austria on May 9 after escaping SS guards. On Oct. 1, 1946, Göring was found guilty on four counts—including war crimes and crimes against humanity—by the International Military Tribunal (IMT) at Nuremberg, and sentenced to hang; he committed suicide by cyanide on Oct. 15, 1946, the night before his hanging.

ABOVE: In the bomb-damaged Reichstag, hundreds of Russian soldiers chalked their names among the stone pillars at the entrance. A newly arrived British soldier is seen adding his name to the list, May 7, 1945, in Berlin.

LEFT: British civilians and Allied service men and women gather in London outside Rainbow Corner, the American Red Cross club near Piccadilly Circus, to hear the final announcement of Germany's surrender in World War II.

Escanaba Daily Press, Escanaba, MI, Wednesday, May 9, 1945

GUNS STILLED IN EUROPE; JAPS NEXT

GERMANS BOW IN DEFEAT TO ALLIED MIGHT

Peace Agreement Is Ratified in Berlin Ruins

By JAMES M. LONG

PARIS, Wednesday, May 9 (AP)—Germany bowed today to the most crushing defeat ever inflicted upon a nation, her abject surrender proclaimed to the world by the United States, Britain and Russia.

The Moscow radio on behalf of Premier Marshal Stalin, whose Red Armies broke the armed might of Hitler's Reich on the eastern front, announced the unconditional surrender to the Russian people at 1:10 a.m. today, ten hours and ten minutes after President Truman and Prime Minister Churchill proclaimed V-E day.

Reich in Ashes

The announcement said the final articles of capitulation were signed yesterday in Berlin, the ruined capital symbolic of the fall of the Third Reich.

Field Marshal Wilhelm Keitel, chief of the German high command, signed the articles in the presence of Marshal Georgy K. Zhukov, assistant commander of the Red Armies; Air Chief Marshal Sir Arthur Tedder, deputy supreme commander in the West; Gen. Carl A. Spaatz, chief of the U.S. strategic air forces in Europe; and Lt. Gen. Jean de Lattre de Tassigny, commander of the French First Army.

For Germany it was a crowning ignominy—Keitel, whose armies all but mastered Europe, forced to sign in the ashes of Germany's first city the surrender articles which stripped the Reich of its last vestige of military strength.

Casualties 40 Million

The guns of Europe, which through five years, eight months and seven days of unexampled war inflicted possibly 40,000,000 casualties, fell silent at one minute past midnight today (6:01 p.m. Tuesday, E.W.T.).

Actually, guns on the western front were stilled yesterday to prevent further bloodshed as the Allied world celebrated V-E Day 11 months and two days after Gen. Eisenhower's armies stormed into France to liberate a Europe in Nazi chains. The last shot on the western front was fired in Czechoslovakia by the 80th Infantry Division of Gen. Patton's Third Army, the last to remain in action. Patton issued his cease-fire order at 8 a.m. today (2 a.m., E.W.T.). The stubborn Nazis in Czechoslovakia—the last to submit—agreed to the terms of unconditional surrender, and a "cease-fire" order was issued in Prague at 1:25 p.m. (E.W.T.).

The final terms were signed at 2:41 a.m. Monday (British Double Summer Time, 8:41 p.m., Sunday, E.W.T.) in a red brick schoolhouse in Reims, which for months had been Gen. Eisenhower's headquarters.

Prisoners Going Home

The fact of this historic signing had been first reported to the world 24 hours before by Edward Kennedy, chief of the Associated Press staff on the western front.

BELOW: Associated Press Paris bureau chief Edward Kennedy sent out this news bulletin announcing the unconditional surrender of the Germans to the Allies on May 7, 1945.

```
D63
     BULLETIN
          BY EDWARD KENNEDY
   REIMS, FRANCE, MAY 7-(AP)-GERMANY SURRENDERED UNCONDITIONALLY
TO THE WESTERN ALLIES AND RUSSIA AT 2:41 A.M. FRENCH TIME TODAY.
     R837ACW
```

German field marshal Wilhelm Keitel, Chief of Armed Forces High Command, signs the ratified surrender terms for the German army at Russian headquarters in Berlin, May 15, 1945. Keitel was also found guilty on four counts by the IMT during the Nuremberg trials; he was executed by hanging on Oct. 16, 1946.

In a ringing order of the day, Eisenhower told his armies that "the crusade on which we embarked in the early summer of 1944 has reached its glorious conclusion. It is my especial privilege in the name of all nations represented in this theater of war to commend each of you for valiant performance of duty," he said. "Though these words are feeble, they come from the bottom of a heart overflowing with pride in your loyal service and admiration for you as warriors. Your accomplishments at sea, in the air, on the ground and in the field of supply have astonished the world."

In a special message to Allied prisoners of war, Eisenhower said they must remain where they were for the present but "your return home will be organized as speedily as feasible."

Eisenhower Saves Pen

German forces which once held nearly all Europe in their iron grip thus knuckled to the "unconditional surrender" formula dictated by Churchill and the late President Roosevelt at Casablanca. . . .

Col. Gen. Gustav Jodl, German chief of staff, signed the surrender document for Grand Marshal Karl Doenitz, successor as head of the prostrate Reich to the dead or missing Hitler.

With the stroke of a pen which Eisenhower long had saved for the occasion, Jodl surrendered unconditionally to "the supreme commander, Allied expeditionary force, and simultaneously to the Soviet high command all forces on land, sea and in the air who are at this date under German control." . . .

The act sealed the fate of Japan, which one day will be forced to sign a similarly harsh surrender, for now the full power of the United States and Britain will be used against the island empire. . . .

In his order of the day, Eisenhower said his armies of the West had put 5,000,000 of the enemy "permanently out of the war" and had "taken in stride military tasks so difficult as to be classed by many doubters as impossible."

RIGHT TOP: Gen. Dwight D. Eisenhower makes a V for victory sign with two pens he used to sign Germany's unconditional surrender instrument at Reims, May 7, 1945.

RIGHT BOTTOM: U.S. soldiers of the 9th Armored Division of the First Army slap one another on the back, shake hands and cheer on hearing the official announcement of Germany's unconditional surrender, in the town square at Weiden, Germany, May 9, 1945.

Des Moines Register, Des Moines, IA, Tuesday, May 8, 1945

SCENES OF JOY COVER NATION

By The Associated Press

The end of the war against Nazi Germany precipitated scenes of rejoicing Monday throughout the nation, although the celebration was tempered by the bitter fighting still ahead against Japan.

The hub of New York City's celebration was Times Square, where police estimated 500,000 gathered. People knelt in the streets to pray. Others stood five-deep in many bars. Confetti and ticker tape littered the streets.

Prayers of thanksgiving were offered in churches and schools in thousands of communities. In many places—as in New York City's financial and garment districts—office workers left their jobs, although war workers continued as usual.

Reaction in New England included the closing of hundreds of retail stores. . . . In Syracuse, N.Y., stores posted signs in their windows which said: "The war is not over—remember Pearl Harbor." . . . In Washington, D.C., there were brief interludes of congratulations and celebration among the thousands of workers in government offices. But routine was soon resumed there. Los Angeles, Cal., a major center of war manufacture, carried on with the job with little evidence of rejoicing at the end of the war in Europe. In San Francisco, Cal., the surrender news got a joyful but quiet reception. Shipyards and war plants remained open. . . . In Seattle, Wash., workmen building giant Superfortress bombers in a Boeing plant rolled out a brand new bomber, named *On to Tokyo*, then returned to their jobs.

New Yorkers hold aloft a youth wearing a mask of Adolf Hitler to cheer the news of the surrender of Germany during the festivities in Times Square, May 7, 1945.

Decatur Daily Review, Decatur, IL, Friday, August 3, 1945

PLANS FOR NEW EUROPE ARE TOUGH ON GERMANY

Potsdam Plan Silent on War Against Japan

WASHINGTON, Aug. 3 (AP)—A master plan for reconstructing a peaceful Europe out of the ruins of war emerged today from the decisions of the Big Three conference at Potsdam. But Russia's role in the conflict with Japan remains cloaked in the same secrecy as ever.

The plan provides for a stripped-down Germany, shorn of territories, wealth and power. The nation that once aspired to world dominion is to be limited to farming and "peaceful, domestic industries." And it is to be subjected to years of Allied control until it earns its way slowly back into the family of sovereign nations.

The plan provides also for a reshaped Poland, augmented by huge slices of Germany and stretching westward to within 50 miles of Berlin, and for the addition to Russia of one-third of the territory of German East Prussia.

Five-Power Council

It leaves most other decisions, however, to future peace settlements. And for these the Big Three agreed on a five-power council, including China and France in addition to the United States, Britain and Russia. Assuming China and France agree to the plan, the five foreign ministers will hold their first meeting in London by Sept. 1. . . .

The big-power pattern of peace for Europe was disclosed in a 6,000-word report on the Potsdam meeting of Mr. Truman, Generalissimo Stalin and Prime Minister Attlee released . . . yesterday evening in Washington, London and Moscow. The conference ended Wednesday night. It began July 17. . . .

The specific accomplishments covered in the Potsdam report fall under a half-dozen headings:

1. PEACE SETTLEMENTS—Mr. Truman, Stalin and Attlee agreed on a U.S. proposal for creation of a five-power council consisting of the foreign ministers of the United States, Britain, Russia, France and China. These are the nations which plan to take major responsibility for maintaining peace in the world as permanent members of the projected United Nations security council. . . .

The council's first job would be to work out and submit to the United Nations a peace treaty for Italy. Then it would work out treaties for Romania, Bulgaria, Hungary and Finland. Once

Territory changes: The black areas on this map, published in the *Decatur Daily Review* on Aug. 3, 1945, are those parts of Germany that the Big Three (the Soviet Union, the United States, and the United Kingdom) proposed to come under Polish rule. The shaded area is that which the Soviet Union took over since the start of hostilities on the continent (Northern East Prussia was a new addition).

these former Axis allies had signed the treaties they would become eligible for membership in the United Nations.

Countries which were neutral in the war against Germany are invited to seek United Nations membership—except for Spain so long as it is ruled by the Franco government. The Big Three barred the Franco regime on the ground of its Axis origins and the present record and nature of the Madrid government.

This leaves territorial settlements as the biggest remaining job in reorganizing Europe, and the foreign ministers council would

A triple handshake between Churchill, Truman and Stalin at the Potsdam Conference, July 23, 1945.

undertake these. The plan is to work out agreements between disputing countries (such as Italy and Yugoslavia) where possible. . . .

2. GERMAN CONTROL POLICIES—Germany is to be administered by the Anglo-American–Soviet–French control council in Berlin until its people are judged ready to rule themselves peacefully. It is to be deprived of all its war-making industries, and allowed only those industries necessary to maintain an average European standard of living for its people. It is to be denied airplanes and merchant ships and to be made so far as possible self-sustaining with agriculture and peaceful manufactures.

The Germans will be permitted political and religious freedom and free speech. They can have trade unions. Control of their local affairs will be put into their own hands, and the political structure of a new German nation will be built on these local beginnings.

Salt Lake Telegram, Salt Lake City, Monday, August 6, 1945

U.S. CRUSHES JAP CITY WITH ATOMIC BOMB

Force Exceeding 20,000 Tons of TNT Hurled

WASHINGTON, Aug. 6 (AP)—An atomic bomb, hailed as the most terrible destructive force in history and as the greatest achievement of organized science, has been loosed upon Japan.

President Truman disclosed in a White House statement Monday that the first use of the bomb—containing more power than 20,000 tons of TNT and producing more than 2,000 times the blast of the most powerful bomb ever dropped before—was made 16 hours earlier on Hiroshima, a Japanese army base.

The atomic bomb is the answer, President Truman said, to Japan's refusal to surrender, Secretary of War Stimson predicted the bomb will "prove a tremendous aid" in shortening the Japanese war.

Even More Powerful Forms in Development

Mr. Truman grimly warned that "even more powerful forms (of the bomb) are in development." He said:

"If they do not now accept our terms, they may expect a rain of ruin from the air the like of which has never been seen on this earth."

The war department reported that "an impenetrable cloud of dust and smoke" cloaked Hiroshima after the first atomic bomb crashed down. It was impossible to make an immediate assessment of the damage.

President Truman said he would recommend that Congress consider establishing a commission to control production of atomic power within the United States, adding: "I shall make recommendations to Congress as to how atomic power can become a powerful and forceful influence toward the maintenance of world peace."

Both Mr. Truman and Secy. Stimson, while emphasizing the peacetime potentiality of the new force, made clear that much research must be undertaken to effect full peacetime application of its principles.

The product of $2,000,000,000 spent in research and production—"the greatest scientific gamble in history," Mr. Truman said—the atomic bomb has been one of the most closely guarded secrets of the war. Franklin D. Roosevelt and Winston Churchill

Col. Paul W. Tibbets Jr., pilot of the *Enola Gay*—the modified B-29 he named after his mother—waves from his cockpit before takeoff from Tinian Island in the Northern Marianas, Aug. 6, 1945. The *Enola Gay*, carrying the "Little Boy" atomic bomb, would soon be en route to the skies of Hiroshima, Japan.

gave the signal to start work on harnessing the forces of the atom. Mr. Truman said the Germans worked feverishly, but failed to solve the problem.

$2,000,000,000 Scientific Gamble Has Won

The president disclosed that more than 65,000 persons now are working in great secrecy in these plants, adding: "We are now prepared to obliterate more rapidly and completely every productive enterprise the Japanese have above ground in any city. We shall completely destroy Japan's power to make war."

The president noted that the Big Three ultimatum issued July 26 at Potsdam was intended "to spare the Japanese people from utter destruction" and the Japanese leaders rejected it. . . . Mr. Truman forecasted that air and land forces will follow up this attack in such numbers and power as the Japanese never have witnessed.

The president said that this discovery may open the way for an entirely new concept of force and power. The actual harnessing of atomic energy may in the future supplement the power that now comes from coal, oil and the great dams, he said. "It has never been the habit of the scientists of this country or the policy of this government to withhold from the world scientific knowledge," Mr. Truman said. "Normally therefore everything about the work with atomic entry would be made public."

That will have to wait, however, he said, until the war emergency is over.

An accurate assessment of the damage inflicted by the bomb is not yet available, however, the war department said. As soon as details of its effectiveness are learned, the department added, they will be released.

LEFT: The Hiroshima atomic bomb explosion recorded at 8:15 a.m. on the remains of a wristwatch found in the ruins. The small hand on the "8" of the watch was burned off from the blast, leaving just a shadow.

BELOW: A mushroom cloud over Hiroshima billows an hour after a 9,000-pound uranium-235 bomb was detonated above the city at 8:15 a.m., Aug. 6, 1945. The cloud rose to over 60,000 feet in about 10 minutes. Although it is difficult to ascertain the total number of casualties because of the destruction of civil institutions in the city, it is believed that an estimated 66,000 died instantly, and another 60,000 were injured. Tens of thousands later died of radiation poisoning and other injuries. A 1998 study found that some 62,000 later died from radiation-related illnesses such as cancer.

ABOVE: Twisted metal and rubble mark what once was the center of Hiroshima, August 1945.

Staggers Imagination

Stimson said in his statement that the explosive power of the bomb is enough to "stagger the imagination." He added that scientists are confident of developing even more powerful atomic bombs.

Stinson said that security requirements do not permit disclosure of the exact methods of producing the bomb or the nature of its action. He did say, however, that uranium ore is essential to the production of the bomb.

Development of the bomb culminated three years of work by Allied scientists, industry, labor and military forces, Stimson said, adding that he was convinced Japan will not be in a position to use a similar weapon. While Germany worked "feverishly" to develop an atomic bomb, Stinson said, the Nazi defeat now has erased danger from that source. . . .

WAR CASUALTIES NOW 1,060,727

WASHINGTON, Aug. 3 (AP)—American combat casualties increased 1,855 during the past week, raising the combined army-navy total to 1,060,727 since the start of the war. Secretary of War Stimson gave his Thursday news conference the current army figures: 197,676 killed, 570,766 wounded, 34,734 missing, and 117,741 prisoners of war, a total of 920,917 casualties as reported through July 29. . . .

Navy casualties reported to date are 51,588 killed, 72,855 wounded, 11,611 missing, and 3,756 prisoners or a total of 139,810. . . .

Stimson said that of the 570,766 army wounded 351,317 have returned to duty and of the 117,741 army men listed as prisoners 95,709 have been since exchanged or returned to military control.

Two people walk on a cleared path through the destruction in Hiroshima resulting from the detonation of the first atomic bomb, Sept. 8, 1945.

He disclosed that development of the bomb was carried out by thousands of persons "with the greatest secrecy." The work has been so divided, he said, that no one has been given more information concerning the bomb than was absolutely necessary to his particular job. . . .

Pasco Plant

Three plants to produce the bombs were started in December 1942. Two of these are located at the Clinton engineer works in Tennessee and a third at the Hanford engineer works in Washington State. . . .

In addition, a special laboratory to deal with technical problems has been established near Santa Fe, N.M. This laboratory is directed by Dr. J. Robert Oppenheimer, whose "genius and inspiration," Stinson said, has been largely responsible for development of the bomb. . . . The secretary added:

"Already in the course of producing one of the elements much energy is being released, not explosively but in regulated amounts. This energy, however, is in the form of heat at a temperature too low to make practicable the operation of a conventional power plant. It will be a matter of much further research and development to design machines, for the conversion of atomic energy into useful power."

★ ★ ★

Roseburg News-Review, Roseburg, OR, Wednesday, August 8, 1945

RUSSIA DECLARES WAR ON JAPS

WASHINGTON, Aug. 8 (AP)—President Truman announced today that Russia has declared war on Japan. Mr. Truman made this announcement to a hurriedly summoned news conference.

He said he only had a single statement to make, but that it was so important he could not delay it.

Then, with a broad grin, he declared: "Russia has just declared war on Japan. That is all."

The disclosure that the Soviet Union at last had pitted its enormous might alongside Britain and the United States against the Pacific enemy had not been unexpected.

Official Washington at once took this development, along with the unleashing of atomic bombing against the Pacific enemy, as a sure sign that Japan could not long continue to resist.

The short announcement brought a gasp from reporters who had rushed to the White House in a stream of taxicabs and an exclamation of "my God" from some.

BELOW: The destruction of Hiroshima's center—only the shells of a few buildings remain after the atomic bomb blast razed the rest.

Joplin Globe, Joplin, MO, Thursday, August 9, 1945

AMERICANS DROP 2ND ATOMIC BOMB, HITTING NAGASAKI

PLANE CREW MEMBERS' RADIO RESULTS WERE GOOD, BUT GEN. SPAATZ GIVES OUT NO DETAILS

Hiroshima's Death Toll Is Appalling

EVIDENCE INDICATES NIPPONESE PERISHED BY THOUSANDS IN FIRST CITY ATTACKED WITH NEW EXPLOSIVE

GUAM, Aug. 9. (Thursday) (AP)—The world's second atomic bomb, most destructive explosive invented by man, was dropped on strategically important Nagasaki on western Kyushu Island at noon today.

Crewmembers radioed that results were good, but Gen. Spaatz said additional details would not be disclosed until the mission returns. Spaatz's communiqué reporting the bombing did not say whether only one or more than one "mighty atom" was dropped.

The first atomic bomb destroyed more than 60 percent—4.1 square miles—of Hiroshima, city of 343,000 population, Monday, and Radio Tokyo reported "practically every living thing" there was annihilated.

A Shipping and Rail Center

Nagasaki, which had 211,000 population 10 years ago, is an important shipping and railway center. It was hit first by China-based B-29s a year ago this month and was heavily attacked by Far East air force bombers and fighters only last July 31 and on the following day.

Nagasaki, although only two-thirds as large as Hiroshima in population, is considered more important industrially. With a population now estimated at 255,000, its 12 square miles are jam-packed with eave to eave buildings which won it the name "sea of roofs."

It was vitally important as a port for trans-shipment of military supplies and the embarkation of troops in support of Japan's operations in China, Formosa, Southeast Asia and the Southwest Pacific. It was highly important as a major shipbuilding and repair center for both naval and merchantmen.

RIGHT: Survivors walk amid the devastation left after an atomic bomb exploded over Nagasaki, Japan, on Aug. 9, 1945, which killed an estimated 39,000 and injured another 25,000.

OPPOSITE PAGE: The enormous mushroom cloud over Nagasaki, Japan, after *Bockscar*—piloted by Maj. Charles W. Sweeney—dropped the 10,000-pound plutonium "Fat Boy" bomb over Nagasaki, Japan, at 11:02 a.m, Aug. 9, 1945.

Decatur Daily Review, Decatur, IL, Tuesday, August 14, 1945

JAP SURRENDER UNCONDITIONAL, MACARTHUR TOP COMMANDER

PRESIDENT SAYS POTSDAM TERMS FULLY ACCEPTED

Fighting Ends

WASHINGTON, Aug. 14 (AP)—Japan has surrendered unconditionally, President Truman announced at 6 p.m., C.W.T., tonight.

General of the Army Douglas A. MacArthur has been designated supreme Allied commander to receive the surrender.

Offensive operations have been ordered suspended everywhere.

V-J Day will be proclaimed only after the surrender has been formally accepted by MacArthur.

President Truman said he regarded the surrender as "unconditional." The Japanese note, however, directly followed one from Secretary of State Byrnes in which the Allies agreed that the Japanese would be permitted to keep their emperor, at least for a time. The Byrnes note prescribed that the emperor should be completely controlled by the Allies; also, that the Japanese people should have an opportunity later on to decide by ballot the kind of government they want.

Mr. Truman read the formal message relayed from Emperor Hirohito through the Swiss government in which the Japanese ruler pledged the surrender on the terms laid down by the Big Three conference at Potsdam.

"Full Acceptance"

President Truman made this statement: "I have received this afternoon a message from the Japanese government in reply to the message forwarded to that government by the secretary of state on August 11.

"I deem this reply a full acceptance of the Potsdam declaration which specifies the unconditional surrender of Japan. In this reply there is no qualification.

"Arrangements are now being made for the formal signing of surrender terms at the earliest possible moment.

MacArthur Supreme Commander

"Gen. Douglas MacArthur has been appointed the supreme Allied commander to receive the Japanese surrender.

"Great Britain, Russia and China will be represented by high-ranking officers.

"Meantime, the Allied armed forces have been ordered to suspend offensive action.

"The proclamation of V-J day must wait upon the formal signing of the surrender terms by Japan."

Simultaneously Mr. Truman disclosed that Selective Service is taking immediate steps to slash inductions from 80,000 to 50,000 a month.

Draft Men Under 26

Henceforth, Mr. Truman said, only those men under 26 will be drafted for the reduced quotas.

The White House made public the Japanese government's message accepting that ended the war which started December 7, 1941.

The text of their message which was delivered by the Swiss chargé d'affaires follows:

"Communication of the Japanese government of August 14, 1945, addressed to the governments of the United States, Great Britain, the Soviet Union and China:

"With reference to the Japanese government's note of August 10 regarding their acceptance of the provisions of the Potsdam declaration and the reply of the governments of the United States, Great Britain, the Soviet Union and China by American Secretary of State Byrnes under the date of August 11, the Japanese government have the honor to communicate to the governments of the four powers as follows:

"1. His Majesty the Emperor has issued an Imperial rescript regarding Japan's acceptance of the provisions of the Potsdam declaration.

"2. His Majesty the Emperor is prepared to authorize and insure the signature by his government and the Imperial general headquarters of necessary terms for carrying out the provisions of the Potsdam declaration. His Majesty is also prepared to issue his commands to all the military, naval and air authorities of Japan and all the forces under their control wherever located to cease active operations, to surrender arms, and to issue such other orders as may be required by the supreme commander of the Allied forces for the execution of the above mentioned terms."

Huge Crowd of Reporters

The president made the historic announcement to a huge crowd of reporters who had been virtually living in the White House for days in anticipation of just such a development.

Smiling and surrounded by his staff, the president told the press that the Japanese had decided to accept unconditional surrender and mentioned that the reporters would not have to take any notes.

Mr. Truman said prepared statements would be available as they left and three were issued, one detailing MacArthur's

BELOW: President Truman briefs reporters on Japan's unconditional surrender and reads them Emperor Hirohito's formal message during a news conference in the White House, officially signaling the war's end, Aug. 14, 1945.

RIGHT: Servicemen and women celebrate the announcement of the Japanese surrender in Washington, D.C., Aug. 14, 1945. Aug. 14 was unofficially commemorated as (the first) V-J Day; President Truman had noted in his speech that day that "the proclamation of V-J Day must wait upon the formal signing of the surrender terms by Japan."

BOWING, WEEPING AT PALACE

By The Associated Press

Domei, the Japanese news agency, said in a broadcast recorded by the FCC today that "on Aug. 14, 1945, the Imperial decision was granted" and that weeping people had gathered before his palace and "bowed to the very ground" in their shame that their "efforts were not enough." The broadcast did not say what the Emperor's decision was.

As recorded and translated by FCC, the dispatch read:

"How shall the 100 million people, filled with trepidation, reply to the Emperor? His Majesty's subjects are moved to tears by his Majesty's boundless and infinite solicitude.

"Aug. 14, 1945, the Imperial decision was granted. The palace grounds are quiet beneath the dark clouds.

"Honored with the Imperial edict in the sublime palace grounds, the mob of loyal people are bowed to the very ground in front of the Niju-bashi (the bridge which leads to the palace).

"Their tears flow unchecked. Alas! In their shame, how can the people raise their heads?

"With the words, 'Forgive us, O Emperor, our efforts were not enough,' the heads bow lower and lower as the tears run unchecked.

"Ever since Dec. 8, 1941, when we received the Imperial rescript, causing his majesty deep anxiety. . ."

It was at this point that Domei broke its transmission to ask editors to hold it up.

Aug. 15, 1945: Schoolgirls and other Japanese citizens weep in sorrow on the plaza in front of the Imperial Palace in Tokyo after learning of Japan's unconditional surrender—"'bowed to the very ground' in their shame that their 'efforts were not enough.'"

appointment and continuing the Japanese note, a second disclosing the immediate cutback in the draft and the third in which Mr. Truman congratulated "one of the hardest-working group of war workers"—the federal employees who were on the job for the past four years.

The president said they were entitled to a holiday Wednesday and Thursday with pay and only skeleton forces should be maintained. . . .

Newsreel cameras buzzed to record the momentous occasion, and flashlight bulbs flickered.

The conference got started on the dot of 6:00 and was one of the shortest on record. Mr. Truman wasted no time nor words making the announcement.

In less than two minutes the conference was over and reporters dashed for telephones.

One of the latecomers to the conference was Cordell Hull, secretary of state 12 years under Franklin D. Roosevelt and a prime mover in the creation of the United Nations organization.

Big Crowd Assembles

Shortly before 6:30 p.m., the president strode out on the lawn of the White House and the big crowd assembled before the north fence cheered, whistled and a few broke into song.

The president waved his right hand and the crowd waved wildly back. Hundreds of people crowded the sidewalk immediately in front of the executive mansion where the broad vista opens across the wooded lawn upon the familiar portico, which most of America knows as the "front door."

Horns of scores of cars let loose with all the noise they could make, people shouted, screamed and threw all sorts of things into the air. Sweating military police in the hot August evening had a strenuous time trying to keep the crowd back from the high iron fence which surrounds the lawn. The crowd spilled over into the street and blocked traffic into a thick mass of screaming horns.

★ ★ ★

Decatur Daily Review, Decatur, IL, Tuesday, August 14, 1945

A GREAT DAY FOR DEMOCRACY

We Must Unite to Preserve Peace—Truman

WASHINGTON, Aug. 14 (AP)—In an impromptu speech on the White House lawn early tonight President Truman told a large crowd of spectators that this was a great day for democracy.

He said it marked the final triumph over fascism and would go down in history as one of its most noteworthy days. The whole country now should unite, the president said, in efforts to preserve the future peace of the world.

Real Task Lies Ahead

America, said Mr. Truman, now can start "on our real task of implementation of free government in the world."

When thousands of spectators who had waited patiently in Lafayette Park across the street from the executive mansion began a chant, "We want Truman," the president appeared on the White House steps with Mrs. Truman. Surrounded by Secret Service men, the president and his wife walked down the steps, across the lawn and around a fountain to the high iron fence which fronts the White House on Pennsylvania Avenue. There the president waved and smiled to the crowd.

As the throng continued cheering, Mr. and Mrs. Truman returned to the White House porch where he spoke into a microphone that had been set up there hastily.

"Day for Democracies"

The text of his extemporaneous speech, as transcribed from shorthand notes:

"Ladies and gentlemen, this is the great day. This is the day we have been looking for since December 7, 1941.

"This is the day when fascism and police government ceases in the world.

"This is the day for the democracies.

"This is the day when we can start on our real task of implementation of free government in the world.

"We are faced with the greatest task we ever have been faced with. The emergency is as great as it was on December 7, 1941.

"It is going to take the help of all of us to do it. I know we are going to do it."

San Francisco Examiner, San Francisco, CA, Wednesday, August 15, 1945

VICTORY CELEBRATIONS LET LOOSE OVER NATION

2,000,000 Go Wild in N.Y.;
Many Turn Solemnly to Church Rites

By The Associated Press

An Allied world that had waited long and sacrificed heavily for this victory gave thanks in its manifold ways last (Tuesday) night for Japan's unconditional surrender, and then went mad in an ecstasy of jubilation.

"It"—the war, the costliest war in blood, dollars and resources in history—was over.

Even as the whistles began shrieking, as the wildly honking automobiles began racing through the streets, as the victory bonfire blazed and the fighting men and their home folks embraced and wept unashamed—even as these things happened, the church bells pealed and the words of the Psalmist were repeated, reverently: "This is the day which the Lord hath made; we will rejoice and be glad in it."

Continued Show

The rejoicing was undiminished for all that it had started, and had been checked repeatedly, last Friday when the enemy of the Western world bared its breast—but asked the shadow of an emperor for armor.

In Times Square, New York, last (Tuesday) night, a crowd of 150,000 that almost lost heart during a day of alternate hoping

In this photo by Ed Westcott, the official U.S. Army photographer of the Oak Ridge, Tennessee, site for the Manhattan Project, residents and workers from Oak Ridge wave newspapers in the air announcing the end of the war, Aug. 14, 1945. Oak Ridge was one of the three main sites of the Manhattan Project, and was responsible (though those most working there did not know it) for refining uranium to be fashioned into atomic bombs in Los Alamos, New Mexico.

and doubting, swelled to a police-estimated 2,000,000 a few hours after the news finally came, and never had there been such jubilation.

Not on Armistice Day, 1918, and not on the day in 1945 when General of the Army Dwight D. Eisenhower came home from the wars to an unparalleled ovation, had there been so thunderous a roar, so joyous an occasion.

All Over the World

So it was to the east and west—to the blood-stained Pacific islands on humbled Japan's doorstep, to bomb-battered London, to the scarred soil of recently conquered Germany.

The veterans of this war, the war of the flame-thrower, radar, the atomic bomb, celebrated if they were able to celebrate, and the cheers that echoed down the long, silent corridors of hospital wards were no less hearty than the cheers in the streets outside. . . .

It reached the staidest farm community and the loneliest island outpost.

Washington blew its top when the official announcement came, and not an instant before. Paper showers burst from the windows and long-hoarded fireworks exploded in a frantic salute. Girls kissed soldiers and sailors, in Washington as elsewhere. . . .

And Pearl Harbor? The mighty naval base, pockmarked by Japanese bombs on December 7, 1941, in a sneak raid that has lived in infamy, sounded its sirens, too; but this time the shouts that broke out were ecstatic, not agonized, and it was confetti, not shrapnel, that littered the streets. . . .

Deep Meaning

There were many causes for jubilation. The end of the war meant the return of 5,000,000 men to their homes, months or years earlier than they and their families had dared to hope. It meant the end of casualty lists, of black-garbed widows, hardly out of their teens. . . .

City fathers of Battle Creek, Mich., forbade a celebration, but the whole city joined in when 10,000 wounded men from the Army's Percy Jones Hospital swarmed into Battle Creek, some on crutches, others in wheelchairs.

These were former comrades-in-arms of the men who sweltered on bloody Okinawa, nearest base to Japan, and could hardly believe there was no more flak ahead, and no more beach-heads.

ABOVE: Three-year-old William Lee throws confetti from his flag-draped fire escape at 31 Mott Street in the Chinatown section of New York, Aug. 14, 1945.

BELOW: Sailors at Pearl Harbor gather around a radio cheering the news of Japan's surrender, Aug. 15, 1945.

195

Joplin Globe, Joplin, MO, Sunday, September 2, 1945

JAPS SIGN SURRENDER TERMS

ACTION FORMALLY ENDS BLOODY WAR IN THE PACIFIC

Capitulation Ceremony, Brief and Solemn, Held Aboard Battleship Missouri *in Tokyo Bay—MacArthur Accepts on Behalf of Allies—Promises Justice and Tolerance in Enforcing Conditions*

USS *MISSOURI*, TOKYO BAY, Sept. 2 (Sunday) (AP)— Japan surrendered formally and unconditionally to the Allies today in a 20-minute ceremony which ended just as the sun burst through low-hanging clouds as a shining symbol to a ravaged world now done with war.

The solemn ceremony, marking the first defeat in Japan's 2,600-year-old semi-legendary history, took place aboard this mighty battleship with 12 signatures which required only a few minutes to affix to the articles of surrender.

Surrounded by the might of the United States Navy and Army, and under the eyes of the American and British commanders they so ruthlessly defeated in the Philippines and Malaya, the Japanese representatives quietly made the marks on paper which ended the bloody Pacific conflict.

That horrible war, which had entered its eighth year in China and had raged for nearly three years and nine months for the United States and Great Britain, was finally and officially at an end with complete victory for the Allies.

Signs for Hirohito

On behalf of Emperor Hirohito, Foreign Minister Mamoru Shigemitsu signed first for Japan. He doffed his top hat, tinkered with the pen and then firmly affixed his signature to the surrender document, a paper about 12 by 18 inches. Shigemitsu carefully signed the American copy first, then affixed his name to a duplicate copy to be retained by Japan.

Following him, Gen. Yoshijiro, of the Japanese imperial general staff, sat down resolutely, and scrawled his name on the documents as if in a tremendous hurry. A Japanese colonel present was seen to wipe tears from his eyes as the general signed. All the Japanese looked tense and weary. Shigemitsu looked on anxiously as Umezu signed.

Gen. MacArthur was next to sign, as supreme Allied commander, on behalf of all the victorious Allied powers.

Two Called by MacArthur

MacArthur immediately called for Lt. Gen. Jonathan Wainwright of Bataan and Corregidor and Lt. Gen. Sir Arthur Percival of Singapore to step forward.

These two defeated Allied commanders, now savoring their hour of triumph, stepped up, and Wainwright helped MacArthur take his seat. MacArthur signed the documents with five pens. The first he handed immediately to Gen. Wainwright, the second to Gen. Percival. The third was an ordinary shipboard navy-issue pen. MacArthur then produced a fourth pen, presumably to be sent to President Truman. Then he completed his signatures with still a fifth, possibly a trophy to be retained by himself.

Generals Wainwright and Percival both obviously happy, saluted snappily. They were followed by serene-faced Adm. Nimitz, who signed on behalf of the United States.

OPPOSITE: A view of the surrender ceremonies, looking forward from USS *Missouri*'s superstructure; Japanese officials stand in a group facing representatives of the Allied armed forces prior to signing the Instrument of Surrender, Tokyo Bay, Sept. 2, 1945. In the front line of Japanese officials, in a top hat, is Foreign Minister Mamoru Shigemitsu, and to his right is Chief of the Army General Staff Gen. Yoshijiro Umezu. Among the officers in the foreground behind the desk are Adm. Chester W. Nimitz and Gen. Douglas MacArthur.

OPPOSITE INSET: Japanese surrender signatories are shown arriving on board USS *Missouri* in Tokyo Bay, Sept. 2, 1945, to participate in surrender ceremonies. Left to right, front row: Mamoru Shigemitsu, who signed on behalf of the emperor, and Gen. Yoshijiro Umezu, who signed on behalf of the Imperial Japanese General Headquarters. Second row in top hats: Japanese government officials Katsuo Okazaki and Toshikazu Kase. Others unidentified.

Gen. MacArthur signs the Japanese surrender documents, Sept. 2, 1945. Standing behind him are Gen. Jonathan Wainwright, left foreground, who surrendered Corregidor, and Lt. Gen. A. E. Percival of Britain, who surrendered Singapore, as they witness—with other American and British officers—the ceremony marking the end of World War II.

Chinese Envoy Signs

Next came China's representative.

Gen. MacArthur acted as a brisk master of ceremonies. He made a brief introductory statement before the Japanese signed, then called upon each nation's signer in turn to step forward.

The United Kingdom's signature was followed by that of Soviet Russia. The Russian staff officer signed quickly, scooting his chair into a more comfortable position even as he was signing.

MacArthur smiled approvingly as the Russian rose and saluted.

Quickly in turn, Australian, Canadian, French, Dutch and New Zealand representatives signed in that order. The Australian general Sir Thomas Blamey happened to sign the Japanese copy first, with an expression that denoted it didn't make any difference.

Rifles Point Skyward

Among U.S. Army officers present were Gen. Stilwell, Gen. Spaatz and Gen. Kenney; Lt. Gen. Robert L. Eichelberger and Gen. Walter Krueger, commanders of the U.S. Eighth and Sixth Armies; and Lt. Gen. Robert C. Richardson, Jr., commander of the U.S. Army forces in the central Pacific.

The 45,000-ton *Missouri*, which less than a month ago was blasting Japanese war industries with her 16-inch guns, had those rifles pointed skyward and her bow pointed toward the heart of Japan for the ceremony.

MacArthur's hand shook slightly as he reached "Dou—" in his first signature. His face twitched but his voice was strong, although he appeared to be under great emotional strain.

198

The ceremony was conducted on the *Missouri*'s gallery deck, on her starboard side, only a few feet from her big No. 2, 16-inch gun turret. A long table was set up for the signing. Every available inch of space was crowded with army, navy and marine spectators and about 200 correspondents, some of whom had been covering the Pacific almost from the war's outbreak.

There were 11 Japanese representatives. All were dressed formally or were in uniform, except one who wore a rumpled white linen suit.

Scene Obscured by Clouds

The scene in Tokyo Bay was largely obscured by clouds which hung fairly low amid the surrounding hills.

The flags of the United States, Britain, Russia, and China fluttered from the verandah deck of the *Missouri*. More than 100 high-ranking military and naval officers of the Allies were in the colorfully uniformed group watching the ceremony.

MacArthur, in his opening remarks, declared:

"It is my earnest hope and, indeed, the hope of all mankind, that from this solemn occasion a better world shall emerge out of the blood and carnage of the past."

Finally, after New Zealand's signature, less than 20 minutes from the start of the ceremony, the sun broke through the clouds, and MacArthur formally and in a firm voice declared the proceedings closed.

The Japanese prepared to depart immediately, their bitter chore accomplished.

MacArthur informed the Japanese that "as supreme commander for the Allied powers, I announce it my firm purpose in the tradition of the countries I represent to proceed in the discharge of my responsibilities with justice and tolerance, while taking all necessary dispositions to insure that the terms of surrender are fully, promptly and faithfully complied with."

★ ★ ★

F4U and F6F fighter planes fly in formation over USS *Missouri* during the surrender ceremonies in Tokyo Bay, Sept. 2, 1945.

Tallahassee Democrat, Tallahassee, FL, Sunday, September 2, 1945

SURRENDER TERMS SIGNED

TRUMAN DECLARES TODAY AS V-J DAY

President Declares Love of Liberty Overcame Tyranny

GLOBE-CIRCLING MESSAGE SIGNIFIES NEW ERA OF HOPE FOR DEMOCRACIES

WASHINGTON, Sept. 1 (AP)—President Truman tonight proclaimed Sunday, September 2, as V-J Day—for Japan a day of "retribution," for America and the world a day of the "victory of liberty over tyranny."

Mr. Truman spoke over a globe-girdling radio hookup that linked the White House with Tokyo, where aboard the great battleship *Missouri* just off the enemy capital, Japan abjectly signed the terms of her surrender. And to the occasion the president attributed a fourfold significance:

1. FOR THIS COUNTRY—a day for "renewed consecration to the principles which have made us the strongest nation on earth and which, in this war, we have striven so mightily to preserve."

2. FOR JAPAN—An end of "power to destroy and kill."

3. FOR THE WORLD—A bright new era of hope for "peace and international good will and co-operation."

4. FOR HISTORY—"the day of formal surrender by Japan."

"We shall not forget Pearl Harbor," he said. "The Japanese militarists will not forget the USS *Missouri*. The evil done by the Japanese warlords can never be repaired or forgotten. But their power to destroy and kill has been taken from them. Their armies and what is left of their navy are now impotent."

For this event of mingled solemnity and joy, Mr. Truman invited members of the cabinet to sit with him in the broadcast room on the first floor of the White House—the White House where Japan once haughtily boasted she would dictate surrender terms. They listened to the ceremonies aboard the *Missouri* and, in the midst of them, the president spoke. . . . There was little of gloating or elation in the president's address. Rather there was sober emphasis on what victory has cost and what it will mean.

"Our first thoughts now," the president said, "are thoughts of gratefulness and deep obligation to those killed or maimed in history's most terrible war, and of their loved ones." He went on:

"Only the knowledge that the victory, which these sacrifices have made possible, will be wisely used, can give them any comfort. It is our responsibility—ours, the living—to see to it that this victory shall be a monument worthy of the dead who died to win it."

Answering thousands of inquiries as to just what V-J Day means, the president repeated previous assertions that it has no legal meaning. Here is what he said on this point:

"As President of the United States, I proclaim Sunday, September 2, 1945, to be V-J Day—the day of formal surrender by Japan.

"It is not yet the day for the formal proclamation of the end of the war or of the cessation of hostilities. But it is a day which we Americans shall always remember as a day of retribution—as we remember that other day, the day of infamy."

Mr. Truman thus adopted the words of his predecessor, the late President Roosevelt, in referring to December 7, 1941. The president had been listening to the radio description of the surrender ceremony when tuned in to the hookup with the *Missouri*. . . .

"From this day we move forward," he said. "We move toward a new era of security at home. With the other United Nations we move toward a new and better world of peace and international good will and co-operation." . . .

The president, after paying tribute to those who died in the war, and millions of other United States and Allied participants, including battlefront and homefront fighters and workers, voiced a eulogy for his predecessor: "We think of our departed gallant leader, Franklin D. Roosevelt, a defender of democracy, architect of world peace and cooperation."

The president said the formal Japanese surrender means a victory of more than arms alone.

"This is a victory of liberty over tyranny," he declared.

OPPOSITE BOTTOM: The battleship USS *New York*, veteran of the Okinawa and Iwo Jima campaigns, returns with World War II veterans to San Pedro, Ca., Sept. 9, 1945, as part of Operation Magic Carpet—during which more than 8 million U.S. military personnel were transported back to the United States from the European and American theaters. Singer and actress Dinah Shore, foreground, accompanied by a piano player, waves from a truckbed waiting to entertain the crew.

NEWS AND THE SUNDAY TRIBUNE

A Sunday Combination of the Morning Capital News and Evening Post-Tribune

VOL. 20. NO. 7. JEFFERSON CITY, MISSOURI, SUNDAY, SEPTEMBER 2, 1945 PRICE TEN CENTS

WORLD IS AT PEACE

U. S. Forces Set Up Headquarters In Japan

Map highlights developments in the Far East as United States Army and Navy forces set up head-quarters in Japan as the occupation of the homeland proceeds. (AP WIREPHOTO MAP)

Robert L. Wilder Released From Japanese Camp

Served on Cruiser Houston Which Was Sunk Feb. 28, 1942

Twenty-three-year old Robert Lee Wilder is the first Jefferson City serviceman to be released from the custody of the Japanese since the war ended, his mother, Mrs. Marjorie Wilder, 905 West McCarty Street, learned Friday when she received word of his liberation from Vice Adm. Randall Jacobs, chief of the bureau of naval personnel.

Admiral Jacobs sent the following message concerning Wilder, who served on the cruiser Houston which was sunk in The Netherlands East Indies February 1942:

"I am pleased to inform you of the liberation from Japanese custody of your son, Robert,

Japan Surrenders Formally, Unconditionally to Allies in Short Ritual; V-J Day Today

Truman Lauds Day of Victory Over Tyranny

Bright New Era of Hope of International Good Will Seen

WASHINGTON, Sept. 1 — (AP)—President Truman tonight proclaimed Sunday, Sept. 2, as V-J Day—for Japan of "retribution," for America and the world a day of the

Surrender Terms

By the Associated Press

Article by article here is what Japan agreed to do under the terms of surrender:

1. Accept all provisions of the Potsdam declaration.
2. Surrender unconditionally all armed forces.
3. Cease hostilities forthwith and preserve and save from damage all ships, aircraft and military and civil property.
4. Command imperial general headquarters to issue orders to all field commanders everywhere to surrender their forces unconditionally.
5. See that all civil, military and naval officers obey and enforce all orders of the supreme Allied commander.
6. Carry out in good faith under Allied direction the Potsdam declaration under which free institutions may be established leading

Sun Breaks Through Clouds as Shining Symbol as MacArthur Proclaims End To Proceedings; Hopes Carnage Over

Nips Quietly Make Marks on Paper That Marks Close to Bloody Pacific Conflict; Gen. Wainwright Is Happy Spectator

USS MISSOURI, Tokyo, Bay, Sunday, Sept. 2—(AP)—Japan surrendered formally and unconditionally to the Allies today in a 20-minute ceremony which ended just as the sun burst through lowhanging clouds as a shining symbol to a ravaged world now done with war.

The solemn ceremony, marking the first defeat in Japan's old semi-legendary history, took place aboard this ship with 12 sig...required only a...the

Revising State's Laws Still Top

Nazi Leaders Now Getting Religious; Still Like Hitler

NUERNBERG, (AP)—About half the leaders held here as war crimes trials are

Staff Changes On News & Tribune

Acknowledgments

BESIDES THE 16 MILLION AMERICAN GIs who served and the 1,600 war correspondents who went with them, there are two contemporaries who made this book possible and what it is: Barbara Berger, executive editor at Sterling Publishing, and Peter Costanzo, Director of Programming & Media Partnerships at The Associated Press. Without them and their remarkable efforts, this work would be just another World War II book, instead of this landmark treatise on a facet of the war that few twenty-first-century Americans know of: the warriors who fought for the Allies with the mightiest weapon of all, the "pen." Peter brought in his own force, too, including AP librarians and researchers Valerie Komor and Francesca Pitaro. At Sterling, we are also indebted to Linda Liang, senior photo editor, as well as Kevin Ullrich, interior designer and creative operations director, who made the visuals into a work of art in its own right. Special thanks also to David Ter-Avanesyan, cover designer, and Elizabeth Mihaltse Lindy, senior art director, covers, for the stunning jacket and case; and Kevin Iwano, production director.

—Les Krantz, Facts That Matter, Inc.

STERLING PUBLISHING IS EXTREMELY GRATEFUL to Les Krantz for bringing this incredible project to us, and being such a wonderful partner in producing it. Peter Costanzo, we were thrilled to be able to work with you and the esteemed Associated Press to tell this epic story of the most titanic conflict in the history of civilization.

We are so grateful to you, and to your team of intrepid colleagues—Valerie Komor, Francesca Pitaro, Sean Thompson, Susan Boyle, and Chuck Zoeller—for all of your hard work under often challenging circumstances during this difficult time.

We are also grateful to historian Alan Axelrod for shaping the framework of the book and for writing such an insightful text that was at once comprehensive and concise.

Thank you all, for your dedication and expertise.

WE WOULD LIKE TO OFFER a *very* special thanks to David Eisenhower for his meaningful and moving foreword, which we are so honored to include in our book.

WE HOPE THAT THIS BOOK—as The Associated Press reported on September 2, 1945, in a recap of President Harry S. Truman's speech announcing V-J Day—in some small way pays tribute "to those who died in the war, and millions of other United States and Allied participants, including battlefront and homefront fighters and workers," and, as Truman said, to "all those who . . . helped in this cooperative struggle to preserve liberty and decency in the world."

—Sterling Publishing Co., Inc.

ABOVE: U.S. paratroopers enter a Douglas C-47 Skytrain at an Allied air base during Operation Market Garden, Sept. 17, 1944. BELOW: Troops of the U.S. Army Americal Division crouch on the sandy shore of the east coast of Cebu after disembarking from navy landing craft, March 26, 1945.

Picture Credits

All photos, newspapers, and maps courtesy of The Associated Press, with the following exceptions:

Alamy: akg-images: 174; dpa picture alliance: 149; ITAR-TASS News Agency: 88; Niday Picture Library: 126; Photo 12/Yevgeny Khaldei: 171; Smith Archive: 77; SPUTNIK: 175; Sueddeutsche Zeitung Photo: 118

AP Images: William C. Allen: v inset, xv bottom, 180 bottom; AP Corporate Archives: xiii, 109 inset; Beatty: 41; Ernest K. Bennett: back endpaper spread; British Official Photograph: 203 inset; Peter Carroll: 139 top; Daniel de Luce: xi; Department of Defense: 72; Max Desfor: 197; John Donwey: front endpaper single; Tom Fitzsimmons: 195 top; FLS: 183 bottom; German War Department: 9; Charles P. Gorry: 165 bottom; Harry Harris: front endpaper spread, 125 inset, 131, 181; Toshio Hashimoto: 48; Hiroshima Peace Memorial Museum/U.S. Army: 185; ja/Yuichiro Sasaki/UN: 185 inset; Ernest King: 83 right; Jens Meyer: 77 inset; National Archives: 58; Jim Pringle: 176 left; Harrison Roberts: xii top; Byron Rollins: 161; Joe Rosenthal: 151, 153; SOVPHOTO: 170; Tactical Air Force, Tenth Army: 155 top; U.S. Air Force: 186 bottom; U.S. Army Signal Corps: 42, 65, 107, 108, 138, 186 top, back endpaper single; U.S. Marine Corps: 152; U.S. Navy: 156 top, 199, 202; Cpl. E.G. Wilbert/U.S. Marines: 116; Eddie Worth: 29 top, 31 bottom

© carenas1/depositphotos.com: 45, 111, 113, 152, 177, 180, 195

Getty Images: alubalish/E+: v inset, xiv bottom, 97 inset; billnoll/E+: 60 inset, 71 insert, 91 bottom; Corbis Historical: 169; George Lipskerov/ITAR-TASS: 82; LoraLiu/iStock/Getty Images Plus: xii inset, 41 inset, 84 inset left, 106, 107, 108, 109; Tolga TEZCAN/E+: i, 55 insert, 73 insert; tomograf/iStock/Getty Images Plus: 19 inset, 84 inset right, 105 inset, 140 inset, 150 inset, 169 inset, 187 inset;

Library of Congress: xi inset; Farm Security Administration/Office of War Information: 55, 59 bottom

National Archives: 115, 157 bottom, 187

Naval History and Heritage Command: 71, 195 bottom; Army Signal Corps Collection/National Archives: ii, 136 top; National Archives: 80; U.S. Coast Guard/National Archives: vi, 111, 112 inset; U.S. Naval Institute: 69; U.S. Navy/National Archives: 68, 74, 84, 136 bottom, 137

courtesy of Wikimedia Commons: 134; FDR Library/National Archives: 165 top; Harry S. Truman Library/National Archives: xi; Charles Levy/Department of Defense: 189; Library of Congress: 125; National Archives: 42 inset, 43, 62, 95 inset, 114, 127, 133, 135, 139 bottom, 143, 145, 164 inset, 188; National Museum of U.S. Navy: 123; U.S. Air Force: 132; U.S. Army/National Archives: 144; U.S. Marine Corps: 157 top; U.S. Navy: 156 bottom; U.S. Signal Corps/National Archives: 141; Ed Westcott/Department of Energy Oak Ridge: 194; WWII Signal Corps Photograph Collection: 102

AP war correspondent George Tucker at work on his typewriter in the Libyan Desert while attached to the RAF, Jan. 18, 1943.